DANCE YOUR WAY HOME

DANCE YOUR WAY HOME

A Journey
Through
the Dancefloor

EMMA WARREN

faber

First published in 2023
by Faber & Faber Limited
Bloomsbury House
74–77 Great Russell Street
London WC1B 3DA

Typeset by Faber & Faber Limited
Printed in England by CPI Group (UK) Ltd, Croydon, CRO 4YY

A CIP record for this book
is available from the British Library

ISBN 978–0–571–36603–3

Printed and bound in the UK on FSC paper in line with our continuing
commitment to ethical business practices, sustainability and the environment.
For further information see faber.co.uk/environmental-policy

2 4 6 8 10 9 7 5 3

'Escapism has always been an adjective used to describe the dance. That's an outsider's view. Solidarity is what it really offers.'

Theo Parrish

CONTENTS

vii

Contents

Contents

Introduction
OPENING STEPS

If you dance, you're a dancer. This is where we begin.

By this I mean that you're a dancer if you've ever danced, even if you've only danced in your imagination, too shy to externalise the movement. The word 'dance' in this book is decoupled from being *good* at dancing.

Consequently, I've included stories about childhood tap dancing and wedding discos, told with a slip-sliding appreciation of the act of moving to music. I'm operating from various corners of interconnected dancefloors, where the ground might be uneven, where a range of people are packed in – occasionally bashing elbows – and where you don't have to learn steps to take part. This is my attempt to explore what ordinary dancing can do for us individually and collectively.

I am beginning in my flat on the edge of south-east London. It has a wooden floor that was originally part of a Scarborough dancehall and which I bought on eBay. I bump, slide and two-step across it to the kitchen in a plain echo of the partner-dancing that took place when north Yorkshire couples danced on these rectangular wooden blocks. This particular dancefloor moved literally from one part of the country to the other, but a dancefloor can also move across time and space symbolically: in this book the dancefloor isn't just the floor of your local discotheque, it's also a work do or a sweaty basement rave. It's anywhere we gather to dance, at any point in history.

Mostly, we'll be meeting dancers like me who are reliant on a basic two-step – a dance you can take anywhere. Occasionally we'll encounter spectacular dancers like Trevor Shakes, who in early-eighties London could spin three times in the air in a packed club without touching anyone. Until I started writing this book I wouldn't have called myself a dancer, given the connotations of training and skill that the word contains. Now I own it, with a few caveats. I am a dancer in the sense that I've spent thousands of hours moving to music in the communal settings of nightclubs, dark basements and house parties. I am mostly untrained. I have a movement palette in my body that reflects my age and life experience. I move like me.

———

I'd spent over two decades on dancefloors when I visited South Africa in 2014. I wasn't going to Soweto for anything explicitly musical. I was taking part in a programme for grassroots social innovators, working alongside people who were inventing school bags that doubled up as light sources so that kids could study after dark, or who were creating township skate clubs where children sat with homework mentors before getting on the ramps. I knew that South Africa contained generations of intellectuals, radicals and visionaries, some of whom had lived through apartheid, and many of whom continue to resist the persistent economic divisions. I also knew I'd be in a situation where there would be dancing, not least because I was aware that chanting and movement had been used during anti-apartheid protests.

Opening Steps

There was a lot of dancing. We'd be out in the evening, and it would begin with a little sidestep or a slide, edged with a tiny hip drop. If the move was nice enough, someone would follow, replicating what had been done and perhaps adding a new element. In this way a routine was built, with none of the 'you do this and I'll do that' that I remembered from childhood choreography. Dance seemed like another language, alongside those spoken by most South Africans. My new friends were fluent in, say, Xhosa, Zulu, Afrikaans and English, as well as being able to converse through shoulder drops and a shuffle.

I saw an ability to share a joke or an observation through movement on multiple occasions, and it gave me a mixture of feelings. I was impressed. I was also hyper-aware of just how basic my basic two-step was, and this had the effect of turning my legs off. I shrank into the background and avoided communing with the moves that I carried in my body from years of dancing to new music in UK nightclubs, whether that was dancing to Roni Size and DJ Krust at a mid-nineties drum 'n' bass night on Bristol's boat-club Thekla, or illicit gatherings in London and Manchester accessed through doorways that had been fashioned between separating walls with a hammer, where people were responding to brand-new music with arms raised, like antennae. I was paralysed by the fear of being a bad dancer and, because of this, became a much worse dancer than I really was, janky and self-conscious. On the plane on the way home I made a decision: if I ever went back, I'd bring the dance I had. All I could do was bring my honest self, and that would be plenty.

———

Introduction

Dancefloors, wherever they may be situated, reflect the times, but also reflect us. Each time we move we share information about who we are, where we've been and where we're going, like the body's version of an accent or tone of voice. Musician and poet Robert Gallagher's collection *The Dance Floors of England* describes the nightclub Fabric, which is adjacent to the historic meat market at Smithfield in east London, and uses the phrase, 'England through the looking glass.' I think this looking glass is present whenever we meet up and dance. Dancing, we can see ourselves and each other reflected with unusual perspective. Just think about how differently we dance depending on whether we're happy or sad, well or sick, old or young. Our dancefloors can also, as Rob Gallagher's words suggest, indicate who we are as a nation. Perhaps dancing together, informally and without too many rules, can also suggest a route through the combined messes of late-stage capitalism, climate change, racism and new nationalism – even if it's simply as replenishment. On the flip, it's worth noting that moving to music isn't inherently good and can cause damage (including, on a very small scale, the knee injury I'm currently carrying).

Dance is somehow hard to value or take seriously, at least in some quarters of British society. Partly that's because people equate dancefloors with hedonism and sex – places to get trashed and pull a partner. Some of the places I've been to were hedonistic, and some of them led to love, sex and partnership. However, I'd say that music and dancing were the primary attractions for most of the people who attended the kinds of dancefloors you'll encounter in this book. People who were just on the pull tended to congregate elsewhere.

Opening Steps

The subtitle of this book describes a journey through the dancefloor, and it is intentionally singular: this would be a different book if I'd been involved in bhangra or heavy metal or any other form of music culture. It's also a journey in the sense of exploration, and I've used dancefloors I've been on, or have a connection to, as a route through the vast subject of moving to music. I'm digging where I stand, to paraphrase Swedish author Sven Lindqvist, who encouraged workers to research the factories that employed them so they could better advocate for workers' rights. I'm using my own experiences for another reason, too, because they help me to navigate the politics of race, class and the other -isms that surround the subject of dance. I decided it was better to dig into Anglo-Saxon dancing or moves that relate to my Irish grandmother than to tell stories with which I have less family connection – for example, historic West African dance. There is a lot of diasporic dance in this book, because I have always lived, worked and danced in British cities. I'm a south Londoner, socialised and enculturated on the dancefloor. I'm also a white, middle-class, middle-aged woman, and I have tried my best to enter each area carefully and with the right amount of respect.

We can't talk about dancing without talking about physical space, since one requires the other – we can't dance mid-air, at least not for more than a few seconds. Music and dancing spiral into each other and become one on the surface of the dancefloor, wherever it exists. Dancing together requires space, and can – at least temporarily – open it up. Dancefloors of all kinds were plentiful across the UK and elsewhere in the decades following deindustrialisation, and they have been gradually removed thanks to rampant profiteering. Consequently I've included overlooked locations like youth clubs and school discos, as well as describing my experiences during acid house and at techno clubs, drum 'n' bass nights and grimy dubstep sessions. I am putting the dancer back in the dance-music story, and I am talking about dance music in its broadest sense – I don't just mean this as shorthand for 'electronic music'.

This is admittedly a very analogue story, but we can, of course, also absorb dance online. My social-media feeds are full of dancers, covering all kinds of styles, whether these are intense young flamenco dancers, women dancing Punjabi wedding styles or young men enacting Irish steps to pop bangers in shopping centres. Online dance allows a breadth of experience that most of our lives can't offer, and the screen acts as a frame that makes movement easier to understand. I find it hard to learn steps at the best of times, but when a dancer puts white tape on the floor in order to demonstrate the Running Man it becomes much clearer. I can imagine the white tape on my own floor and have a better chance of getting my feet in the right place, at the right time. The frame assists. This book, though, concentrates on physical interactions, on real-life dancefloors. My hope is that this amassed information will spark layers of feeling – and ideally, further exploration of these spaces, too.

Context is everything, and before we move on I should declare that this book was researched and drafted during the pandemic, revised as I recovered from long Covid, and edited as I re-entered dance spaces, watching people's feet with new interest. The subject wasn't just an abstract choice of something I found interesting; it gave me a foothold into communal life when none was possible. The process of researching, writing and editing it brought felt knowledge from the depths to the surface and clarified previously submerged perspectives. I began seeing dance as culture, comedy and information. I understood it as medicine, communication, a source of strength and solidarity. I recognised it as alchemy, in the sense of allowing individuals and communities to take the raw material of their lives and stamp it into the precious metal – or perhaps mettle – required to make it through another day. Moving together to music, I realised, allows us to form new relationships with ourselves and with the wider world. Through writing, I became aware that the dancefloor is a portal, a container, a drum; a lens and a repair shop; an open university and a laboratory. It's a sorting hat that can help you find where you belong. It is protest and celebration.

———

Finally, I know that dancing can be embarrassing and that it can have a shameful or hesitant quality attached to it, at least for some people on these islands. You might be a confident dancer or you might be conflicted, seizing up when the very idea is raised. Either way, I want to end these opening steps by explaining what happened when I returned to South Africa, eighteen months after my first visit. This time we were in Langa, Cape Town, and I had a secret sub-plan. I was going to dance, and I did, just being me, just being basic London, just feeling the music and moving. I'm a shy dancer and I like to dance in a small space, arms close to my body as if I'm dancing within a glass rectangle of my own making. I found my moves and I joined in.

One of the guys I'd met in Soweto was there too, a hilarious and brainy man called Sifiso. He'd grown up working in his family's fish-and-chip shop and now created durable carts for local rubbish collectors, who earn a pittance recycling trash, often using rickety string-and-pallet contraptions. We'd got on well in Soweto, spending long evenings laughing about all sorts. He approached me one evening when we were all out, music blaring in a bar. 'Emma,' he said, flopping down onto one of the white sofas. 'You're a much better dancer than last time. What happened?'

The fear of being a bad dancer stops many of us dancing. The day-to-day art of moving to music is not about quantifiable excellence; it's about coming as you are and contributing to the dancefloor. So if you ever worry about being a useless dancer – don't. We bring what we have, and we have to start somewhere. If you're dancing, you're a dancer.

DEFINITIONS

Dancing

The rhythmic movements we make in response to sonic stimulation. Much of the dancing in this book is to music provided by expert DJs or musicians, and in these situations movement can also affect the music.

The Dance

A place where people gather to dance to the specific music they collectively know and appreciate. The prefix 'the' arrived from the Caribbean, and it suggests importance, a centrality. The dance can be comprised of 20 people or thousands, as between the 1970s and the 2000s, when tens of thousands of UK youth gathered multiple times each week across the country to dance to reggae, soul, funk, house, techno, drum 'n' bass, garage or any sub-genres thereof.

Dancers

The people who inhabit the dance. Professional training is not required, but the presence or absence of skill, technique and confidence means we can organise our dancers into three main groups:

1. Everyday Dancers

These dancers have a few basic steps in their repertoire. They have a collective rather than individual effect on the music and

9

the culture – unless they're the everyday dancer who is first on the dancefloor and therefore gives permission and energy to the rest of the dancers, even if it's the energy generated by a dismissive eye-roll. The majority of the dance will fall into this category, although 'everyday' is relative. Everyday dancers at the *festa junina* I went to in São Paulo would probably be considered skilful at a drunk Cornish wedding. I am an average everyday dancer, with an above-average experience of the dance.

2. Skilful Dancers

Dancers with enough skill and technique to manipulate their movement to the moment – and who can also manipulate the music by tuning into and acting in concert with the person providing it. This category includes people who have noticeably more confidence, technique or style than the everyday dancer. It also incorporates people with incredible levels of skill, such as the jazz dancers who lit up dancefloors in cities across the country in the mid-1980s – bar those who fit into the following category.

3. Pro Dancers

Individuals with high levels of officially sanctioned, certified training who take part in compensated work as dancers and who perform their work to audiences. This book is minimally about pro dancers, although it is influenced by my pre-teen obsession with the 1980s TV show *Fame*, which was about trainee pro dancers at New York's High School of the Performing Arts. Top-flight musician-dancers like James Brown, Prince and the Jacksons (Janet and Michael) would also be in this category, along with a surprising number of DJs and producers whom we'll meet.

The Dancefloor

The ground upon which the dancers dance. In my case, mostly nightclubs, but also youth clubs, community centres, crossroads, kitchens, backyards and churchyards.

The Everstream

A phrase I use to describe the always evolving and interconnected undercurrent of culture that reflects and responds to our lives.

Part One

BEFORE THE DANCE

Photo on previous page: tap and ballet class at
Shirley Cox's Dance School, circa 1981
Photo credit: Meg Warren

1: DANCE YOUR HISTORY

Toni Basil's 'Mickey', pre-school tap class,
and front-room dancing to *Top of the Pops*
circa 1982

The first dance is at home. You're small, a toddler, and you're being danced around the kitchen. A song has come on and someone is feeling happy, so they scoop you up and stand you on their slippered feet. Small arms are reaching up, fingers held in grown-up hands.

Later, when you're taller and stronger, but still too small for school, siblings and cousins might have encouraged you into performances at family parties. The adults sit around drinking, dancing or talking, and the kids scurry about creating a top-secret show. The kindest child bends down, offering teacherly instruction to the smaller ones: 'You're going to stand here and do this, and then you need to stand there and do that. OK?'

Those of us lucky enough to grow up in homes or neighbourhoods that were at least sometimes warm and funny will have experienced something similar. It's human nature to express ourselves through movement, and this often begins at home. It starts as soon as we're big enough to be danced about by a grown-up, or earlier, as a babe in arms being rhythmically soothed to sleep as a tired person performs a slow waltz around a dark bedroom, dancing to the invisible music of new parenthood. Ultimately it begins inside, to the low-frequency quartet of heartbeat, blood flow, digestive rumble and maternal voice.

15

The ways we move in our families help us develop our beliefs about ourselves and each other, expressed in the character short-hand that we all use: this one loves to dance, that one has two left feet. Dancing generates feelings of familiarity and belonging. Moving to music with our families and neighbours bonds us and may have deep purpose. Author Barbara Ehrenreich gathers up the evidence in her beautiful book *Dancing in the Streets* and includes the idea that prehistoric communities would ward off attackers by giving the impression that the people dancing in formation were one big, unidentifiable creature. I imagine them now, 150 men, women and children fighting for their lives with an ancient and terrifying iteration of the Electric Slide or a caveman take on the lairy wedding-party chaos unleashed by Bad Manners' spiralling version of the 'Can Can'.

Dance is unstoppable expression. Each gesture, flex, slide or shape we make in response to music contains communication and history. We absorb or reject each other's movement in order to signify that we're part of a community or to indicate that we're not. It shapes us, as we make shapes. Movement is bound to music, not separate from it. The Greek root of the word 'music' related to all the arts of the muses, and this included dancing.

————

I was at primary school in February 1982, when Toni Basil hit the charts with 'Mickey'. It went platinum across the world and came with an equally famous stomp-style cheerleader video which she choreographed and which I attempted to mimic with my friends in the playground.

It is a particular pleasure, then, when Toni Basil agrees that I can ring her at home in LA. She's a highly skilled and technical dancer and choreographer, of course, but her real rarity rests on a lifelong connection to art and culture built by young people dancing on street corners and in nightclubs, and she has spent decades combining grass-roots artistry with establishment dance. 'I would always be in clubs where there would be a small amount of people – in every era – who would take it to a bigger level.' I ask her what she means by the phrase 'bigger level'. 'Art!' she says. 'It's not just party dancing or partner dancing. It becomes something else. It becomes art.'

Toni Basil is also a significant dance historian. She carries endless knowledge and context from her embodied memories of watching Fred Astaire from the side of the stage that her orchestra-leader father ran; through her lived knowledge of cheerleaders as pre-internet spreaders of new social dance; from working with James Brown in 1964; from co-founding the pioneering street dance group The Lockers with Don Campbell and bringing the crew onto the internationally influential TV show *Soul Train* – ensuring that the whole of the US saw street dance; and from choreographing the video for Talking Heads' 'Once in a Lifetime'; as well as having had a long working relationship with David Bowie, and much more. She went newly viral in 2016 after a gorgeous, unplanned and improvised couple of minutes at the end of a house-dance workshop.

What does street-level dance give us, I ask, over and above the simple pleasure of doing it or watching it? 'For me, it's been my life and my career. I'm a historian not because I do homework but because I've experienced it. I love it. I'm obsessed by it. As far as the public goes, the pop culture – it's dictated fashion, it's dictated so much.' When I push into the question and ask her to tell me more, she slows right down. 'It's a question that I emotionally understand, but it's really hard to articulate,' she says. 'When you're a great street dancer [in] the act of improvising to the music, you're outside of your body and you're inside your body. You're both places simultaneously.' Dance, she says, is a drug, and it's her drug of choice. 'Once you get that high you want to keep going back, back, back. In ballet class, if you're spinning and you start to really spin and you spin more than you've ever spun before, you want to go back there. It's immortal. There's a sense . . .' – she pauses – 'of going beyond the realm of the norm.'

Our early-morning phone call is a fast-paced, wide-ranging conversation, and at one point she tells me about Henry Link, of hip-hop dance crew M.O.P.T.O.P., who showed off their collective grace and groove on the front porches of their homes in the 1992 PBS documentary *Wreckin' Shop: Live from Brooklyn*. 'I said to him, "Oh my god, I wish I could improvise like you. I wish I could dance like you." He looked at me and said, "Dance your history," and it was one of the best things anyone has ever said to me. It was incredible.'

We finish up our call with pleasantries. 'I love that phrase, "dance your history",' I say, scanning through the conversation in my mind. She pulls me up. 'Yes, but if you use these quotes, please . . .' Her voice takes on an uncharacteristic pleading quality. 'You've got to give them to me and you've got to give them to Link, otherwise we lose our history and it goes somewhere else.'

I assure her. This exploration of movement is about respecting and recognising the valuable raw material of personal history. To me, the phrase 'dance your history' is a call to express where you're from and where you belong. It indicates community, because history is collective. It also asks that you look forward, into the histories ahead, and express where you're going, where you might belong in the future.

I dance my own history too, of course. My parents, Meg and Rick, met on the dancefloor at the Sailing School, just off the Barbican in Plymouth. My dad lived in the city with his teacher dad and housewife mum and was starting out as a petroleum geologist. My mum was visiting with one of her friends from nursing college in Birmingham. It was 'nicely amateur', according to my mum: a dark and dingy upstairs room accessed via steep stairs, always packed, with a DJ playing rock 'n' roll, Motown and pop songs. There was jive dancing and smoochy dancing. My mum was eager, badgering her friends – or anyone, frankly – to get on the dancefloor, lacking the confidence to start the dancing, even though that's what she really wanted. I exist because this square two-storey building was used for dancing – although this fact also makes me loath to record that the Sailing School was known locally as 'GX', or 'Groin Exchange'. My parents were married within months. I'm their eldest, arriving two years into their marriage.

Meg is now 74 and is a woman in perpetual motion. 'Oh, before I forget . . .' she says. I'm sitting in my mum's back garden; she disappears inside her bungalow and brings out a small square photograph. She's smirking, although that might be harsh. Perhaps another way of putting it is that she is filled with the time-travel pleasure of being a mother who can see her three-year-old child crystal-clear in the adult sitting in front of her. I think she's also remembering what it's like to love your

19

child but also be able to indulge in the comedy of their existence in a way that involves gently mocking them. I once took
part in a dance show at Catford Broadway Theatre when I was
five or six, in a generic chorus-line role of Leaf Pixie. We wore
brown costumes and carried a light which was a box with a torch
in it, and our short contribution to the performance involved us
floating around and collapsing into a pile before skipping off. I
distinctly remember looking at my parents from the stage and
recognising that they were willing me on and attempting to
conceal their laughter, all at the same time. I was dancing my
history – enthusiasm outstripping skill – which may not have
exactly matched the steps we'd been taught.

Meg hands me the photograph. I have seen this picture
before, but not for years, and it's not exactly how I remember
it. It shows two small girls holding hands outside someone's
house, ready for class at Shirley Cox's School of Ballet and
Tap, which was located above a row of shops a few minutes'
walk from our house. My best friend Jessica looks cute. She
is taller than me, with curly brown hair, and her white dress
looks neatly pressed. She is serene, a little shy. The red waist-
band sits nicely in the middle of her body, making the skirt
puff out a little, nearly a tutu.

Frankly, I am a mess. I'm grinning, with my chin down,
so it looks as if I have no neck. The red bow in my hair is
wonky. My dress is taut and twisted around my baby pot belly,
which makes the bottom of the dress ride up at the front. The
hem is coming undone. I have one sock up, one sock down,
and my red slip-on pumps show evidence of scuffing or shuffling around in dusty gravel. On the upside, I look eager and
happy, like I'm about to run out of the frame just to get to

class quicker. I look like I've been pinging up and down in the seconds before the image was taken and that I'll be jack-in-a-boxing up and down again the second my mother puts the camera down and walks us along the road to class. The whole idea of tap and ballet for children is strange, when you think about it. Tap involves phenomenal physical movement and rich, layered cultural material. Ballet is anti-gravitational impossibility. I wonder how these dance styles ended up being shoehorned away for pre-schoolers, made childish.

Ballet began, say the history books, in Italy in around AD 1500, when the Italian Catherine de' Medici married the French King Henry II and brought her courtly dance styles with her. I found scant information on ballet before this courtly Year Zero, although the dances that ended up with Italian aristocrats would have come from somewhere. Mid-twentieth-century New York dance critic and poet Edwin Denby claimed it began as a community dance that was gradually 'theatri-cized', first for Greek theatres and later for those of the Roman Empire: 'Ballet began as the kind of dancing current at village festivals around the Mediterranean from the times of King Minos and Daedalus to those of da Vinci.' Everyone grew up knowing the sequences and the tunes that went with them, he wrote, 'and knowing from having watched it the harmony that the dance could show'. Perhaps, then, children skipping around in dance schools contains a hint of ballet's roots, with the rest of the community cut out of the picture.

Dance classes for tots often involve examination, as if learning to dance, even for fun, and even if you're only five years old, requires the imposition of quality control. My small child self knew that other children were being put in for dance exams and I wasn't. The rationale for this? I was too heavy on my feet.

Tap and ballet classes choreographed us into certain ways of moving and certain ways of being. We absorbed gendered cues about how we should move our bodies, and accepted that boys moved differently to girls – and that this was simply normal, correct. Ballet contains hallmarks associated with the ideals of femininity, including grace, control, poise, a skinny frame and a certain type of physical beauty. The exams didn't just measure how good you were at tap or ballet. They measured how good you were at being a girl, and, apparently, I failed.

A paper by Egil Bakka, a professor emeritus for dance studies at the Norwegian University of Science and Technology, claims that interaction is the 'core value' of dance. I like this, not least because my five-year-old dancing self – and perhaps most five-year-olds – would have passed an examination on interaction with flying colours. In the paper, he describes Erik, a toddler who cannot yet speak fluently. The adults at a family gathering begin singing a song that most Norwegians know and which has actions that go with it. Erik immediately begins stamping his feet when he hears the word 'stamping'. 'He cannot sing the song nor understand the words,' Bakka writes, 'but the "dance movement" gives him a tool to participate and interact with the grown-ups.' Bakka believes that participatory dance shows a basic way to learn, in the shape of imitation. It also shows a basic reason for *wanting* to learn – interaction. 'I believe it is an instinctive urge in humans as well as animals to imitate others,' he writes. 'In this, they find the key for interaction, which opens the way for them to be part of the community.'

I carried on interacting by making up dances at home, either putting on my ballet costume or, once I'd grown out of that, my swimsuit, which in my mind and limited wardrobe came close. I'd dance with my siblings to the songs that were played each week on BBC TV show *Top of the Pops*, which brought each week's top 40 chart to life with performances, videos and a very exciting countdown that ended by revealing the current top-selling song in the country. There is a family photograph of me, mid-dance. I am captured in the moment, swimsuit facing the telly, face at the camera, looking a bit annoyed to be distracted. In an early prefiguring of my later working life as a music writer, I'd review the songs as they occurred in the chart rundowns: thumbs-up for favourites; thumbs horizontal if I didn't know the song; thumbs down if I didn't like it. Basically I just really liked moving my body, and *Top of the Pops* was a great opportunity to do this, from the theme tune to the end credits. I was exploring what choreographer Rudolf von Laban called the 'kinesphere', or the space around the body that can be easily reached by extending the limbs, and I recognised that this was highly enjoyable, very social and often very funny.

My parents would sit around and soak up the energetic comedy of three small kids leaping around the front room to pop music. They probably needed some respite. My dad Rick had a genetic condition that presents differently in every person – usually mild to the point of invisibility and occasionally disabling. He was at the extreme end of the scale, requiring regular and often experimental spinal surgery, and would eventually make an unwilling shift to life as a wheelchair-user. My mum was a nurse and therefore understood what was going on. She's beautifully idiosyncratic, or 'crackers', as my dad used to say.

Viv Albertine, fomerly of punk band The Slits, could also be described as idiosyncratic. I interviewed her a few times when her first book came out, including a talk at the Port Eliot literary festival in Cornwall in 2014. At the end, a man in the audience asked a good question: 'What is your advice for bringing up girls?' 'Let them get messy,' she replied. 'Don't buy them nice dresses that they have to keep clean. Encourage them to roll around in the mud. Let them move.'

I don't think my mum was following a punk philosophy, but the end result was the same. I was allowed to move and I was allowed to get messy. I was accepted, even though I naturally defaulted to scruffbag. Meg came from the rock 'n' roll era but, in many ways, she remains an under-the-radar punk, picking her own route through the dancefloor of suburban life. She grew up as part of a doctor's family in a small mining village in the Midlands, with 'a very English father and very Irish mother', absorbing the shock of being left behind when her aunts, uncles and cousins migrated to Australia. Her family had planned to go too, but then couldn't because her father had tuberculosis. She danced these histories through Latin and ballroom classes as a young teenager and then as a young adult, through the medium of the jive, loving dancing and enjoying it the most when the room was full, everyone together. Now, in the absence of suitable dancefloors, she dances her history through another form of movement. She is a rare septuagenarian cyclist, haring around the lanes on her Raleigh racer just inside the M25, where concrete folds into fields.

———

When I was six we moved to a mock-Tudor semi-detached house in the far suburbs of south-east London with my two younger siblings. The housing detail is important because a lot of the dance I encountered later was made by people who didn't grow up in semi-detached houses and instead grew up in environments with plenty of everyday opportunities to hear new music and learn new dances. My childhood neighbours weren't blaring out soca, electro or gospel, although the teenage mod next door might have wished they were. There were moments of dancing in our house growing up – one of us kids making up a move or expressing a moment of excitement in a limb-chucking dance-spasm; my dad dancing me around the garden on his wellington boots or grabbing my mum in the kitchen for a twirl – but nothing regular or embedded in our family life. The radio would often be on, and my parents had their respective musical loves – Motown (my mum), The Beatles and Elvis (my dad) – and a box of records that I mined in my teens. Family gatherings were focused around eating and drinking. Dancing happened away from home, at special events. I have a photograph of my parents dancing together, mid-jive, in the mid-1980s, in front of a drummer who is wearing a bow-tie, on a stage that looks like it's been cut-and-pasted from any hall anywhere in the country. My dad is concentrating, mid-step. My mum, in a polka-dot dress, is smiling and looking out of the frame into the space on the dancefloor next to them.

I think more of us could take up space on a dancefloor, if only to show some solidarity with those who need it. Dancing is a basic need which has somehow been hived off from everyday life, at least for some people. Academia now offers interesting and rational explanations of why dance can be good for us: there are studies which reveal things about dancing that dancers know intuitively – for example, that dancing increases opioid production in the brain, especially when people move in synchrony. It uses more calories than cycling, swimming or running. There's good evidence that dance stimulates the brain, and not just because of the oxygen-rich blood that dancing pumps throughout the whole body. It reduces feelings of fatigue, improves emotional states and has an overall energising effect. Other studies have unearthed remarkable results, as is the case with PhD student Carine Lewis at the University of Hertfordshire, who showed that 20 minutes of improvised dancing improved divergent thinking. It doubled the amount of ideas people came up with in response to a problem.

My siblings and I were brought up Catholic, which ensured that we had some specific problems to solve. We would troop up the road every Sunday and every Holy Day of Obligation to Mass at Holy Innocents church in Orpington, in the London borough of Bromley. The priest, and the altar boys in their white robes and scruffy trainers, would process down the aisle, knocking incense out of a silver ball that dangled on a heavy chain, moving in time to organ drone and the opening hymn. There wasn't any dancing, but there was movement. The machinery of 1980s Catholic Mass required a constant shifting of position: stand, sit, stand, sit, kneel. All rise for the gospel.

We dance our histories, back in time. My maternal grandmother Máire was Irish and Catholic, arriving in England as a teenager to train as a nurse, at a point in the mid-1930s when the Irish church and state were clamping down on jazz and new forms of dance. My grandfather Donald was a newly qualified doctor and the son of a top Anglican cleric, in whose house there was no music, let alone dancing. Máire and Donald fell in love, then decided to separate because their relationship was untenable, given the intersecting red lines of nationality, status and religion. They soon realised they couldn't live without each other and were married in a side aisle of my grandmother's Catholic church in Coventry, because their marriage was deemed unacceptable in the eyes of God. The couple moved 65 miles north, to Mansfield. He became a lay preacher at his local church. She attended Catholic Mass above a betting shop, which was upgraded to a site above a garage, before the community raised enough money to build their own church.

I have some old newspaper cuttings, edged in small triangles from the pinking shears Máire used to cut them out of the *Catholic Herald*. One contains a letter signed by 'Despairing Mother', who wrote asking for help on the subject of mixed marriage between Catholics and Anglicans. 'Our different religions have put a cloud over our marriage,' she wrote. 'All the occasions that should be happy events are dreaded . . . Is it any wonder that in all the mixed marriages I know there has been a weakening of faith all round?'

Máire wrote back, offering to put Despairing Mother in touch with her local Association of Inter-Church Families. 'We have found our faith increased and strengthened through our marriage,' she wrote. 'We have experienced sadness and difficulties at times, particularly when our Communion separates us. We have also experienced great joys.' Inter-faith families, she explained, have 'unique opportunities', especially to bring up children who know and love two churches while appreciating their differences. It was possible to belong to two communities, she thought. Amalgamation, she believed, involved addition, not subtraction.

My own movement communicated family history through kitchen choreography and childhood cartwheels in the garden. It offered a bedrock, which I built on with a push–pull combination of reserve and enthusiasm: I love to dance, but I like to dance small and mostly unnoticed. Ancestry can affect us in ambient ways, and mine is discernible in a desire to step into togetherness on packed dancefloors, to commune through gesture and to understand in my body something of the complex interplay between the new and the established. I know in my bones that movement can be a way of welcoming someone, or of being welcomed.

The Sisters of Mercy nuns who taught alongside the lay staff at St Anne's Catholic primary school shaped us with Scottish sword dancing. One of the more volatile nuns ran the class, which was about right for a dance with warrior roots. I stand in my kitchen, thinking about Scottish dancing at primary school. I wonder: do I still know the basic steps? I feel my way into it and stand up straighter, shoulders back. I put one hand on my waist, the other curved above my head, and I leap and step to either side, then turn so I'd be dancing on the next quarter of the imaginary crossed swords, if I were in the dinner hall at school rather than at home. It strikes me as curious that Irish Catholic nuns taught Scottish sword dancing rather than, say, Irish dancing. Perhaps it was easier for Irish nuns to teach Scottish dancing than to inhabit Irishness in a country in which there was historic discrimination against Irish people.

Dance Your History

We dance our histories directly and indirectly. We also dance them on a species level. Edwin Denby made some intriguing comments on the way other animals move. He noted that birds gather in flocks in the evening, suggesting that both birds and humans enjoy social movement when the work of the day is done. He also wrote about the ways people move on the street, with as much care and detail as he'd apply to a review of the New York City Ballet. He observed that youth in Italian cities lolled differently to Americans (Italians more likely to rest on a central point; Americans tending to shift their weight to the periphery, therefore taking up more space than their body actually occupied). He described Parisians carrying their bodies 'like a large parcel of dishes: sort of low', while in Copenhagen 'the crowd has an easy stride, strong in the waist, light in the feet, with a hint of the sailor's roll'. We move within our cultural framework, and we can also step outside of it. Some Manchester youth in the 1990s adopted the Happy Mondays' rolling swagger. Others walked as if one leg were injured, perhaps by gunshot, in a controlled gangsta limp. We belong to ways of moving that are rooted in location, lineage, self-image and family.

2: NATIONAL DANCE

Anglo-Saxon rave-ups, lost English step dancing,
and a biography of the Electric Slide (b. 1979)

People must have moved to music in the far past. Dawn-to-dusk shifts in the fields or at home would have had a corollary: gaps in the working week, month or season when the community could connect with friends and family and where everyone could release the pressure. A rave-up around the hay bales in mid-summer however many hundreds of years ago isn't that different to a rave-up around the hay bales at any one of the outdoor festivals that punctuated summers in the early decades of the 21st century. A sweatbox in a barn is a sweatbox in a barn whatever the century, air cooling the face when dancers emerge for the trans-centurial version of a quick smoke or not-so-quick kiss. People in this country still dance to the cadence of the season, whether it's at Notting Hill Carnival, a summer wedding disco or a New Year's Eve house party.

The Fuller Brooch allows us a peek into Anglo-Saxon dancing. Believed to have been made in around AD 800, it is a small engraved piece of jewellery held by the British Museum that shows the five senses. According to the official text, the image that depicts hearing shows someone 'running, perhaps answering a call'. Professor Martha Bayless, director of Folklore and Public Culture at the University of Oregon, wrote a paper on the brooch, arguing convincingly and with disarming warmth that the engraving depicts dancing. In getting there, she pulls evidence out of clerical edicts, illustrated manuscripts and fragments of helmets that show that many ancestral country-folk danced regularly, in different locations and in different styles. Dancing was then, as now, an everyday part of life. Her paper describes martial men dancing with swords, and skilful erotic dancers. It depicts lairy late-night round dances, line dances in alehouses and at fairs or festivals, and women dancing in the woods, all girls together.

Everyday dance is about release, but it's also an expression of strength when you don't have much statutory power. Bayless suggests that Anglo-Saxons at the end of the first millennium used their dancing bodies to make a point, even if the point was just to revel in rudeness. After all, the word 'stance' suggests both posture and perspective. She quotes the eighth-century King Edgar, who refers to the widespread condemnation of corrupt clergy – 'soldiers shout about these things, people mutter them, performers sing and dance about them'. King Edgar's observation reminds me of a song from a different context: St Vincent's soca maestro Skinny Fabulous's Carnival classic 'BTW (Behaving the Worst)', which repeatedly exhorts listeners to show their worst behaviour. He's asking for the kind of serrated, high-energy, nose-thumbing, ass-waggling rudeness that would no doubt have fired up any Anglo-Saxon dance and sent shady clerics running for their condemnatory quills.

In her essay Martha Bayless mentions recurring objections 'to what appears to be a longstanding tradition of dancing near churches' and within the churchyard itself. When I think about an Anglo-Saxon church I imagine a small building, maybe a tower, with toothy gravestones covering most of the grass. Surely they didn't dance in a graveyard? I emailed her to clarify. 'By all accounts the churchyard was indeed like a village green,' she replied. 'They didn't have gravestones of our modern type, and it seems as if the graveyard part of the churchyard may have been restricted to one part of it, so the rest would have just been an expanse of grass, perfect for dancing.'

There's no evidence, she told me, that people used the church itself as a dancehall, as I did in my teens in the crypt of St Paul's, just off Deptford High Street, in the late 1980s, or at London jazz gigs in St James the Great, in Lower Clapton, in the late 2010s. Dancing women were singled out for criticism in the distant past; those who danced, vaulted or sang amorous songs outside the church during feasts threatened with excommunication. Pope St Leo IV urged the clergy to forbid women from singing and dancing in the churchyard. Caesarius of Arles was outraged by leaping dances known as *saltātiōnēs*, which were linked to seasonal feasts, and by 'contortions and bawdy songs praising vice performed by soldiers in women's clothes'.

There is something about Englishness in particular that can make questions about dancing slightly embarrassing, as if the subject is filed alongside nudity or personal bathroom habits. It's a nonsense to talk about whole demographics as if they were one amorphous mass, but allow me a moment to make a very general observation: there's a contingent of people who'd describe themselves as English who are slightly embarrassed by dancing. The Anglo-centric awkwardness I'm talking about expresses itself in a number of ways: the need for drink or drugs as a precursor to movement; or a cloak of 'silliness' that allows for more flexibility. It's cultural.

Part of this cultural disconnect may relate to language. Asking someone if they dance contains a suggestion that the question relates to skill, as if enquiring, 'Do you dance?' is the same as asking, 'Are you a good dancer?' This is a constraint of our language, comprised as it is from a mish-mash of German, French, Latin and their Indo-European roots. In Italian, for example, there are two words for dancing: *ballare* and *danzare*. *Ballare* connotes the everyday dancing that you'd do with friends and family. *Danzare* relates to high-quality dancing that requires a lifetime of formal training. In translation, we lost some important nuance.

'Dance' is, of course, a loanword from the French, and it arrived with the Duke of Normandy, aka William the Conqueror. As any GCSE historian knows, the French became the people of nobility, the judiciary and commerce, and their word *danser* absorbed extra connotations of skill, class and courtliness. The Old English words it replaced were active: *tumbian* (to tumble), *hoppian* (to hop) and *sealtian* (to leap or jump), which borrowed from the Latin *saltare*. This last one makes me wonder about the roots of the word 'salutation'. Does it contain a grain of movement, that to greet someone is to move, synchronously? Our language is full of arrivals and departures. Linguist Lorenzo Dow Turner believed that the English word 'shout' relates to movement, and that it derived from the word *saut*, which was used by West African Muslims to describe moving in circles around the central building in Mecca – the Kaaba – during *hajj*.

Cecil Sharp House is a short walk away from Camden Town. It is famous in certain circles as the home of the English Folk Dance and Song Society, which opened in 1930 as a memorial to the folk collector who had died six years previously. Sharp had worked as an organist, composer, conductor and lecturer, and, in his late fifties, he embarked on a crusade to capture and codify what he considered to be 'real' English song and dance, and to build a lineage of his choosing. He cherry-picked rural songs and dances from across the country and from the descendants of English migrants in the Appalachian region of the United States, preserving those that fitted his taste and perspective. This is, of course, what all collectors do: collect according to preference and intention, whether that intention is explicit or not.

Sharp's work was an attempt to bend the national narrative towards an imagined past unpolluted by urban life. Dance can liberate, but it can be – and repeatedly has been – manipulated in the service of a particular view of the past or future. He believed that studying folk song would 'stimulate the growth of the feeling of patriotism'. And so in 1911 he founded the English Folk Dance Society and began running weekly folk-dance classes, with over a thousand people attending. Historian Sharif Gemie writes that Sharp 'dominated the organisation . . . [he] decided what counted as legitimate folk dance and what could be ignored'. What remains of Sharp's work is a version of Englishness told through his collection of 5,000 songs and around 500 folk dances, as well as ongoing debates about the ethics and impact of his work, some of which take place in the spacious archives and meeting rooms in north London that bear his name.

'Stepping On' was a conference that took place in 2019 at Cecil Sharp House, in the wood-panelled Kennedy Hall, which has a sprung dancefloor. The organisers were attempting something new: to bring together invited practitioners, researchers and 'all who are interested in the diversity of traditional dance' to share ideas and information on the rich, interconnected histories of percussive step dancing. Experts shared fascinating work on 'street' clog dance, hornpipe stepping or the use of hand-dancing as a transmission method in Irish dance. Speakers would step away from the lectern to dance-demonstrate a point, and in the evening there was a céilí, where everyone got to show and share their skills in the dance, reel-time.

There was a lot of talk about street dance, although the speakers weren't referring to hip hop. They meant the kind of people-generated, local, improvised step dancing that might get a sailor a ten-shilling fine for drunkenly breaking out moves on Union Street in Plymouth, or northern factory workers clacking their clogs in time to the kling-klang of the machinery. The speakers and audience had a shared understanding of street dance, which differed from mine in terms of the detail but was the same in the sense of dance as an everyday part of community life, in which learned-not-taught movement contains embodied information and expression. Over lunch I pulled out my phone and showed some ladies a video of Chicago footwork dancers King Charles and Pause Eddie demonstrating a few steps from this hyper-fast 160bpm movement style, which evolved from 1990s house music in the city. The dancers were demonstrating moves with names like Erk 'n' Jerk, Ghost and Mop 'n' Glows. It wasn't really a tutorial in any practical sense, because these guys are some of the best practitioners on the planet and they move so fast that you have to double-check the video is not on fast-forward.

'Oooh,' said one of the ladies, leaning in over her buffet sandwiches better to identify the moves. 'That's a Lakeland clog step.'

'Only so many things you can do with your feet,' added her husband, drily.

The community of practitioner-researchers attending the conference were attempting to illuminate the deep past. They have spent years, sometimes decades, trying to catch steps that only existed in the moment. These steps were enacted in bodies that moved according to freedoms and constraints we can only imagine, which perhaps makes this archiving task as slippery as attempting to archive one family's laughter. I recognised the intended generosity: a desperate desire to ensure that precious and hard-won knowledge is passed on, either by writing it down or by demonstrating it so that others can carry the gestural information with them and, in turn, pass it on. I was also reminded of the schisms and irritations that exist in every tight-knit community, whether that's gardeners on an allotment or this niche community of researchers digging into a region's lost footwork. The Q&A sessions elicited disagreement and questions to which the asker clearly knew the answer. There was some snappiness within parts of the audience, which I interpreted – judgementally – as a need to control the narrative and pin things down. The undercurrents were clarified over tea. People were writing their own histories, said an elegant gentleman holding a biscuit. They're wedded to them. People hang on tightly to things they claim as their own.

I learned a lot from these experts in lost steps. There was percussive dancing in every county in England until at least the first part of the twentieth century. Footwork-based dance styles had strong local flavours that were made distinct by the types of shoes people wore – clogs, for example – or the kind of floor that was available. The steps were simple enough for everyone to take part, and contained enough room for complexity so that really good dancers could use them as a bedrock for incredible skill and style. Dances happened everywhere: on raised stages at parish picnics, on farms, in pubs and at home. In Devon they danced on carts; Cornishmen danced on local slate like tap-dancing beatmakers. Religion destroyed Welsh clog dancing, because clerics were anti-pub and were especially against 'mixed' dancing, where men and women might have a chance to put hands around waists. A lady tells me, in the informal hanging out that naturally happens between speakers, that Norfolk steps came in with the herring fishermen.

I imagine a far-future version of this conference, when people peer back into the past to deconstruct raving. I wonder about researchers making sense of the school-disco slow dance or young mods shuffling to The Who, and I wonder what would be visible through the enclosure of time. Something is inevitably lost when you cut a dance out of context, like a person scissored out of a family photograph. The thing that has been cut out is always there, at least partially visible through its absence.

Cecil Sharp and I have something fundamental in common: a shared belief that dancing is valuable, powerful and worth recording. We have very different ideas, though, about what to do with this abundant collective material. I imagine what would happen if I were able to travel back in time to meet him, and quickly come to the conclusion that we would fall out, fast. He looked selectively into the past in order to bolster a version of Englishness that he believed in, in which the true heart of the country was rural and uncorrupted by modernity. Consequently, he ignored songs and dances that evolved in the city, positioning urban moves as predatory. The introduction to his 1909 publication *The Country Dance Book: Part I* reads: 'In the village of today the polka, waltz and quadrille are steadily displacing the old-time country dances and jigs, just as the tawdry ballads and strident street-songs of the towns are no less surely exterminating the folk songs.'

I have versions of Englishness that I believe in too, and which are visible on the dancefloor. I'm talking about dances in community centres; packed warehouses where thousands of young people dance stresses out and resilience in; rollerskaters on public plazas extending movement into new shapes; or kids with a wide movement vocabulary from internet-learned dances who throw forward to a dance-rich adult population. An England where we recognise the cultural riches that state action diverted to this small collection of islands off the coast of mainland Europe – and one in which we accept what this diversion cost. An England where ordinary dancing is valued, and not just because it indicates an understanding of who we are.

———

Tradition is a river, not a glacier. Folk dances aren't something that existed just in the past, ready to be sucked into the present, fully formed and ripe for presentation. They are constantly shifting forms through which we express ourselves in celebration and in protest, in the school playground, at weddings or at work dos. They're always evolving, only 'folk' when they've receded far enough into the past to be reconvened when someone needs a cultural lift or wants to prove a certain political point. Traditional dances grow from ordinary steps, the kind people do at home with friends and family. Rules and regulations are imposed on a movement language in order to teach, perform and judge it. At this point, a dance becomes fixed – until the steps are enlivened by new use. Dance is a generous kind of virus that enters our bodies and changes itself as it changes us. Like a virus, it mutates, better to spread.

This is what happened when 20-year-old Morgan Bullock went viral. The Virginia-based dancer was doing highly skilled Irish dance steps, but she wasn't doing them to old jigs or reels. She was doing them to Houston rapper Megan Thee Stallion. Her re-application of the steps to a new context brought Irish dancing into a hip-hop context – and no doubt gave existing Irish dancers new ideas and new permission regarding what their steps could convey. Culture is always being built and regenerated like this, and it does so away from the realms of financial or political profiteering – although profit-making bodies will inevitably get involved once new culture has emerged. The past is never a solid unit. It is always changing, like a step dancer's percussive taps and kicks, improvised and altered over lifetimes.

So when I talk about folk dance I'm just talking about the dance styles that most people in a certain demographic or interest group know how to do, whether that's waltzing, a basic-geezer two-step, internet-spun dances like the Renegade or gesture-based dances like the YMCA. I'm purposefully steering away from ideas of dance as ritual, not least because Professor Theresa Buckland pointed out back in 2002 that the idea of dance sharing primitive origins with ritual practices 'emerged quite specifically from traditions of European thought during the eighteenth and nineteenth centuries' – particularly what she describes as 'colonialist inequalities' – and that this idea has been 'soundly criticised' by anthropologists of dance and human movement.

I decided to ask a few friends from across the UK a clumsy question, which is clumsy because of a collective lack of fluency in the subject: 'What is the national dance where you live?'

Northern Irish writer Wendy Erskine is the author of *Dance Move*, and her answer involves line dancing inspired by Billy Ray Cyrus's 'Achy Breaky Heart', the Time Warp and the YMCA. 'I remember going to a supermarket and hearing the Macarena,' she said, 'and I noticed how many people were either consciously or unconsciously doing the moves as they were doing their shopping.'

My friend Scott is from Greenock, outside Glasgow, and I've been in his dancing company for a long time, from 1990s techno nights at the Complex in Islington to a local night he runs with friends called the Hither Green Super Social. He mentions jigs, reels and strathspeys. 'Most people don't have a clue which is which and only ever do them at weddings or céilís,' he said, adding that it's complicated because Scottish culture is rooted in a way of life that was decimated during the Highland Clearances, when large numbers of tenants in the Scottish Highlands and Islands were evicted. For 90 per cent of the population, he said, that world is like *Brigadoon* – a memory of a memory of a memory. He adds some more contemporary candidates, including the dances you do to indie pop, northern soul and techno. Another Scottish friend describes the Slosh, which is a simple line-dance staple of middle-aged Glaswegian weddings and hen dos. 'It is usually danced to "Beautiful Sunday" by Daniel Boone,' they said. 'And the men would desert the floor.'

Ffion, who is from west Wales, referenced 'jumping up and down to Stereophonics' "A Thousand Trees"' and the traditional *dawnsio gwerin*, which can be learned at school and through Eisteddfod festivals. I also asked Dave, who grew up in a china-clay-mining village near St Austell, because I knew there's a rich history of Cornish community dance. He cited the Furry Dance, which happens on Flora Day in Helston, where everyone dances in the streets, weaving in and out of their neighbours' houses. 'Then there's the one we know as the Greebo,' he said. 'It's the thumbs-in-the-belt-loops dance people did in the 1980s to Status Quo at local discos. I just searched that to see if that's what it's called anywhere else, and a video came up of my brother leading people in it at a mate's wedding ten years ago.' He sends me the link, and I watch it. There's a drum roll from the live band and someone shouts, terrace style, '*Greeeeeee-bo!*' The women move to one side. Someone stands in front of the Greebo instigator and mimes putting his thumbs in belt loops. They mirror the moves at each other briefly, instructionally. The band strikes up an introduction, and the two men step into full oppositional mode and prepare by moving their hips side to side.

The movement is kind of stiff, but it still looks fun: thumbs in a belt, chest out, pushing each shoulder forward down towards the opposite belt loop, then repeated, in whatever time signature suits the drunken wedding hour. There's cheering from the small crowd watching the men line up. It's a ragged kind of crew, but everyone knows the steps and everyone in the Greebo crew responds to the Greebo call. Someone does the air guitar while hopping with one leg outstretched like a rock guitarist. Another one adds in a tiny suggestion of some bodypopping, or at least the kind of robot mime that would have been popular at a youth-club disco. The Greebo reaches a point of completion, and everyone is happy. I feel happy just watching it through the remove of my laptop.

When I've asked English friends and acquaintances about national dance, they've mostly laughed and shrugged and said something tentative about morris dancing. Ask it differently – 'What are the dances that everyone can do?' – and the answers flow like a river of remembered moments. Answers include internet-learned dances like the Floss, the Milly Rock and the Ney Ney, and the specific moves which are instigated by the opening notes of Kylie doing 'The Locomotion', Beyoncé's 'Single Ladies (Put a Ring on It)' or Cameo's 'Candy'. Others describe mass miming to David Bowie songs in Manchester clubs in the early 1980s, or headbanging, or the conga. Someone offers 'formation dancing to certain jazz-funk tracks known as the Essex Barn Dance', while another offers 'a scally finger-twirl plus swagger, aka dialling the tall telephone', which was commonplace in house and techno clubs.

The description of 'dialling the tall telephone' is a perfect example of the daily gestures that make it into our everyday dances, as dancer Simone Sistarelli explained to me: 'Mimicking the action of bringing a phone to your ear with your thumb and little finger made sense when phones were old-school. When kids now want to mimic talking on the phone they bring their whole palm to their ear.' Dance, he says, is a product of the context. For example, people could only do the moonwalk after the Moon landing. 'When robots did not exist, no one could dance like them.' Collective movement can reflect the present and nod towards the future, even if it's drawing from the past. It's present continuous.

Before we head into the biography of an emerging national dance, let's consider the idea that there is power in stillness, too. The Romans understood this, as Barbara Ehrenreich noted in the aforementioned *Dancing in the Streets*. She quoted the historian Cornelius Nepos: 'We do not need to be told that, by Roman convention, music is unbecoming to a person of prominence, and dancing is thought to be positively vicious.' It is still considered broadly unbecoming for 'persons of prominence' to dance – European ones, at least – unless they're performing a formal dance, as Vladimir Putin did when he waltzed with Austrian Foreign Minister Karin Kneissl at her 2018 wedding.

Prominent, powerful people in the UK are disproportionately white and male, often coming from backgrounds that encompass the holy trinity of home ownership, historic land possession and expensive private education. (I'm purposefully avoiding the phrase 'upper class' because 'upper' requires 'lower', and I don't believe there is such a thing. The old-fashioned phrase 'officer class' will have to do.) I dance like me, but I might have found it harder to dance like me if I'd been a white man of my generation or older, particularly if I'd been embedded in the demographic described above.

Why? There are plenty of examples of white working-class men dancing to ska at mod clubs or performing silky technicalities to northern soul. There are also examples of middle-class people dancing, as with Cecil Sharp's hugely popular folk classes, or dances and balls in the 1950s and 1960s, which were often based around Scottish reels. It's about what music writer and academic Caspar Melville described to me as 'the burden of the powerful'. Elements of the middle classes, he said, wanted to 'exude the authority and "backbone" fitting for an imperial master – "I am in control of my body, my wife, my estate, my colony. I have mastered my body and my base nature."'

Professor Maxine Leeds Craig explores this area in depth in the brilliant *Sorry, I Don't Dance: Why Men Refuse to Move*. It focuses on the US, although the European roots of many North Americans expand the relevance. Her book establishes that in 1914 it was completely normal for young white men to dance, and to do so confidently, but that by the sixties and seventies 'the truism that white men can't dance became firmly established'. She describes the way that a disturbing idea of 'natural awkwardness' emerged, and goes on to nail a powerful thought: 'White middle-class men are rarely reduced to their bodies and the price many of them pay for that privilege is dancefloor awkwardness.' I wonder if certain men and women in Britain, especially those who come from a demographic which once controlled many millions of bodies across the world, absorbed the idea that moving freely presents a risk to status and social standing. Stature through this lens sounds a lot like 'statue'.

Dance alone can't redistribute power but, as Craig suggests, deciding to dance can be powerful individually and collectively, chipping away at the idea that only women, people of colour of all genders and feminised men can move to music. Hesitant English dancers: finding your feet can be an act of solidarity.

I wonder, what is 'English' anyway? The root of the word nods to the Germanic tribes of Angles, although it was Saxons and Jutes who also arrived to settle on these islands. This country is Angle-ish, which suggests a parallel universe in which it's alternatively Saxonish or Juteish. The English are the ancestors of Anglo-Normans from the time of the French invasion, of Romans who stayed, and of African–Roman legions stationed in the north. DNA sequencing of people buried in the east of England in the seventh century showed that three-quarters of their ancestry came from northern Europe, specifically Germany, Denmark and the Netherlands. We have been seen by visitors from afar, including the Bengali Muslim cleric and diplomat Mirza Sheikh I'tesamuddin, who arrived in 1765 with his servant Muhammad Muqim. He wrote *Shigurf-nama-i-Wilayat* about his experiences. The title translates as *The Wonders of Vilayet* – 'Vilayet' being an Urdu word for a foreign land – and in it he noted that English dancers were beautiful. We collectively dance to the tune of these broad diasporic realities. Perhaps there's another parallel universe in which we're Vilayettish, too. We dance to the reality of our cross-cultural stories.

Like many kids, I made up dances with my friends. We did this in preparation for youth-club or school discos and often based them on what we'd seen other people do on TV or in the school playground. My friend Nicky and I created our own very basic choreography to Colonel Abrams's proto-house record and top-five UK hit 'Trapped', which was released in 1985. We stood side by side and stepped our right foot forward, bringing it back home on the beat, then sending it out to the right, repeating the sequence to the left and to the back, before switching sides, then swivelling to the right and beginning again. It was a very basic formation dance.

Formation dances appear all over the world, often using a series of steps known within the dance world as a grapevine. The term refers to a series of steps where the dancer walks one way or another, crossing one leg in front of or behind the other, often based around 'four walls', so that the dancers begin each new phrase – or section – of the dance facing in a new direction. Grapevine dances include the Israeli Mayim Mayim, which is also danced by schoolchildren in Japan, and the Irish Walls of Limerick, with tendrils of grapevine visible in the foxtrot, polka and the Hustle. Also in this category is the Cha Cha Slide, which was built by DJ Caspar in 1998 for his nephew's fitness class in Hyde Park, in Chicago's South Side. It comes with instructional lyrics and is truly simple and, therefore, extremely popular. More complex is the Electric Slide, which is a group formation dance based on grapevine steps. It allows for a range of skill levels, from relatively simple – once you've mastered the pesky foot-slide hop-turn – to complex, individual and deeply communicative.

The Slide is familiar to many families across what sociologist and Fellow of the Royal Society of Literature Paul Gilroy referred to as the 'Black Atlantic', a term that describes shared African-diasporic culture that is transnational: African, Caribbean, British and American. The Electric Slide has become increasingly common outside of Black Atlantic families. I've seen it used on a TV show about two Irish sisters living in London; it is taught during PE at a primary school near me; and I joined in with a group of teachers and support staff aged 23 to 60 at my friend Maria's workplace leaving party. One explanation for the spread can be found in the weddings and family gatherings suggested in 2011's UK census data, in which nearly one in ten of the 63 million people in England, Northern Ireland, Scotland and Wales were living as part of a couple in an 'inter-ethnic' relationship. Some Electric Slides require a high level of skill from participants, but weddings can be safe places to join in and be shown the ropes in a friendly and non-judgemental way. Just remember that standing at the back won't save you, because the back will inevitably become the front, and beginners might want to find themselves within the body of the dance. In the UK, it is also known as the 'Candy Dance', because it is generally instigated when the opening bars of Cameo's low-slung, Prince-inspired 1986 mega-hit 'Candy' is played at a social function.

It began life as the dance to a different song. 'Electric Boogie' was originally released as a DJ promo in 1976 by Neville 'Bunny Wailer' Livingston, and was inspired by Londoner Eddy Grant's paean to Brixton, 'Electric Avenue'. In 1982 it was re-released, with reggae royalty Marcia Griffiths on vocals, and went to number one in Jamaica. At this point, the song and the Electric Slide dance had become entwined, but news of this coupling had not yet reached Jamaica. Things reached critical mass in 1989, and when Marcia Griffiths played Washington DC that year, everyone got up and danced the Slide, and she had to learn it on the spot. Naturally, this required another re-release, and the dance was committed to celluloid on the beautifully colour-saturated choreographed promo clip.

The hot new dance showcased in the Marcia Griffiths video appeared because it had become popular on the dancefloors of the United States, initially in New York. Enter Portuguese–American dancer and choreographer Richard 'Ric' Silver. In June 1976 he choreographed a four-wall, grapevine-based dance using a promo copy of the original Bunny Livingston tune, and later filed a successful copyright claim on the choreography.

It's important to pause a moment here and ensure we're not singularising collective events, because there is rarely a true Year Zero when it comes to a dance. Sometimes a dance style can be traced to an individual: for example, Sex Pistols bassist Sid Vicious sprang up and down like a boingy jack-in-a-box and inspired the punk pogo. But movement is never truly new, and there are shades of the punk pogo in any kind of jumping dance. Sid Vicious didn't invent the jumping dance that became the punk pogo; he just presented that kind of movement in a context where it could take on new life. While there's a trademarked version which places Ric Silver at the centre of the Electric Slide story, he didn't invent the human movement of stepping to one side and then to the other, and then turning so you can start again in another direction.

I found an interview with Silver through his website, which has rotating text and dancing smiley emojis. He tells the story of the Electric Slide to presenters on the YouTube channel SEC-TV. In late 1975 or 1976 he was working at a New York disco, where the DJ gave him a one-sided promotional copy of 'Electric Boogie'. Later in '76 he got a job at a new club run by Manhattan restaurant chain Beefsteak Charlie's, tasked with throwing parties and ensuring that only top-quality dancers got through the door. Six months later, management felt the clientele was 'slipping' and asked him to create a dance to premiere at the reset party. He went home, pulled the one-sided white label off the shelf and went to work.

His choreography went down well, and every night he'd teach the dance so that new people could join in, and so that experienced people could add more style and flow. It slid into their bodies and spread out through the club doors and into the city. Three months down the line, with queues around the block, the owners decided to drop the dancer-only entrance requirement – a decision Silver is clearly still annoyed about: 'I told them this was a bad idea, but they did it anyway. Once they opened the doors to the general public, I had to dumb down the dance. There were double pirouettes, double tours in the air, triple tours in the air. I had to cut all of that out and go back to the basic first and second section of the dance. Now they weren't for dancers, they were just Average Joes coming off the street.' The choreography had taken on a life of its own, which also involved dropping four additional steps Silver had added in. He wanted a 22-step dance because his birthday fell on the 22nd. The people decided otherwise and created a desire line through the dance, trimming the fat and making it fit.

The Slide received an international boost after it was used in award-winning romantic comedy *The Best Man* in 1999, which was written and directed by Malcolm D. Lee and produced by his cousin Spike. The final scene takes place on the dancefloor, at a wedding party. The characters have been through all kinds of dramas – the wedding nearly didn't happen – but now all is resolved. Everyone's beginning to relax as they dance, mostly in couples, while tiny bridesmaids show off their moves. The opening notes of the song roll out, apparently from the wedding band onstage, and the camera zooms in on the character Uncle Skeeter, played by Jim Moody, who also appeared in the film version of *Fame*. He announces his intention – 'I'm gonna get it going on, y'all . . .' – and takes four steps to the right, then four to the left. The characters closest join in, and by the end of the back step everyone's got the message and they dip collectively, before taking the little hop-step that turns the dancefloor congregation around 90 degrees, ready to start again.

Something in the boundary between actor and person fell apart as I watched the scene. The actors are smiling because they're dancing, no longer the 'uptight college friend' or 'long-suffering girlfriend' or 'womaniser who finds the errors of his ways through prayer'. They're people engaged in the joyful feeling of moving together and seeing their neighbour add a little flourish or a gesture-as-joke. I feel like I'm watching a home video from the wrap party as much as watching the final scene of a polished movie. It looks so enjoyable that I get up and join in, by myself, on my own wooden floor – although

I quickly realise that I need some assistance from one of the many YouTube tutorials on the subject. All dancing is learned, just like any other social skill.

Director Malcolm Lee remembers people 'Electric Sliding to all kinds of music' when he was at college in the late 1980s and early 1990s, including a variation inspired by Black fraternities and sororities. 'I definitely couldn't do that variation on the dance,' he tells me. 'It took me a while to learn how to do the Electric Side, really.' Cameo's 'Candy' had already been used in the film to introduce Regina Hall's character, who is a student paying her way through college by exotic dancing, and Malcolm wanted to reprise it at the end of the film despite cast members and crew querying his musical selection. 'I'll tell you the truth,' he says. 'It almost didn't happen. We were over time that day, and I was getting pressure from the line producer – we have to cut that scene. My director of photography was like, "No, no, no. We'll put a camera here, a camera over there, and we'll cover it, we'll just have fun."'

There was another issue that nearly scuppered things, when a union rep said that if the crew made everyone dance, they'd have to be paid as principals. The director got around the issue by making it optional: if you wanted to dance the Electric Slide, you could; if you didn't want to, you didn't have to. Of course, most people wanted to. He recalls the actors bringing their steps to the scene – Sanaa Lathan taking off her shoes; classically trained Alvin Ailey dancer Melissa De Sousa freestyling towards the end – 'having their own thing, within the dance'.

'Twenty years later, every cook-out, wedding, what have you – when "Candy" comes on, people do the Electric Slide,' Lee says. 'I was at a US track and field event in Ohio, honouring the 1968 Olympic team. It was a bunch of people – old, young, Black, white. They played "Candy", and everybody did the Electric Slide. I was pretty amazed.'

The bride and groom in *The Best Man* had got married and so had these two elements: the Electric Slide and Cameo's hit record. For Millennials in the UK, it's as if they've always been together. 'That was the first time. My recollection of college days is that I don't remember us dancing to "Candy" for the Electric Slide,' says Malcolm, pausing. 'I think we started something.'

The Electric Slide moved towards the mainstream through MTV, cinema, the internet and our increasingly diverse relationships and wedding ceremonies. In the future it could well be as ordinary as basic rave dancing is to people who grew up in the 1990s, or as widely known as the 'Gangnam Style' dance is to anyone who was under 35 when it came out. And, of course, it might just slip away again into a back room where only those who were young at the time know how to do it, like Baby Boomers doing a joyfully rusty Frug.

———

Parliament Square, the week after George Floyd was murdered by a Minneapolis police officer. It's impossible to social-distance in this sea of young Londoners wearing masks and holding sharpie'd banners. There's a powerful combination of undercurrents going on, the twin pandemics of Covid-19 and white violence feeding into each other. This response, a protest, is happening right in the middle of this shifting double helix. There's music, banners, families, teenagers, a few middle-aged people like myself and the two friends I'm with. We are crammed sardine-style and funnelled through the tight exit out towards Westminster Bridge. Something happens nearby which we can't see but which I watch later online. Someone takes four steps to the right, then to the left. The signal is picked up, immediately, and the people around the initiator join in. A group of protesters are doing the Electric Slide outside 10 Downing Street, articulating a political stance. This is movement in the sense of gesture in action, and in the other sense too: a movement. Movement is communication, dance is language, and both exist so that people – the folk – can say what needs to be said, in the now.

3: DOWN WITH JAZZ

Priests and politicians try to control the foxtrot
and the shimmy in 1930s Ireland

Stories of dancefloors are surrounded by stories of people trying to shut them down. The unwanted arrival of controlling
forces hovers in the background and can sometimes erupt
into the clattering of batons or the invisible brutality of forced
venue closure. Not all dancing is considered dangerous, of
course. In December 1989 then Scotland secretary Malcolm
Rifkind wrote to the home secretary, cautioning that the anti-
rave Criminal Justice Act might accidentally affect 'entirely
innocent events such as a barn dance'.

In between pandemic lockdowns I went to an exhibition about electronic dance music at the Design Museum in
London, which concluded with a section on the state regulation of dancefloors. Material relating to the Criminal Justice
Act, which criminalised groups of more than 20 people moving
to repetitive beats in unlicensed premises, had been placed
in vitrines for us to peer at. There was a requisitioned police
riot shield redesigned into an acid-house smiley by Jimmy
Cauty from the KLF. Another panel described violent raids
on Bassiani and Café Gallery, two queer-friendly techno clubs
in the Eastern European country of Georgia, and showed the
public protests that followed. There was a 'No Dancing' poster
from Tokyo, which laboured under the Businesses Affecting
Public Morals Regulation Act between 1948 and 2015. New

York had it too, with the Cabaret Law, designed to control jazz clubs and speakeasies in the 1920s and used against whichever demographic group was troubling the authorities. That law was finally repealed on Halloween 2017, courtesy of tireless work by the Dance Liberation Network.

When Jeremy Deller's 2019 film *Everybody in the Place: An Incomplete History of Britain* was broadcast on the BBC, a friend messaged me. The programme made a link between ravers dancing in derelict industrial spaces and political struggle – in particular, the Miners' Strike – and my friend was irritated. It wasn't political, he said, that's not what we thought we were doing. He may be right, but the state machine responded to the two entities – miners and ravers – in the same way: with legislation (changes to welfare benefits in 1984 which affected the dependents of striking miners and the later Criminal Justice Act respectively) and, on occasion, with violence. The state thought it was political, in the sense of requiring a political response, even if we didn't.

Vested interests have long attempted to control dancing bodies. At the time of writing, it is illegal to dance in public in Kuwait (although slow and gentle clapping is allowed at concerts); the authorities in Iran impose strong restrictions on dancing, particularly for women, with imprisonment and lashes for those who disobey; and dance was being explicitly quashed in Saudi Arabia. A woman was charged with violating public morality by 'shuffling' in her abaya and niqab at a concert in Riyadh in 2019. There is no doubt some people will continue to dance, secretly and away from view, even in the most oppressive situations, because moving to music is normal – and, in some cases, necessary.

The Irish experience, which culminated in a pre-war equivalent of the later Criminal Justice Act, gives us an unusually illuminating perspective on ordinary dancing – and it relates to my family experience because it fits with the time frame of my grandmother's departure from her home country. But first, some background. The history of Britain's occupation of Ireland lies beyond the scope of this book, and so instead I will offer some glimpses into the past. Writer, musician and magazine editor Breandán Breathnach offered examples of colonial-era Irish dance in his slim 1971 volume *Folk Music and Dances of Ireland*. He used accounts from English visitors during centuries of occupation to illuminate 'rude' dancing at wakes; *báire* sessions where couples danced to win a cake; pantomime dances (the Droghedy, described as 'very objectionable'); Cossack-style *damhsa na gCoinín*, which translates as 'rabbit dance' or 'dance of the rabbits'; and dances performed by butchers. Colonial travellers also noted a game called the Clap Dance. I'm immediately reminded of two things: playground games in which people make up a dance using body percussion; and South African gumboot dancing, which developed in the late 1800s, when miners used the sides of their rubber wellies to communicate because they were forbidden to speak. By the 1930s the latter had become formalised into a dance language, and in the early 2010s I saw children performing it in Langa, Cape Town.

Dance communicated underground messages in Ireland during the long haul of occupation. It's too vast a subject to discuss in detail, but it is important to briefly explain a series of government decrees that culminated in 1695's Penal Laws. Irish Catholics (the majority of the population) and Protestant dissidents who refused to convert to the Church of Ireland were disenfranchised. Laws made many aspects of community and family life illegal, including the Gaelic language and Irish music. Catholic religious services were banned, but there were, of course, secret gatherings, because prohibition is never entirely effective, especially when it comes to matters of faith. Dance historian Mark Knowles wrote in *Tap Roots: The Early History of Tap Dancing* that a child would sometimes wait outside Mass, ready to indicate imminent danger by tapping out certain rhythms with their feet.

Until the start of the 1900s, people living in Western Europe and North America mostly danced in homes, whether that meant a small cottage or a residence large enough to contain a ballroom. In Britain, historian James Nott described dancehalls starting as 'impromptu get-togethers in public houses, and other public places, where singing, pianos and other simple instruments would provide the music for working-class people to dance to'. Some early examples were small community-built structures, while others were spacious and glamorous. All types of dancehall proliferated on both sides of the Atlantic in the years leading up to World War I, and again after World War II.

In most countries these new, public dance venues sprang up in cities and large towns. This was not the case in Ireland, where dancehalls proliferated in rural towns and villages. Dr Méabh Ní Fhuartháin is the Head of Irish Studies at the Centre for Irish Studies at the University of Galway and is an expert in post-independence dancehalls. One example from her research shows the ubiquity: in 1946 the village of Ballindine had a registered population of just 231 people, and it had two busy dancehalls. 'The public social dance spaces that developed in Ireland in the first half of the 20th century reflected the centrality of dance to the country's society,' she wrote in 'Parish Halls, Dance Halls and Marquees: Developing and Regulating Social Dance Spaces, 1900–60'. I learn from her work that Irish dancers would step out in a range of venues, which included privately owned commercial dancehalls – themselves ranging from barely fixed-up barns to New York-style spaces like the Atlantic Dance Hall in Tramore, County Waterford, and church halls. Motivated individuals ran touring pop-up dance marquees, while others temporarily transformed primary schools, libraries and army huts into dancefloors. I sent Dr Ní Fhuartháin an email with a handful of questions about dancehalls, and later that day she replied. 'Spaces are really important in all this,' she wrote, 'but that cannot be decoupled from the "danger" of the dancing body and its perceived associations with emotionality, sexuality and hyper-feeling (not to say a potential for lack of control).'

By the mid-1930s two important things happened. One was the arrival of the Public Dance Halls Act, which put dancehalls under strict legal controls. It followed a sustained moral panic about jazz dancing that had spread across multiple Eurocentric countries in the early decades of the 20th century. The other was important only to me, in that my grandmother Máire left Ireland. The family story goes that Máire's mother decided that her teenage daughter would be a nurse, bought her a one-way ticket to Birmingham and told her to attend an interview at the General Hospital – all of which was announced with immediate effect. Máire left with an overnight bag, and the matron put her up for the night because she didn't have anywhere else to stay. She completed her training and worked as a nurse throughout World War II and in the earliest days of the NHS.

She was one of just under 10,000 women who emigrated around this time. Consequently, I'm one of an estimated six million people in the UK with an Irish-born grandparent, something which came in useful when Brexit happened. Now I'm Irish too, officially at least, with an Irish passport and a new Irish name given to me by my young nieces at the unofficial backyard citizenship celebration that I hosted after my paperwork arrived. My nieces couldn't decide between their two favourites, so I came away with an unusually hyphenated name: Aoife-Aíne. It was a nice choice. Aíne relates to the pre-Christian sun goddess on whose celebration day, it was said, people could dance themselves into different forms.

The legislators behind the Public Dance Halls Act of 1935 didn't want young Irish people dancing themselves into different forms, especially those suggested by swing jazz. The law responded to the way in which unlicensed and commercialised dances were being blamed for shameful illegitimate births and the loss of Irish futures through the unpatriotic emigration of young women like Máire, whom the media cast as having been unthinkingly beguiled by foreign dancehalls. The Act aimed to control dancing spaces – and the women within them – by introducing a licensing system and a tax on tickets, and it came into being under the deeply conservative Taoiseach, Éamon de Valera. He had taken part in the 1916 Rising and remained a dominant power in Irish politics, first with Sinn Féin, then Fianna Fáil, before serving as president until 1973.

There were some reasonable concerns behind the legislation. Worries about dancehall ventilation existed in the context of tuberculosis, which was the third leading cause of death among children in Ireland. John Porter's research for an article for *Irish Historical Studies* sent him digging through files in the Irish national archive. He came across reports sent by the Garda Síochána – the police – to the Department of Justice. An officer in County Waterford reported that six out of seven dancehalls were not suitable or safe, including the Royal Dancehall, which had only one exit. Another didn't have enough exits and no men's toilet. Two others were located over garages in which petrol and other combustibles were stored. In fact, many pre-Act dances took place in old schoolhouses or timber structures with tin roofs and were often lit by large paraffin lamps suspended from the ceilings. Paraffin was sometimes smeared on the floor, to offer dancers better slip and slide as they moved around the room. Controls aren't always negative: the horrific fire at Dublin's Stardust Club in 1981, in which 48 people died and 214 people were injured, underlines the importance of such concerns at every moment in time.

Back in the 1930s widespread fears about dancing and dancehalls escalated beyond legitimate matters of public health. If it was just about ventilation and fire safety, why were crossroads dances in the firing line? They took place outside, on wooden platforms, but were attacked by empowered clergy, who reportedly set them on fire and drove their motorcars backwards and forwards over the timber dancefloors. The Act effectively allowed socially powerful individuals – judges, priests, easily irritated neighbours, the police – to clamp down on anything they didn't like, with varying degrees of success. 'The Act passed on the back of a moral panic about jazz undermining traditional culture,' wrote Simon Price in *The Rabble* newspaper, 'but implementation undermined that very culture as it was used to stop country dances too.'

The panic and negativity was focused on new and imported music, including the foxtrot and dances like the shimmy, which was a partnered two-step dance with a close embrace and lots of body wiggle. The anti-jazz contingent, which included priests, press, politicians and the Gaelic League, which promoted Irish language and culture, was remarkably unclear about what it was railing against. Dr Eileen Hogan dug around for a contemporary definition and found one in records of the Dáil, the Irish parliament, for her paper *Earthy, Sensual and Devilish: Sex, 'Race' and Jazz in Post-Independence Ireland*.

In 1936 parliamentarian, or Teachta Dála, Mr Kehoe spoke in the Dáil and described jazz-dance disparagingly as 'a cross between a waltz and all-in wrestling'. Hogan also found a useful letter to the editor of weekly newspaper *The Anglo-Celt* in 1926. The writer referred to 'scandalous conduct' in the dancehalls, which were, they believed, a disgrace to any Catholic country. 'There appears to be no control whatsoever. I was an eye-witness to these dances, namely the jazz, foxtrot, the shimmy dance and the "Blues" and my opinion is that not alone are they are immoral and vulgar, they are disgusting.' Hogan's interest in the dancefloor, and particularly women's experiences on them, spans the centuries: in 2014 she co-curated an exhibition about influential Cork nightclub Sir Henry's (1978–2003), and recently led a conference on the 'Fag-Smoking, Jazz-Dancing, Lipsticking Flappers in Post-Independence Ireland'.

One of the biggest musical entities inducing the foxtrot and the shimmy was Phil Murtagh's band. They were based in Dublin but had a residency at the Atlantic in Tramore, County Waterford (as well as a summer stretch at the first and only Butlin's holiday camp in Ireland, in Mosney, County Meath). They were renowned as one of the best in the country, and in 1941 they played until 3 a.m. at the Atlantic with Miss Peggy Dell, a jazz singer and pianist famed as the first woman in Ireland with her own dance band. They were 'tip top', according to the *Waterford News and Star.* The band featured saxophone, trumpet and drums, and played 'jazz in all its moods', from Jimmy Dorsey's 'The Breeze and I' to Count Basie's 'piping hot' 'Doggin' Around' and Cole Porter's 'Begin the Beguine'. 'Perhaps their best number is a splendid arrangement of [big band songwriter] Stephen Foster's melodies, brilliantly played . . . they are also heard effectively in a medley of popular foxtrots . . . Miss Dell cannot escape without singing "Mush Mush".' The youth of Waterford, like youth across the country, were dancing the times and dancing their story, like young people will always dance the times and will always sketch out a new story with their feet. They were perhaps also dancing their futures, making their mark on the state through movement.

A catch-all conflation of disparate newness had become concentrated in the word 'jazz', and the dancing had become merged with the music, all of which was described in almost entirely negative and frequently racist terms. Dancing spaces were regularly described as evil, anti-national and pagan, although the latter term was also used to describe anything foreign or English, which was fair enough after hundreds of years of living under a colonial oppressor. In November 1929 the tradition-focused Gaelic League issued a jazz ban and wrote to all branches warning them as to their conduct with regard to attending or promoting jazz. Known as Rule 29, clubs were forbidden to host 'non-Irish dancing'.

Shocking and extreme statements were widespread in 1930s Ireland when it came to jazz. There is voluminous evidence of Irish priests proclaiming from the pulpit and of moral campaigners kicking off in the constrained rectangle of a newspaper leader, although you could easily take almost anything from the following examples and find a similar version offered by a bishop in Chicago or a magistrate in London. This was a transnational phenomenon, which played out in particular ways in Ireland. It's worth remembering that making sense of the controls placed around dancers by listening simply to people whose job it was to have extremely conservative opinions is like understanding acid house by reading the *Sun* in the summer of 1988, apart from – or perhaps especially – when the newspaper was selling acid house t-shirts for £5.50 each in October of that year.

As early as October 1925 the bishops of Ireland released a statement titled 'Evils of Dancing', which described 'imported dances of an evil kind' as causing 'the destruction of virtue in every part of Ireland', and instructed parishioners to condemn them. The statement was to be read at the principal Mass on the first Sunday of each quarter of the ecclesiastical year, and priests would confer with responsible parishioners with regard to 'the means by which it will be fully carried into effect'.

A County Leitrim priest named Father Conefrey energised an estimated 3,000 people to march in Mohill in January 1934.

They famously carried banners which read 'Down with Jazz' and 'Out with Paganism' (which reminds me of some graffiti I once saw on a Cornish hay bale that contained the phrase 'Witches Out'). Father Conefrey and his followers marched with five pipe bands, before gathering for speeches at which they were no doubt very careful not to move their bodies in non-Irish ways.

Dancing – and specifically women dancing in new ways to contemporary music – soaked up the blame for the social, cultural and economic difficulties faced in the 1930s. A shorthand explanation of Ireland's hardships might include centuries of occupation, the catastrophe of famine and the aftermath of the Irish War of Independence, also known as the Anglo-Irish War (1919–21). The civil war which followed between June 1922 and May 1923 carved the pain deeper as friends and family split around the Anglo-Irish treaty, which established a Free State of Ireland within the British Empire, and which allowed the six counties of Northern Ireland to remain British. Partition followed. Dancehalls responded to the austerity, grief and division that spilled out in the twelve years between the war ending and the Public Dance Halls Act being passed. Youthful dancing became a container into which all kinds of Irish troubles were stuffed, regardless of their true source.

It was perhaps useful to dance the pain away. It may also have been useful for the state to refract public anger through the doors of the dancehalls. It's worth adding that the only Irish citizen ever to be deported from the country was the socialist Jimmy Gralton, who built a dancehall that doubled up as a community education centre, which also ran successful campaigns to overturn evictions. He was himself permanently evicted from Ireland in 1933, later becoming the subject of both Ken Loach's 2014 film *Jimmy's Hall* and a state apology which recognised that he had been illegally deported from his own country for his political beliefs. His commitment to community dancing amplified both his message and the degree to which he was considered dangerous by the authorities. There is now a monument to this dancehall hero in his home town of Effrinagh, County Leitrim.

Enter the legislators, who set up a commission, membership of which was kept secret, to examine apparent moral degeneracy in the still-new Irish state. The Carrigan Committee was tasked with reviewing amendments to the Criminal Law Act and laws around what was then called juvenile prostitution. They came to the conclusion that unlicensed dances were 'orgies of dissipation' leading to 'pernicious consequences' and required separate legislation, which in turn led to the Public Dance Halls Act. Their findings were considered over the top. 'This section of the report wanders some way from the terms of reference,' wrote a civil servant, with an eye roll that is visible through the decades. 'The committee might equally have concerned itself with housing, education, unemployment or any other matter which might have had an indirect effect on prostitution and immorality. Their suggestions amount almost to a suppression of public dancing.' The report was also embarrassing to the government because it painted a picture of an Ireland which had lost its moral compass when it came to youth and chastity. The report was suppressed and the Act was passed without being debated in the Dáil, and was still in place at the time of writing. Documents relating to it weren't released to the national archive until 2000.

By 1999, 'dance music' meant electronic music, and *Muzik* covered the scene extensively. In June that year it ran a cover story titled 'The Country Where Clubs Are Illegal'. The article doubled up as a campaign to change Ireland's licensing laws, which stemmed from the Public Dance Halls Act, with readers encouraged to cut out a coupon stating support for reform and post it to the relevant minister. The magazine claimed that Ireland's club laws were 'a disgrace', describing the cost and stress of maintaining the complex web of restrictive licences that clubs required in order to operate. 'The whole country breaks the law,' said John Reynolds, who owned internationally respected club the Pod, and who was the nephew of former premier Albert Reynolds, who himself ran a network of dancehalls across the country in the 1960s. 'It's the party capital of Europe but we have these laws which are almost 100 years old.' The laws remained, despite the best efforts of *Muzik* readers, and two decades later another campaigning group – Give Us The Night – was making another concerted attempt to undo what the Carrigan Committee started.

Even at the time, one member of the Carrigan Committee warned against excessive measures. 'Legislation should avoid the kind of New England Puritanism which forbids dancing of any kind,' said Father Gildea, in one of his submissions to the report, although he did also describe dancehalls as a 'crying evil', stating that the five dancehalls in his parish of Charlestown (population: 670 families) held 'dances of a disgusting character'.

The legislation required almost anyone running a dancehall to apply to licensing hearings, at which priests or other people of supposedly good character were invited to object.

Justices were required to consider the suitability of the applicant and the location. Closing times were also up for grabs. Unsurprisingly, many priests wanted the congregation in bed early. The *Irish Times* has two examples from the same edition in May 1935. 'Dance halls should be closed at 11 p.m. at latest – otherwise they [are] a menace to morality,' said Bishop Patrick McKenna of Clogher, outside a confirmation in Bundoran, County Donegal. Elsewhere in the day's news, there was a report of priests bringing noise complaints to a licence hearing at Carrick-on-Shannon. 'At 3 or 4 in the day people began punching and kicking the walls of the hall and beating a drum, and it was like bedlam,' they said. The priests might not have approved of the noise, but the dancers were clearly approving of the music – banging the walls remains a timeless response, observed on intense dancefloors, as we'll see later.

None of this stopped a mammoth hall-building exercise by local clergy, in an attempt to move the dancers from unsuitable locations into new parochial halls where there might be supervision; although whether or not supervision actually occurred remains unclear. Ironically, dances then became necessary in order to meet the construction and maintenance costs of these halls – and in some cases, according to Dr Méabh Ní Fhuartháin, to 'defray the running costs of the parish'. Black-and-white footage in the RTÉ documentary *Down with Jazz* shows a priest collecting cash at the door of a dance. He holds up a note and kisses it.

My grandmother was from Dungarvan, a small portside town in County Waterford, but her Irish-dwelling relatives – my mum's cousins – live just outside Nenagh, in County

Tipperary. In the mid-1930s the local paper, the *Nenagh Guardian*, regularly reported on anti-dancehall declamations and judgements. In October 1935 it relayed information from the new licensing session at the Roscrea District Court, where some licences were granted and others were batted away. One applicant, the Dromakeenan Fianna Fáil Club, applied for a dance licence for Sundays and holidays, and a weekly practice dance that would be attended only by locals and finish by 10 p.m. The programme was self-consciously Gaelic, consisting of céilí dances, with 'no English dance' permitted. Their solicitor's argument stated explicitly what many people believed: 'The Act was not against Irish dancing at all,' he said in court. 'It was directed against jazz. If there were no jazz the Act might not have been passed.' The concept of 'foreign' dancing conveniently forgot that Irish jigs and sets had absorbed movement material from across the world, including French quadrilles.

Underneath the dancefloor lay deep and complex histories that had caused pain and trauma to generations of families. Every family would have their own. Máire told me that her father's farm in Kerry had been 'taken by the British', and that he stayed – or was left – in Ireland when all of his brothers and sisters emigrated to America. She also remembered him 'nearly' being shot by the IRA, but not being shot because he was pushing her in a pram. Her father, John, was a member of the Royal Irish Constabulary, who were the face of colonial rule in Ireland. This made him a target for the IRA, who escalated their campaign against the force during the War of Independence by attacking barracks and ambushing patrols. Police and their families were shunned. John left in the summer of 1920, along with over a thousand of his colleagues. Many of them were replaced by unemployed British soldiers known as the Black and Tans, who brought with them additional levels of violence and brutality.

My grandmother grew up and left. She stepped into a new life in England as the dances around her were being squashed. Her teenage peers who stayed weren't going to give up their new freedoms easily. The volume of dancers kept promoters busy regardless of the Act. Some dances took place in golf and tennis clubs and in volunteer halls that didn't require a licence, and were often described as short dances or practice classes to get round regulations. Five years after the Act passed, surrealist author Flann O'Brien wrote about dancehalls in the literary magazine *The Bell*, claiming that there were 1,200 licensed halls and estimating, in journo-maths style, that 10,000 dances were being held a year. This meant, he said, that a foxtrot was in progress 'in some corner of Erin's isle throughout the whole of every day and night'.

The Irish authorities – and authorities worldwide – surfed the anti-jazz wave while staking out cultural territory through so-called traditional dance. O'Brien had the measure of the contradictions, which saw dancing as both the ruin of the newly independent state and its saviour: 'They believe that Satan with all his guile is baffled by a four-hand reel and cannot make head or tail of "The Rakes of Mallow",' he wrote. His essay provides a pen portrait of the everyday dancers in Ireland at this time. Dress dances were 'run by those of the white collar and the white soft hand' and were 'not very interesting', with Irish dancing getting similarly brusque treatment. The real thing, he wrote, was the cheap dance.

His description will resonate with anyone who found themselves in a smoky, strobe-lit basement or ram-jam warehouse in Glasgow, Liverpool or Bristol at some point before the end of the 2000s – or later, if you were lucky. 'No cheap dance can be said to have succeeded if the door of the hall can be readily opened from without after the first half-hour,' he wrote. 'When you do enter, you find yourself in air of the kind that blurts out on you from an oven when you open it . . . Whether standing or dancing, the patrons are all *i bhfastodh* ('in a clinch') on each other like cows in a cattle truck, exuding sweat in rivers and enjoying themselves immensely. Nobody is self-conscious about sweat. It rises profusely in invisible vapour from all and sundry and there is no guarantee that each cloud will condense on its true owner.'

Dance is an absorbent medium, shifting and expanding in response to what's in the cultural ether, whether that's Flann O'Brien's cheap dance or a diasporic céilí. Migration is movement in the most literal sense. New arrivals affect how established communities move to music, but migration also affects the diaspora, with the two elements engaged in a complex partner-dance. I emailed Dr Méabh Ní Fhuartháin again to ask about her observation that moving to similar music on different dancefloors created connection and a feeling of transnational togetherness between those who left and those who stayed. 'It let them connect with their loves ones' perceived lives,' she replied. 'Whether that was emigrants' lived experience or not, and indeed more generally the lives imagined as lived in cosmopolitan spaces. Images of those spaces were disseminated through popular culture – film, for example – layering those remote places onto the lived experience of those dancing in Ireland.' Dancing became a portal which allowed imagined access to dispersed family and friends, everyone moving to similar music on similar wooden floors, whether they were in Borrisokane or Bridgeport, Chicago.

The Gaelic League in London used dance to improve the reputation of their countryfolk, as if highly disciplined and respectable dancing would cancel out centuries of anti-Irish sentiment in England. The League ran the first céilí in London's Bloomsbury Hall in October 1897. They decided what steps it contained – in short, a heavy dose of Scottish dancing, which may explain my primary-school nuns and their sword dances – and the name of this new traditional dance. The word 'céilí', with all its various spellings, did exist in the Gaelic-speaking parts of Ireland, but it referred to a group of people visiting, not dancing. The London Irish had a word for day trips to Epping Forest – '*séilgí*'. From these roots a new word emerged, with a meaning unknown in Ireland. The céilí was born in London. It was ballast; it offered something to hold onto.

Dance contains information about migration and human movement between countries and continents. Mark Knowles's *Tap Roots* suggests the word 'jig' links to the Hindu deity Lord Jagannath, whose week-long annual celebrations in Puri include huge chariots, a vast procession, chanting and dancing. He suggests that the word probably arrived with 'the Crusaders, through Syria', or with people of Romany descent and gradually became attached to a specific style of dance. He goes on to describe the percussive nature of traditional Irish dancing, stating that jigs were performed in triple time, with dancers generating beats with the heels, toes and tips of their hard shoes. A good jig dancer, he said, could make at least 15 sounds per second with their feet – skills that went on to inform tap dancing as it emerged under the feet of innovators like Master Juba. In the RTÉ documentary *Steps of Freedom*, choreographer Dewitt Fleming Jr described the connections between tap dance and Irish dance through the 'straight line' that can be drawn on a map between Ireland, the Galician region of Spain, Portugal and West Africa: 'The Spaniards traded with the Irish through West Ireland, and with the Africans and the Arabs. Personally, I think that's where you find the connection.'

———

A documentary was transmitted on RTÉ Radio in 2006, titled *Heel Up*. It told the story of *sean nós* – a term used to describe both song and dance. The latter involves fast footwork, with the feet staying close to the ground, battering steps that mark out the music, and free movement of the arms, in contrast with the rigidity of competition-style Irish dancing. The documentary described *sean nós* as 'the jazz of traditional Irish dancing'. There is a delightful arc of history evident in that description, which recognises the similarities between traditional dance and jazz, and which would have been inconceivable to the 1930s anti-jazz crew. The programme notes continue: 'It is performed alone in short bursts of exuberance as dancers respond to the music in their own unique way. Dancers start with a few basic steps and improvise and refine them over a lifetime. No two performances are ever the same. There are no set pieces, no costumes, no rules. It is essentially a pulse.'

This improvised dance style is now taught around the world and has been given new life online, with millions of shares through viral videos. Back in the 1960s, though, *sean nós* was almost extinct. Dr John Cullinane is a marine biologist and champion dancer. He's also a dance historian, the author of 11 books about Irish music and dancing – including the one which details the London Irish and their invention of the céilí – whose collection of dance-related material was recently acquired by the Irish Traditional Music Archive in Dublin. Six months prior to our interview he was 'nearly dead and buried' after cancer treatment. When we speak he's thankfully in fine form, aged 81, and is recently returned from South Africa, where he introduced Irish dancing two decades ago.

The young John Cullinane began dancing at the age of 11, following in the footsteps of his mother, who had been taught by the famous dance master Cormac O'Keefe. His own teacher 'played the piccolo for dancing class', said Cullinane. 'We hadn't ghettoblasters or anything like that.' Our conversation was delightfully warm and involved him singing me a few lines of an old song, 'The Blackthorn Stick', which almost instantly and very unexpectedly caused my eyes to leak tears onto my laptop. In the mid-1960s he was employed by the Irish government to do a seaweed resources survey along the West Coast. Daytime, he looked for dulse and carrageen moss; evenings, he'd go and find the dancers. 'I became familiar all along that coastline with what we now refer to as *sean nós* dancers. There were very few of them at all. In Connemara there were about six or eight.' The dancers didn't use the phrase *sean nós* to describe themselves; it was a name that was given to them. Cullinane says that the style was named by the Gaelic

League to fit into their competition framework in the mid-1960s; before that it didn't have a name, it was just dancing. It's a process familiar to many street-up dance styles, especially ones that developed before the internet. People dance locally in a certain way for one reason or another, and it's just dancing. If it spreads, it needs a name, which is usually bestowed upon the dancers regardless of whether they like it or not. The words that became attached to this kind of Irish dancing translate to 'old style', which was indicative of the Gaelic League's intentions: to present the rural past as a blueprint for national perfection, just as Cecil Sharp had done in England. To the dancers it wasn't necessarily old style. It was *their* style.

Times were changing. New music was entering Ireland on stations like proto-pirate Radio Luxembourg, which began broadcasting to the UK and the Republic of Ireland in 1933. Between 1935 and 1945 there was an unofficial ban on jazz at Irish national broadcaster 2RN (renamed Radio Athlone and then Radio Éireann), which ensured that local listeners turned elsewhere for their dose of new music. On Sundays at 1 p.m. Radio Luxembourg would broadcast 'the latest dance music' on a show sponsored by Zam-Buk, a medication for cuts and bruises, playing jazz, operetta and what was known as 'light music'.

The Down with Jazz movement had helped cut off the remaining blood supply to improvised rural dancing, which was already weakened by changing social circumstances. It was squashed by priests trashing dancefloors, by promoters having to argue their case in court and by the young people listening to new music from Europe and America that spoke to their realities. Things changed, even though dances in rural homes had provided movement that stretched back hundreds of years, holding history stashed under the floorboards like the horse skulls that people would bury to improve the resonant quality of their battering steps.

Kitchen dances provided a regular opportunity to meet and socialise and to celebrate big moments in the lives of families. East Limerick dance master Pat O'Dea grew up dancing the Ballycommon Set and remembers the last few years of the hoolie, when neighbours from the nearby eight or ten houses would gather to sing, play the fiddle and dance. 'My house was one of the last houses that was known for the hoolie in the kitchen,' he tells me. 'It always happened after Mass on the first Friday of every month. You could not run a hoolie in the kitchen until that Mass was said first.'

Pat is a charming man who now teaches Irish step dancing to people with Parkinson's disease, and he's telling me a story in shifting tenses, reflecting the way memory works. 'There were eight of us siblings, and we'd be sent to bed before the hoolie starts but we wouldn't go to bed, we'd be up at the bannisters, looking through the bannisters, watching all this go down,' he said. 'I remember seeing a guy playing the fiddle, and a lady got up, pulled up the apron, and I see her boots and I can still see her tan socks and she just freestyle dancing. It was absolutely one of the most amazing things I ever saw in my life. It was nothing pre-planned. It was just something that came to her head, and she was able to feel the music.' I'm touched by his description, not least because I remember being very young and sitting on the stairs, looking through the bannisters while my parents played music. I wanted to join in, but the door was closed. Looking back, the door seems like a symbol of the distance between suburban life and a more communal way of living, even within a family unit.

'As adults, we have to make sure we allow the kids to have that start,' adds O'Dea. 'It has to start somewhere.' His work teaching *sean nós*-style dancing to people with Parkinson's obviously fulfils this idea that the dance must be passed on, and that it contains health benefits, but it also relates to control in the muscular sense. There's a whole subsection of treatment for the disorder that relates to dance. The English National Ballet has a programme around dance and Parkinson's, while in south London Simone Sistarelli's Popping for Parkinson's flips the muscle contraction that is common in the illness in service of the early b-boy style. A team at Washington University found that Argentinian tango also held up well against traditional physiotherapy.

Back in the summer of 2010 Italian neurologist Dr Daniele Volpe had a revelation during one of his regular visits to Ireland, where he'd indulge his side interest in jigs and reels. He visited Pepper's Bar in the tiny village of Feakle, County Clare, for a session of traditional music and dancing. He clocked a man shuffling in who looked, to his expert eye, very Parkinsonian. But when the music started, the man danced the reel step just like everyone else. He couldn't walk well, but he could dance, mimicking the neurological idiosyncrasy of stroke patients who retain song while losing language.

Dr Volpe realised that this particular step required almost constant transferral of weight from one leg to the other, so therefore mitigated against the 'freezing' that people with Parkinson's sometimes experience when walking. In 2012 he presented his findings – that Irish dancing offered better results than standard physiotherapy – to the International Congress of Parkinson's Disease and Movement Disorders in Dublin, before publishing them, the following year, in the peer-reviewed *BMC Geriatrics* journal. He's now looking into how Irish dancing might have a positive effect on Alzheimer's disease.

———

I'm visiting my friend Dawn at her home in Kent. She's standing at one end of the kitchen, and I'm on the other side of the breakfast bar, leaning on it. We've known each other since attending the same Catholic primary school, and we're reminiscing, engaging in the kind of shorthand you can use only with people you've known for a lifetime. She and I have a shared history in the classroom and on the dancefloor, going to the same under-18s night and subsequently to many London clubs throughout the 1990s. Her ability to go out dancing became limited when she developed ME and had to navigate the harsh, invisible obstacles that an energy-limiting condition brings in its wake.

'Hold on, how did we dance?' She stops, remembering it not just in her mind's eye, but in her body. She reorganises her frame to try to find the right starting point, then clenches her fists, moving her hands down, staccato. Her body is remembering for her. She moves, and for a split second she's 14 again and she's on the spot, dancing in a tight square of her own kitchen-turned-dancefloor, balls of the feet connecting so that her heels can move side to side like windscreen wipers in opposition to each other, fists punching down across the body on one side and then the other. Her hair is extending the shape she's making in a kind of counterpoint, an upside-down metronome, rocking out to the reimagined sounds of air sirens and sampled drum breaks. Dancing relates to release and repair, to controlling your movements and to being controlled. Here in Dawn's kitchen it's also time travel.

4: DEEP ROOTS

Shuffling and skanking in the reggae dancehall,
1976–1982

Between the mid-to-late 1970s and early-to-mid-1980s many thousands of young people across Britain danced to reggae and lovers rock. This music had been generated and was predominantly danced to by Caribbean diaspora communities in church halls, community centres and terraced houses – using such locations because existing white spaces often operated an informal colour bar. The dancing stamped out a strong foundation for the globally influential UK dance music that followed, something author Lloyd Bradley described to me as 'the soundman revolution'. The physical space of the reggae dancehalls, the bespoke sound systems through which the music was powered and a widely disseminated body of expertise ensuring high vibes supported what came next in practical and concentric ways. Dancing in these rooms did more than just provide recreation in the form of six straight hours of bopping and skanking. It generated the alchemical processes that occur in what Linton Kwesi Johnson called the 'electric hour of the red bulb' in his poem 'Dread Beat an' Blood'.

I should say here that I didn't dance under these particular red bulbs, and might not have done so even if I'd been the right age. I believe strongly that it's useful to tell a story from a perspective of lived experience, if only to avoid the errors of nuance that inevitably follow when you write from a cultural remove. However, reggae dancehalls were the mother and father of the subsequent generation's electric hours – including mine – making it important for me to attempt to include this part of the collective dancing story. I've tried to square this circle by keeping it local wherever possible, hence the focus on the London borough of Lewisham, where I live. What follows is just one version of the story.

———

Let's look at this initially through a few key personnel, just to establish the overlapping interconnections between my generation, who came of age in the late 1980s and early 1990s, and the reggae dancehall. Many of the influential figureheads in our world came through sound-system dances and carried the influence with them, refracted. Jazzie B has sold over ten million records worldwide with his Soul II Soul collective, which he started as a reaction to the reggae systems run by people half a generation older. He and his friends took the format of the reggae dance and applied their own music to it, including funk, soul, hip hop and electro. I once made a BBC radio documentary titled *Classic UK Clubs* and interviewed Jazzie, who told me that their Monday-night residency at London's Africa Centre between 1985 and 1989 was 'the first time reggae sound systems had gone uptown'.

Norman Jay built a reggae sound system with his brother Joey, through which Norman would play imported soul, funk and disco at his Shake 'n' Fingerpop warehouse parties and on pirate-era Kiss FM. He picked up many of his records in New York while visiting family – who also ran reggae sound systems.

His uncle operated the Dr Wax Roadshow, which Norman told me in an interview for the Red Bull Music Academy was 'the largest Caribbean sound system in New York at the time . . . he used to do all the big Afro-Caribbean events in the five boroughs'. By the end of the decade his sound system was being used by early acid-house night Shoom, which I attended during my own underage nightlife explorations.

When Goldie started his Sunday night Metalheadz session at London's Blue Note in the summer of 1995, he requested sonic assistance from the reggae-schooled Eskimo Noise sound system. He also invited Cleveland Watkiss to host the night. Cleveland is a world-class vocalist, conservatoire lecturer and legendary figure in UK jazz. In the 1970s he was a teenage dread, skanking to reggae at Hackney's Four Aces. He has a perspective that spans decades and understands – as Goldie did when he hired Eskimo Noise – the power of sound. Phebe's in Dalston on a Friday was the spot, back in the reggae era, when Fatman HiFi's sound system was playing in the basement. 'I remember being there one night, being next to the speaker, this big 18-inch bass speaker, and I put my head right inside the cone,' he tells me. 'There's no way on earth you could ever do that today at any sound system now. You'd fry your brain. I'm telling you, the sound of the bass was vibrating my brain and my body. I was like, [sounds rapturous] "*Ohhhhhh myyyyyy godddddd.*" These were some of the best experiences I've ever had in my life.'

Cleveland also helped me understand something important, which was invisible to me from my cultural perspective. I was asking him about the reggae skank, and how it became a universal way of moving. I knew it was a dumb question, but dumb questions can sometimes help you get underneath a subject, so I asked it anyway – how did people *know* how to do that type of movement? – and was rewarded with one of those moments when realisation sinks in.

'Because it's in the sound,' he said. 'Because the dance is the music and the music is the dance. It's really that succinct. When you hear a sound it has a dance, it has steps, it has movement. There is a movement to that sound. When you see a dance it has a sound – and there's only a thin Rizla paper between the two.'

It's worth noting that each of the cultural figures I've just mentioned has also been recognised by the official state honours system. Jazzie B is an OBE, and all the others are MBEs, with Norman Jay being the first DJ to receive the award. The connections are intergenerational and overlapping. Fabio, of early-1990s jungle pioneers Fabio and Grooverider, told *Resident Advisor* that Jah Shaka was 'without doubt the greatest influence on me'. Jungle producer and DJ Shy FX was the grandson of pioneering Jamaican sound system Count Shelly. Late-nineties garage outfit So Solid Crew began life in a sound system called Killawatt and first performed at their MC Romeo's uncle's sound system at Notting Hill Carnival. Reggae's dancefloor substructures went deep, and this allowed for extraordinary levels of creativity in the styles of music that followed. Huge commercial success could also be built on reggae's foundations: Ed Sheeran first found success in 2011 by collaborating with grime artists including Wiley (whose dad ran a sound) on the *No. 5 Collaborations Project*.

Mainstream styles of music and movement benefited from what Lloyd Bradley described to me as the 'logic and ambition' of sound-system culture. Some of these outcomes are structural, like the soundclash, where rival sound systems would compete for the crowd's attention, and which provided the basslines and a baseline for jungle and drum 'n' bass, and cemented a central role for the lyrical host or MC. The influence and impact has been co-opted, even by politicians, including a Conservative minister who was congratulating contributors to a conference at the end of the 2010s. He didn't say 'well done'. He used a phrase that was popularised through the microphones at countless reggae dances: 'big up'. The incongruity, of course, lies in the fact that the minister's government had a long-standing commitment to a 'Hostile Environment' that led to threatened and actual deportation for thousands of Commonwealth-born citizens and their children, many of whom would have had some connection to the reggae dancefloors that built contemporary British music culture.

————

The story of Music House offers just one example of the deep, layered ripples set off by reggae dances. Chris Hanson played lead guitar in the band Black Slate, performing extensively to dancers across the country. They had a big hit in 1980 with 'Amigo', which also made the top ten in New Zealand. When tour bookings started to dip in the mid-1980s, Hanson moved from music-making to the vital supporting role known as 'cutting dubs', a process which involves mastering music so it sounds as good as possible and manufacturing vinyl records, often as one-off or strictly limited 10-inch dubplates, aka dubs or 'slates'. The dancers non-verbally and collectively demanded that DJs and producers had their own bespoke copies of new tunes before they were released, and Chris opened a space in which these special one-offs could be mastered and manufactured.

Music House has a comparably foundational relationship to British dance music as Abbey Road Studios does to British guitar music. It began in Chris's home, before he moved into a series of rooms on the Holloway Road in 1985, mostly serving British and Jamaican reggae artists, including Jah Shaka, Sugar Minott and Ninjaman. House and techno arrived in the late 1980s, and Danny Rampling would be there every week cutting slates, as was the influential rave-era DJ Grooverider, who was the only person allowed to breach Music House's legendary 'first come, first served', no-bookings rule.

Artists, producers and dancers responded to house and techno with a music known as hardcore, which gathered speed in the early 1990s. DJ Slipmatt was one of the first people to have a chart hit with this music – 1992's 'On a Ragga Tip' – which was cut at Music House. A staggeringly high percentage of the jungle and drum 'n' bass tunes that caused havoc on mid-1990s dancefloors were cut at Music House after Leon Chue joined his sound engineer dad, Paul, and began engineering and cutting dubs. I can attest to the legendary waits and parade of greats, as one afternoon in the late 1990s I sat on the waiting-room sofa with the artists Ed Rush & Optical, under fading posters for reggae shows. Producer Teebone later filmed a half-hour conversation with Leon, laughing and joking about the number of UK garage or grime producers who used the place, including Leon's brother Jason, who became known for his inventive garage productions under the name Wookie. Leon was mastering drum 'n' bass, reggae and jazz and working with local bands until he passed away in November 2020, and you can still see the letters 'MH' scratched into the run-out grooves of many reggae 7-inch reissues. The influence endures.

———

One spring afternoon in 2018 I joined a 'Reggae Walk' with two academics, who were then working at Goldsmiths University. Professor William 'Lez' Henry was born and grew up in Lewisham, south-east London, although on the basement dancefloors of the early 1980s he went by another name: Lezlee Lyrix. By the late 2010s he was digging into his own history with papers, books, conferences and these walk-and-talks alongside Croydon-born professor Les Back, who has a similar length of service in the dance.

The walk began in the university car park, before crossing the petrol-soaked arterial road, where we stopped at the end of a tiled pathway. Time-peeled paint had dropped off the red front door, revealing the undercoat, and in the driveway a car was wrapped in grey plastic like a forgotten gift. This was the location of a basement known as 51 Storm, which was named in memory of the devastation caused by Hurricane Charlie when it hit Jamaica in 1951, and where sound systems would run a dance. Professor Lez stood at the end of the path and explained. Every Saturday, young people would carry speakers, amplifiers and record boxes into the basement for a shebeen – or shubeen or shubz, depending on your spelling preference, or *síbín*, to use the original Gaelic. Initially the word referred to illegally brewed whiskey, and it came to mean any kind of unlicensed premises that sold alcohol. It travelled out of Ireland with the waves of migrants from the 1800s.

In the early 1980s Professor Lez had his own up-and-coming 'yout' sound system, Ghettotone, which was part of the junior network feeding into what the grown folks had built. A bigger local sound, Saxon Studio International, had created a platform for soon-to-be-famous names like Smiley Culture, Papa Levi, Maxi Priest and Tippa Irie, and they also created opportunities for Lez. On New Year's Eve 1981 he stepped off the dancefloor at 51 Storm and up to the mic, to share the wordplay he'd been practising at home in readiness for this moment. He recited the same lyrics to us, on the reggae walk, standing by the path leading up to 51 Lewisham Way, and time collapsed. It felt like he momentarily inhabited his teenage self, by pushing into the floor and pulling up the feeling, and that he brought us with him – or at least he brought me with him, back onto the dancefloor we were standing outside of. The rest of the walk was similarly deep and rich, and I came away with a strong feeling that we take the dancefloor with us; that we carry it in our bodies and that, in the right circumstances, the essence of the experience can be transmitted from one person to another.

Similar-but-different chapters of this national story exist behind doorways in Birmingham, Coventry, Huddersfield – anywhere British Caribbean communities rebuilt lives for themselves after responding to the UK's post-war request for labour. Some sounds were tiny and local, just for friends, family or neighbours; others were nationally known. The *NME*'s 'Big Big Sound System Splashdown' issue in February 1981 listed over a hundred top players. These included Kendra the Young Lion and Sledgehammer from the Bridge in London, with another 27 top sounds listed under the heading 'Country', including Count Ton Hi-Fi in Hastings and Wellingborough's Mr Entertainer. The reggae dancefloor was widespread, reaching many thousands of individuals. There were many women involved, including individuals like Sister Culcha, Bionic Rhona, Olive Ranks, Ranking Ann and Sister Candy, along with sounds like Ladies Choice, Silhouette and Nzinga Soundz, many of whom are included in photographer Anna Arnone's fabulous book *Sound Reasoning*.

Daddy Colonel was part of the Saxon Studio International sound system, who formed in Lewisham in 1976, and provided a key part of their 'fast chat' arsenal. He talks about the dancefloor's reach in IG Culture's documentary *Two Big Sound*. 'We play out seven nights a week, sometimes two dance, three dance a night,' he tells the camera. The screen cuts to Blacker Dread in his Brixton record shop, who continues: 'In 1977, every Monday we go Wolverhampton, we play in a club called Club 67. Every Tuesday we play Derby, Havana Club. Every Thursday night we play Bristol,' he says, emphasising the numbers by counting off the fingers of his open palm, which is raised and tilted towards the camera like an abacus. 'Every week for several months straight we would do that.' The camera cuts to another interviewee, Trevor Saxon, who describes playing 'seven nights a week . . . venues holding two, three thousand people. It was always rammed,' explaining how they'd play from 7 p.m. until 11 p.m. in one hall, then dismantle the turntables, amplifiers and speaker boxes and reinstall – 'string up' – all these elements in the next venue.

We're not talking about a mobile DJ set-up here, because the reggae sound system is as different from a standard PA as my old Nissan Micra is from a Bugatti. Dancers benefited in distinct ways from music transmitted through pre-amps and speaker stacks that had been built and carefully placed in the room by cliques of experts with a high-level overview of maths, physics, sound engineering, acoustics and much more. Music is vibrational instruction, and the information contained in a bassline – 'Move! Pause!' – became unavoidable under these circumstances. I felt this in environments that were built, decades later, on reggae's sound-system foundations, like mid-1990s jungle or drum 'n' bass nights, or in the dubstep dances of the mid-2000s. It's impossible not to move, and to feel, when the music is powered in this way.

The skills required to create sounds were passed between individuals in informal 'each one teach one' apprentice-ships. 'Sound-system building, both the carpentry and the electronics, was always passed down the line,' said Lloyd Bradley when I emailed him to check. 'So the old guys that built an original sound would pass their skills on by teaching the youngsters that were graduating from being box boys. Which is exactly how things would have worked in Jamaica, where people applied trades they had learned – carpentry and electronics – or went to somebody who did. In Jamaica and the UK there were a few well-known amp builders, while boxes would be made to order by carpenters, with the sizes and shapes developed as to what sounded best.' The young Rastas of the reggae era were tech innovators and engineers, although this was entirely invisible to mainstream society.

I was outside my friend's house in Catford, in the London

borough of Lewisham, when I met Janice. She was visiting his neighbour, who used to run Prince Melody, which was another of Lewisham's hyper-local sounds. Janice – she prefers to be known just by her first name – was out and about in the early 1980s, following Saxon and queuing up with the crowds to gain entrance. 'Anywhere Saxon went you couldn't get in, and if you did get in, you're squashed,' she says. 'We used to call it "shubeen", them times, underground. You go downstairs. It's dark, that's shubeen. Saxon could play anywhere, any single where. When Saxon and Coxsone had their battle . . .' She pauses for effect and for the energy levels to bubble up with the memories. '*Oi!* The foghorns, the whistles. Buss out your air jabs, mate!' Janice is happy to slip back in time with me, and I'm grateful for the perspective she's transmitting through her memories. If you imagine yourself on the dancefloor, I ask, what do you see? 'It's vibes, just people, everyone bubbling and vibesing out. It was lovely. Lick up the speakerboxes, trample, stamp hard. Oh my days.' She saw soon-to-be-famous artists, including Smiley Culture, at Saxon dances. 'We all used to sing and dance along. Whenever he did his shows it was full.' It was difficult getting permission to go out, but sometimes her older brother would ask her parents if she could come with him, and knowing she'd be safe with her sibling, she was allowed out, to pile up the stairs of Moonshot in Deptford or to a now-forgotten spot in Catford near where the Lidl is today. 'The vibes was just amazing,' she remembers. 'I loved it, I really did.' The vibe stayed with her, and she remains actively connected to music and culture, most recently contributing Bible verse to a Sunday neo-soul show on Deja Vu radio.

Before the Dance

Janice and the rest of the everyday dancers on the dance-floor were an important motor through which the music evolved, and they were the reason the sound-system operators hauled their bespoke bassbins into terraced basements, community centres and church crypts. Naturally, there was a range of dance styles inside the dance, just as there was a range of people. One of these was the style known as 'the skank'. 'It's like a marching army, knees coming up, marching to and fro,' says primo producer Dennis Bovell in his deep baritone. 'There's a step forward, step back, steps to the left, steps to the right, and over again during the whole piece. A jigsaw puzzle of steps that had been fitted in, like something choreographed but in your own style. You could see the difference in people who were accustomed to dancing to calypso, people who were deep-seated in reggae, people who were born and brought up in London. You could see it in how they danced.'

Dennis ran a high-ranking sound system called Jah Sufferer, released dub records as Blackbeard, formed and played in the band Matumbi, helped develop the genre of lovers rock, produced reggae and post-punk records for Madness, The Slits, Maximum Joy and Orange Juice and has a long-standing working relationship with poet Linton Kwesi Johnson, among many other things. You'll have seen him in a cameo in the lovers rock episode of Steve McQueen's *Small Axe* films, joining a house party in an extended dancefloor singalong to Janet Kay's 1979 pan-European hit single 'Silly Games', which he wrote and produced. He also composed the score for the 1980 film *Babylon* – working as the musical director. He knows about the dance. 'The reggae skank was about freeing yourself,' he says. 'This wasn't music for cuddling up to each other. It was the music of

90

revolution. It was music for making a stance. It was love, but it was love of your people, love of your kind. The love of those interested in what they were saying. A kind of oneness.'

I've interviewed Dennis a number of times over the years, and he's one of the best storytellers I've ever had the pleasure to encounter. One of the first times we met, in the early 2000s, he was drinking red wine and regaling everyone with vignettes in a beautiful 15th-century courtyard in the centre of a former monastery in Rome. I've heard him tell stories about making tape loops at school, before the technology was easily available to make tape loops, by using a broom handle to create the required tension and roping in the music teacher to hold the broom. I've sat in his north London kitchen while he brought to life long-lost dubplate cutting houses, and I've followed him as he breezed into a Soho pub with the kind of high-energy charisma that most people never have, even when they're in the high altitude of maximum youth. He has endless stories because he has been at the centre of the universe – the singularity in which culture is made – on countless occasions. He knows what the dancing built because he lived it.

During his reign as a top sound, Dennis's Jah Sufferer would end every night with a shuffling competition, where dancers would show off their skills. Dennis's cousin Andy was Sufferer's star dancer, able to drop a hanky on the floor, do the splits and pick it up again. 'He'd carry a couple of sachets of salt from Wimpy to sprinkle on the floor and make it easier to slide on,' he says down the phone. 'He'd mash the place. He looked like he didn't have a bone in his body.'

'Shuffling was a real big deal at dances in the 1960s and early 1970s, mostly to ska,' said Lloyd Bradley when I emailed him – again – to find out more. 'Everybody, including me, had a go at one time or another.' Top shufflers were celebrities, he explained, adding that most reggae dances featured at least a couple of competitions. 'It's impossible to describe on paper,' he added. 'Splits were commonplace, and a killer move involved picking up a handkerchief from the floor with your teeth. You'd have to get somebody to demonstrate some of the moves if you really want to understand it. The problem is the original shufflers are now in their sixties, and it wasn't a skill that got passed down.'

I had the chance to ask for a demonstration when multi-instrumentalist and renowned rollerskater Orphy Robinson MBE appeared as a guest on my Worldwide FM radio show. He often watched the dancers shuffle, usually when a ska record like Dennis Alcapone's 'Guns Don't Argue' came on towards the end of the night. The shufflers tended to be older, some of whom would have been born in the Caribbean and had brought home-style moves with them. 'Toe, heel, toe, heel is what you're using,' he told me after we'd finished broadcasting. 'It might be snaking or circular or it might move forward. If you'd stuck tap shoes on them, you'd probably have got some sounds.'

He described the moves and illustrated them at the same time with the relevant gesture. 'You know how in Irish dancing the arms are still and the legs go? Here, the arms were out, but they were kind of still.' He lifted his arms forward a little and bent his elbows slightly, like unfinished triangles. I was standing next to him and I followed, attempting to make the same shape so I could get a sense of the basics in my body. Circles would form, he said, and individual dancers would move into the middle to show off their best moves, with the top dancer being decided by the audience. On the most powerful dancefloors, I think, there are opportunities for everyone. The ordinary dancers can allow their simple steps to lead them through the night, and the accomplished ones can explore the upper limits of their skills and style by entering the circle and expressing themselves.

The dancers could sometimes be the starting point for a whole new sound, not least because of the symbiotic relationship between the two art forms. 'Dance is yeast or starter culture, adding the bacteria and liveliness something needs to grow,' says Dennis Bovell, picking up the theme in our phone conversation. As already mentioned, he'd played a significant part in evolving lovers rock (as did guitarist John Kpiaye and sound-system operator Lloydie Coxone, who'd play soul records at his events), and the naming of this Black British music form involved dance moves, according to Bovell. 'I was exploring the possibility of lovers rock not only becoming a genre of music, but a dance . . . I noted that's how every mood changed in the reggae world,' he says, referencing two influential songs that contained dance instruction and which helped fix styles of music and movement into the cultural consciousness. The first was Alton Ellis's 'Rocksteady', which was released in 1967 and contained lyrics that encouraged listeners to do the new dance of the same name and explained how to do it. The second was 'Do the Reggay' by Toots and the Maytals, released a year later, which referred to a passing dance fad and is credited as an early use of the word that would come to define a genre. A circular process was at work, with the dancers influencing the music and the musicians influencing the dancers. The act of moving to music, collectively, is at the heart of it all.

'I was attempting to depict lovers rock as a dance,' says Bovell, before singing his tune 'Lovers Rock' down the phone, complete with lyrics that describe shaking shoulders and wining (aka winding) waists. In the decades that followed, all kinds of UK youth began to shake their shoulders and wine up their waists – and not just the ones who had reggae dancers in their family. I ask him what role did the Caribbean diaspora have in how UK youth dance now? 'Use of the ass,' he replies, without missing a beat. 'I'll just say that. Previously you didn't go there, but now – *woah*. The ass has become such a feature.' There's a pause and a resonant chuckle. 'It's ass-tronomical.'

Film director Menelik Shabazz told the story of lovers rock and the dancing that went with it in his inventive 2011 film of the same name. The film featured choreographer and author Dr Kwame 'H' Patten, who described the mechanics of a slow dance that had evolved alongside the range of movement styles that occurred in the reggae dancehall. The style is sometimes referred to as 'the rub-a-dub': couples making a tiny and continuous figure-of-eight motion with the hips, intermittently and slowly 'dipping' vertically, knees bending before slowly pushing back up to standing. Its popularity at house parties left evidence in the form of worn sections of flock wallpaper just below waist height. Another of the interviewees, actor and singer Victor Romero Evans, who appeared in *Babylon*, is filmed reclining on a sofa, dressed in a bright blue shirt. 'When a child is hugged, it instils confidence,' he says, an observation backed up by established molecular science that explains how the hormone oxytocin helps create feelings of warmth and attachment. 'We used to go and get a hug every weekend. You felt nice, especially if you found a partner and you and her gelled. It might not lead to anything, but the fact you had a wicked dance, you were glued to that partner . . . You felt good if you had a dance.' New dance styles, perhaps, evolved in response to need, especially in the context of the cold violence of British institutions.

Finally, in this description and discussion of dance styles, let's consider the remarkable dancers that followed Lewisham's Jah Shaka. Shaka's outsize influence on UK music was largely established through his powerful sound system and highly individual way of selecting, recording and presenting music. In the early days of his ascent this involved using one turntable in the traditional Jamaican style, playing with his back to the audience, better to let the music flow uninterrupted. The teenage dancers who flocked to his events certainly believed in him, and the spaces he created allowed for remarkably expressive moves. Musician and journalist Vivien Goldman was writing for the *NME* when she described the dancefloor at a Shaka dance for the 1981 cover story about sound-system culture. A dancer, she wrote, 'cuts a complicated caper, freezing on the offbeat'. Jah Shaka inspired the dancers in specific and notable ways, she added. 'When his [Shaka's] turn comes round, the music hits a new intensity and the youths launch into gymnastic feats. As much mime as dance. The motions of stepping on stones over river currents . . . of finding your way from a fortress to freedom. These are guerilla movements to complement Shaka's warrior style.' The idea of moving from 'fortress to freedom' explains so much about the power of moving to music for everybody, not just the teenagers who found that Shaka's 'warrior style' allowed them to express themselves. Your body might be a fortress, holding stresses caused by hostile or traumatic experiences, in which case dancing can allow you to shake off at least some of the armour. The fortress might be the world outside, keeping you out. Either way, the right music in the right environment can allow a person to move through the constraints. To exhale.

The *NME* cover story had been initiated and co-ordinated by Paul Bradshaw, who went on to found *Straight No Chaser* magazine, among other things. I know Paul from being out and about at the same gigs, and so I knew that he'd also experienced Jah Shaka playing at Club Noreik in Tottenham in the late 1970s, because he'd told me about it. I called him to find out more. He described the 'tension and release, and the steppers, deep into it, responding with their moves' and a movement style that drew from kung fu and Shaw Brothers movies – 'praying mantis-type stuff . . . militant and out there'. He recognised the importance of the space, and that his whiteness brought a complication into the room. 'To tell the truth, I didn't stay long. Shaka's followers were young – 16, 17, 18 – and I felt I'd stepped into something and had no business being there. We were between Carnival going off in 1976 and the riots of 1981. This was their world, their creation. Their space away from discrimination at school, unemployment and the police.'

Rare footage from Club Noreik in 1979 illustrates the point. A dancer is leaning forward at the waist and exploring the space around him as if underwater, while Jah Shaka is speaking on the voiceover. 'There are a lot of things that make Black people not really free, not even in this country,' Shaka tells the interviewer. 'But just by hearing a certain record or by hearing that drum knocking – *bom, bom, bom* – you have to move your body. It's automatic . . . They don't know no other way to be free, except for music, in this country.' It's my view that downward pressure can create the dance, like pressure turns carbon into diamond. I think that whenever you find oppressive circumstances you'll find dancing, because squashing a person's prospects and opportunities results in the need to create prospects and opportunities, and if this can't be done directly, it will be done sideways. I think this is true even when oppressive governments or religious leaders – or strict families or abusive partners – think they've shut down people's bodies and stopped them moving to music. The need to dance will remain, and often people will find a way. A dancefloor created like this gives us a clue to what is emerging, a gestural alarm call that conveys the emergencies.

Some of the emergencies in the early 1980s related to unemployment. The reggae dance created a substructure that would hold new culture as it developed, but it also had real benefits at the time. Work isn't always about money. It is also about the profound economies of belonging, contribution and collective improvement, as well as earning necessary cash. There was a practical need for employment, even if it wasn't conventionally salaried, at a time of disproportionate unemployment. The Runnymede Trust found that when the recession was at its peak in 1982, unemployment for Black, Pakistani and Bengali people reached nearly 30 per cent, compared with 12 per cent for white men, and this would undoubtedly have been higher for identifiably Rastafarian men, who were at the centre of this particular universe.

One of the professors we met on the reggae walk – Les Back – wrote a paper titled 'Marchers and Steppers: Memory, City Life and Walking', which describes the effect of understanding social history by walking, as he and Professor Lez Henry did around Lewisham's citizen-built dancefloors. In it, Back uses the phrase 'thinking on the move', and I believe that the same can be said of what happens when we dance. We're doing a kind of cognition that occurs in the knees and hips as much as in the brain, and it's a kind of reasoning that can only happen on the move. Perhaps we can literally shake or slide new ideas into being when we shift positions.

Dancing, then, can be an education. June Reid, aka Junie Rankin, has been running the Nzinga Soundz sound system with Lynda Rosenoir Patten, aka DJ Ade, since the 1980s. She is now writing a thesis about female sound-system operators for her MA at Goldsmiths University, and we're chatting over Zoom. 'It goes back to young people learning about who they are, about their identity, their history. Any of those pan-African tunes like Burning Spear's "Columbus" prompted you to find out more. You were young Black people and you were in a safe space with other like-minded people where there were tremendous dancers. It was uplifting, it could be a real education,' she says. 'It was a time when you were being discriminated against in terms of school, jobs or whatever. It was something you looked forward to.'

Creating spaces from scratch required a community of skill and contribution. You needed people who would find the location – a task made more difficult because many of the usual locations back then were unavailable, not least because of proprietors' unwillingness to do business with communities of colour. Some spaces were easier to navigate. 1980s house-music pioneer Kid Batchelor grew up in an environment where a number of people built sound systems, and remembers the role of the Keskidee Centre: Britain's first arts centre for the Black community, founded by Guyanese architect and cultural archivist Oscar Abrams in 1971 and located near King's Cross in London. It was purpose-built and included a library, gallery, studios, theatre and restaurant – 'a major hangout-cum-youth club where we built homemade bass-heavy speaker sets and DJ equipment,' Batchelor told Paul Byrne for music and culture website Test Pressing. Like Batchelor's speakers, the dances sent out an amplified message of being here and of digging into here, step by skanking step.

Young people across England had to bend reality in order to access the reggae dance, getting around obstacles that ranged from over-policing to family resistance. Rastafarianism and reggae were seen as interlinked, a notion which contained some truth, at least in the foundational role of devotional nyabinghi drumming in reggae music. Both were seen as anti-social and dangerous, a hazardous inaccuracy solidified in John Brown's *Shades of Grey: A Report on Police–West Indian Relations in Handsworth*. The 45-page document had been published in 1977 and played a key role in 'creating the popular sentiment that Black people were much more predisposed to criminality, and that it was their culture which produced this behaviour', according to author Derek Bishton, who helped edit and design a community response to the report. *Talking Blues* was published in 1978 and contained interviews with young people, parents and church ministers on the subject of police harassment – including testimony from interviewees who found themselves subject to violent and discriminatory behaviour on their way to dances, during dances and after dances.

Mothers like the one portrayed in Winsome Pinnock's brilliant Deptford-based play *Leave Taking* (premiered in 1987) desperately wanted their children to be seen as respectable. 'I don't want people saying we lazy,' says the character Enid to her daughter Del, whom she has discovered has been out all night. 'All I did last night was dance,' replies Del. 'What's wrong with that? I like dancing. I been following that sound system for years. The bass is mad. You wanna see it pounding the walls, like one big pulsing heart. When the bass gets inside you and flings you round the room you can't do nothing to stop it.'

———

The film *Babylon*, directed by Franco Rosso and written with Martin Stellman, was released in November 1980. It has now become widely available, but for a long time it was out of print, and the only way to see it was by going to someone's house to watch an old VHS copy, which is how I first saw it. The film tells the story of a group of music-loving friends in southeast London who are living through the everyday realities of racism and police brutality, and it features Aswad's Brinsley Forde in the lead role. The characters have built their own sound system and they're preparing for an important clash, where two sounds will battle and the crowd will decide the winner. Here the film fuses fiction and reality. Their nascent sound, Ital Lion, is fictional (with the real-life Rootsman HiFi and the Mighty Observer named in the end credits). The sound system Ital Lion is clashing in the final scenes couldn't possibly be fictionalised because it was Jah Shaka and, as we've seen, he was already legendary.

Stellman and Rosso could get the script to a certain point, but they needed specialist expertise to make it iconic. Rosso had moved from Turin to south London when he was a child, with all the challenges that came with being Italian in Streatham in the 1950s. Stellman was ten years younger, a reggae-mad 25-year-old youth worker of Jewish parentage who was running a drama programme at the Albany in Deptford. He replied to me when I got in touch to ask about the relationship between the film and the many reggae dancefloors that took shape in south London. 'Sandra Marsh, who was later to have a few lovers rock hits as Cassandra and whose tune features in the engagement party, was the girlfriend of Billy Currie of Ital Rockers. I see her very much as the one who opened the door to the whole sound-system world,' he said. 'This led to a wider network of friends who could help us with the script.' The end credits also thank Moonshot Youth Club, Lewisham Way Centre, Lewisham Youth Centre, Riverside Youth Club, St Marks Centre, the Albany and 'all the people of Lewisham who made this film possible'.

The people of Lewisham and the dancers across the UK demanded that even experienced operators like Shaka stayed on top of their game. The dancefloor was part of a structure in which sound systems could evolve and mutate, learn through being beaten or occasionally rise superior in the kind of David and Goliath scenario that Rosso provided in the final scene of *Babylon*, which was shot in the old Albany on Creek Road, a building that was subsequently firebombed by a far-right group.

The cinematic clash in *Babylon* between the fictional Ital Lion and the very real Jah Shaka is the equivalent of some up-and-coming hothead trying to best James Brown's footwork in 1965, or attempting to manhandle the mic from Stormzy while the star was power-jumping onstage in the late 2010s. This final scene concentrates the dancefloor into an intense centrality. Not just the reggae dance, but the dance as you might have experienced it in any sweaty room where high-calibre selectors or musicians are playing their best sounds to audiences who have a strong connection to their community, and who, in various ways, need what the dancefloor is offering. Moments of this kind are marked by an intensification of energy, the cold heat of the stillness you find when you're in the zone, front left, by the speaker. By the release that happens when you tune into the feeling of the music and find that this allows your own feelings to surface and take shape. When you feel the bass not only in your chest, but under your cheekbones, and when your feet mark out the music on the floor and your hips circle. When you're packed in together, shoulder to shoulder, chest against back when the unit moves forward, like a wave; when the music lifts you collectively, like something growing, but fast, so that you're an entity and don't need to think about where your feet go or where your arms should be or what your shoulders are doing. You have passed over control of your next movement to the music, and you're just doing what is communicated in the basslines and drums and the spaces in-between, and suggesting what it does next. You have become part of the music.

The final scene of *Babylon* communicates a moment that I recognise, even though my life experience differs from that of the people represented on that dancefloor. I understand something of the decisions you make on the dancefloor about how much of the moment you will allow yourself to absorb, and what opening up to the moment can cost, and what it can do for a person. I see this, too, in the men who express their need through the most minimal of movements, standing at the back where it is safe and where they can survey the dance. Perhaps this is a place where there is a tiny window of opportunity to release, to relax, to become less guarded, to be soft and sensual and to feel the music, or perhaps just to feel. I see the energy of the ones who can let go, and who will let go, using the music to power the movement, to take up space, to exist.

The film ends – of course – with a police raid and with Ital Lion's refusal to turn off the music. Brinsley Forde's character Blue remains on the mic. He repeats a phrase: 'Can't tek no more.' The character Beefy, in a red tracksuit, dances behind him, in a tiny space, in the small square of space created by the other young men around him, staying in the refusal while the police knock through the red door that separates the dance from the outside world. The film ends with Forde's voice echoing outwards. He has the last word.

———

There are histories of resistance that are essential for understanding the context within which this dancing took place. In 1981 the New Cross Fire took the lives of 13 children and young adults who'd gathered to dance; another young guest died 18 months later, and others experienced horrific long-term injuries. It was widely believed that the fire had been started deliberately, because other racist attacks had happened before, repeatedly, without anyone ever being charged. The Waterloo Action Centre, a few kilometres north, was so aware of the peril of firebombing that it didn't even have a letterbox. The postman might not have been able to deliver their letters, but neither could fascists easily slip an incendiary device into the building. The local Moonshot youth club, which regularly housed dances, had been gutted in a firebomb attack, as had the nearby Albany in Deptford – where, of course, the final scene of *Babylon* had been filmed. *Time Out* reported at the time that neo-Nazi organisation Column 88 had claimed responsibility.

In 1976 the National Front and a breakaway faction known as the National Party achieved a combined vote of 44.5 per cent of the electorate in a Deptford council by-election – an area adjacent to New Cross. The National Front argued in their manifesto that all Black and Brown British people should be thrown out of the country, even if they were born here, and Prime Minister Margaret Thatcher spoke in supercilious soft tones about the country being 'swamped'.

On 13 August 1977 the National Front marched from New Cross to Lewisham town centre under the pretext of protesting against street crime, specifically 'muggers', a term which operated as a racist synonym. The proposal to do so was considered so provocative that Lewisham council asked the home secretary to intervene. The council also applied to the High Court to force the Metropolitan Police to ban the march, but they were turned down because the judge agreed that the force was well capable of maintaining control. There was context, of course, including support for the far right in the borough – activists sold their newspaper in the town centre – and, as the *Sunday Telegraph* reported, an awareness that the date chosen for the march was significant. They quoted Front leader Martin Webster discussing a forthcoming by-election in Ladywood, Birmingham, and the fact that a demonstration in Lewisham would offer their candidate publicity. The paper reported Webster directly: 'Of course,' he said, 'there is only a fortnight to go to the West Indian carnival in Notting Hill, where we do not plan to take any action. But we realised that a demonstration now would serve its purpose.' The subsequent violence became known as the Battle of Lewisham and is an example of the degree of racist and statutory peril people were facing at the time in that part of London, and countrywide, and demonstrates how necessary the dance must have been.

The police had agreed a route for counter-protesters, which would allow a show of anti-racist solidarity at the top end of Deptford High Street. This was important, given the multi-cultural demographic of the area and the Front's showing in the previous year's local elections. A few days before the event, the police changed the route, but feelings about marching in Deptford were so strong that a large group took the original route anyway. They were led by drummers sat in the back of an open truck, and by the mayor, 30-year-old Roger Godsiff. This led to a remarkable confrontation, captured on film. Mayor Godsiff, who had thousands of people behind him, stood face to face with chief of police David McNee, who informed the mayor that anyone who proceeded further along the original route would be arrested. A stand-off ensued, before protest-ers were re-routed. Frustrated, many people walked the back streets to New Cross to join the crowd that had amassed to try to stop the Front marching as planned in the afternoon. A few hundred members of the National Front were gathered behind police lines in Achilles Street, a road whose very name suggests weakness. Thousands of people of varying age and ethnicity – *Camerawork* magazine estimated 10,000 protesters – waited nearby in the unofficial blockade, occupying the main road through which the march was due to pass. There were speeches, including one by British broadcaster and campaigner Darcus Howe, outside the Harp Club (now the Venue), an Irish dancehall that also hired out rooms for reggae nights. Photographer Syd Shelton remembers an 'old lady' putting two big speakers up in a window and playing Bob Marley's 'Get Up, Stand Up' at full volume – although other people who were there recall the tune being Junior Murvin's 'Police and Thieves'. It was, recalled Shelton in a podcast for Goldsmiths University, 'something of a party atmosphere, people dancing . . . a great mix of people and attitudes'. Professor Lez Henry, aka Lezlee Lyrix, was there too. 'We weren't going to fight them [the National Front] because we fought them anyway,' he told the podcast. 'We were going to observe, to see what was going to happen.' A photograph by Paul Trevor, printed in the *Cameraworks* special issue that followed the battle, captured a stretch of New Cross Road, showing hundreds of people packed into the space, with a crew at the front of the image, arms raised, mouths open mid-chant or song, jackets moving in response to the wearers' movement.

Footage from another perspective shows a man with a megaphone instructing Front members before they began moving. There was to be 'no backchat' with the police or 'the opposition', and no leaving the column for fights. The group marched out, fast, chanting a most basic slogan – 'National Front! National Front! National Front!' – to an angry beat. They were led by flag-bearers holding Union Jacks and the George Cross, closely followed by embroidered banners from the Coventry, Bristol and Birmingham branches. There weren't many people behind each one – Syd Shelton suggested the National Front numbered around 200 in total – so the banners followed each other closely, like gappy dominoes. The column was flanked by tightly packed lines of police, each line radiating outwards four or five deep like rungs on a broken ladder, greatly outnumbering the Front. A placard read 'Start Repatriations', but it looks to me, from my remove, as if they were really saying something else: 'This is our manor, and we can do what we want, because everywhere is our manor, even if we've come from Coventry, Bristol and Birmingham.'

All kinds of missiles – dustbin lids, corrugated iron, bricks and flares – were thrown at the National Front and the police who'd been instructed to escort them, in a very physical confrontation. The police charged the protesters, on horseback. The Front limped – sometimes literally – towards Deptford Broadway, harangued by counter-protesters. 'At one stage the left-wing demonstrators held up a National Front Union Jack and did a short tribal dance,' wrote the *Sunday Times*. While the Front did reach Lewisham town centre, where they were allowed to hold a rally in a side street, Lez Henry believed that something had changed. 'Normally you saw these dudes, chests out,' he told the Goldsmiths podcast. 'Seeing that air of invincibility eroded – it empowered a lot of people. In the context of south-east [London], they just weakened after that.

People that were afraid of them didn't seem to be so fearful any more.'

Huge police resources were poured into the march, with the *Observer* reporting that 4,000 police were deployed throughout the day – a quarter of the Met's workforce – along with the entire mounted division. The battle continued once the National Front were escorted by the police to special trains that were waiting for them, in what the *Sunday Times* described as a 'secret arrangement' between police and the Front. Then it was just police versus protesters, and the use of riot shields brought England in line with Northern Ireland for the first time. Front-page coverage the next day focused on injured policemen.

The Battle of Lewisham was, in fact, plural: there were battles, ongoing, and they give us a tiny view into the pressurised context within which the reggae dance occurred. That, as well as the uprisings that lit up the country a few years later in 1981, which were another form of communication.

By 1982 reggae was considered of great interest to a broad British audience. Channel 4 began transmitting in November that year, and the third programme to be shown on day one was a six-part history of reggae titled *Deep Roots* that explored the Jamaican origins of the genre. The music and the dancing were moving from powerful foundation to a supporting wall of British cultural life. A pop-reggae song by Birmingham's Musical Youth reached number one that year. 'Pass the Dutchie' sold over four million copies, and the music video turned a Thames pathway into a dancefloor, right opposite the Houses of Parliament. The band played and lifted their knees in front of bespoke sound-system speakers painted in red, gold and green, although judging by how easily the band lifted them into place in the opening seconds of the clip, they were empty plywood, purely props. The video showed a truancy inspector landing them in court, where they were found not guilty. The band leapt over the witness stand and turned the town-hall courtroom into the centre of the dance. There was energetic, exuberant stepping, dance moves with knee lifts and high kicks taking up space between the witness stand and the jury – owning the space.

A couple of years later, Smiley Culture was in the charts with hits like 'Cockney Translation' and 'Police Officer'. He and fellow Saxon MC Asher Senator contributed to the then-emerging art of the 'fast chat' vocal style that had been supercharged by Papa Levi's 'Mi God Mi King'. It expanded British reggae's lyrical form, with artists writing, improvising and speedily spitting lines about bus routes, relationships, the police and other daily realities, just as grime MCs would a generation later. As with grime, the lyrics were sometimes funny, sometimes pointed, and sometimes dense with rage.

At 7 a.m. on 15 March 2011 Smiley Culture's Surrey home was raided by the Metropolitan Police. He was due to stand trial for conspiracy to supply cocaine, but within hours he was dead. The death of the 48-year-old musician, real name David Emmanuel, was covered widely by the press, including the *Daily Mail*, which wrote: 'Smiley Culture died of a single stab wound to the heart, the police watchdog confirmed today, amid claims by the reggae star's family that officers let him make a cup of tea following a raid. The Independent Police Complaints Commission is probing the circumstances of the death, which happened at the singer's home in Surrey on

Tuesday after officers swooped. His family say they have been told that he stabbed himself while making a cup of tea in his kitchen while police were still inside his home.'

In November that year the IPCC concluded its investigations and found no evidence to justify criminal proceedings against any of the officers who were in the house when Emmanuel died. The *Guardian* reported that the summary of the final report 'condemns the raid as significantly flawed and compels the MPS to overhaul the way they plan and execute future drug seizures', noting that the coroner requested that the full report not be made public or shared with Emmanuel's family. I wondered how common a move this is, so I emailed the solicitor who represented Smiley's daughter. 'Generally speaking,' she replied, 'it is very unusual for the IOPC (or IPCC as it was then) to keep a report from the public or the family.'

An inquest took place two years later, over a fortnight in June 2013, in Woking borough council's civic offices, in front of a jury. Jermaine Haughton covered it for the *Voice* newspaper, noting that four Metropolitan Police officers involved had been granted anonymity and would be giving evidence from behind screens. He reported on proceedings: 'While other officers looked around the property, Witness 2 had the sole responsibility of supervising Emmanuel for large parts of the search, while also filling out a premises search book, recording items found by his colleagues. "He had got both hands up in the air and in his right hand he was gripping the knife," said Witness 2, who has been a police officer for 11 years. "I have shouted 'knife' to alert Witness 1 because of his close proximity to where we were. As I'm shouting that, Emmanuel screamed at me, then in the same action has driven the knife into his chest."' The report then described legal cross-examination, before continuing: 'The court was told Witness 1 and 2 then restrained him and put handcuffs on as he struggled and reached for the knife. Emergency services were called to Emmanuel's home but [he] was pronounced dead at the scene despite attempts to resuscitate him.'

The inquest heard evidence over a fortnight and deliberated for 12 hours. The jury could not reach a unanimous decision, so the coroner agreed to accept the majority view that this was suicide, although the inquest verdict did find that 'the way in which Mr Emmanuel was supervised following his arrest materially contributed to his death'.

In the days immediately after Smiley Culture's death there was a protest march from Vauxhall, past the Houses of Parliament, to Scotland Yard. It was organised by Smiley's nephew Justin Boreland, who had his own creative life as MC Merlin a decade earlier. He found himself in the position of family spokesperson, able to find the capacity to organise and be organised, even in his grief. 'I sought to protect his legacy, to really let people know about the person he was, because there were a lot of allegations being spun at the time,' he told me. 'He was more than an uncle. He was a big brother.'

The BBC reported that 'about a thousand' people attended the Justice for Smiley march, and I was one of them. Markie B of the Celebrity Showcase sound system organised the music, which was played through speakers stacked in the back of a truck at the head of the march. It stopped outside Scotland Yard, and the DJ played Chaka Demus and Pliers's 'Murder She Wrote', pulling the tune up again and again and again. The crowd added whistles and shouts to the speeches, which were punctuated by the airhorns usually reserved to show approval of a big tune. This was a wake in motion. This was the dancefloor on the move.

———

William H. McNeill was professor emeritus of history at the University of Chicago, where he began teaching in 1947. In 1995 he produced a small book, *Keeping Together in Time: Dance and Drill in Human History*. His thesis was simple: that moving together in time 'arouses warm emotions of collective solidarity and erases personal frustrations as words, by themselves, cannot do'. He argued that moving together to music could be political in the sense of building community – collective movement being 'an efficacious way of consolidating distinct sub-groups within larger communities'.

At the heart of his book is a powerful idea: that dance-like behaviour created and maintained connections and strengthened 'emotional bonds associated with that sort of behaviour [which] were critical prerequisites for the emergence of humanity'. He believed that moving to music created human-sized communities and, much later, sustained them once settlements developed into cities and – as cities do – began attracting individuals and families from diverse locations.

Dancing, perhaps, is the mother of the most basic human invention: humanity.

Part Two

THE DANCE

5: UP THE YOUTH CLUB

A short history of the youth-club disco, including
early-1980s Sheffield and the Civic in Orpington

Today, teenagers frequently absorb and transmit dance moves through screens, whether that's scrolling through a phone or watching on a laptop. Youth-club disco offered a similar schooling in the decades before the internet. There were youth clubs everywhere, thanks to a network of state-funded clubs built on the back of a 1960s Conservative government report that were then dismantled under subsequent Conservative governments. Such spaces offered teenagers the opportunity to take part in loosely defined communal movement, whether that was an indie pogo or a disco shuffle to music selected by one of their contemporaries. Youth clubs operated as an informal, peer-led classroom where specific dance styles like northern soul or breakdancing could be learned, practised and adapted. Weekly discos created a familiarity with dancing together, and this would nourish an everstream of music culture in the UK as the youth-club dancers moved up to the networks of nightclubs, discos and community centre dances that also existed countrywide. It wasn't all utopian, of course: one friend remembered their local youth club as 'a more violent version of school'. I consider youth clubs to have been a central, if almost entirely overlooked, motor of UK music culture.

As with the sound systems, these spaces allowed for the constant mutation and evolution of the raw life material from which personal progress and culture develops. Youth-club stories have been lost or obscured, perhaps because journalists and academics who became the keepers of the story didn't go to a youth club, or perhaps didn't need them. Lisa Rutter of Space Youth Services in Devon attended a youth club in late-1970s Dorset. It was well furnished, with a disco room, a wall which doubled up as a screen for showing films, a snooker table and full-size trampoline, and a fitness room with bits of gym kit in it. Understandably, it was 'really busy', open every night, with different age groups attending. 'I didn't realise that there was a local perception that this was where the naughty kids or the street kids went.' That perception, she adds, was unfounded, because the club had young people from all walks of life: 'The mix of backgrounds among young people broke down class barriers, and music was a strong cultural link,' she told me. 'Identity and belonging came from shared interests, not adults' perceptions of class and status.'

Youth clubs were predominantly working-class spaces, and had proximity to emerging culture, direct from the source. 'Disco areas within youth centres were key to shaping many young people's lives,' says Kev Henman, CEO of Space Youth Services. 'They were zones for experimentation, learning, sharing, persuading and expressing. Often youth-centre attendees were made up of musical tribes: ska, heavy metal, goth, New Romantic, reggae. All of these shaped behaviour, dress, friendship groups and, often, values.' Crucially, he says, these centres were accessible to young people from households that couldn't afford structured dance classes or activities. They offered a safe place to explore, where there was a lower risk of being ridiculed.

Youth clubs suffered the erasure that often happens to culture made by and for people who are young, are of Global Majority ethnicity, are queer or poor or otherwise marginalised. Our society fetishises youth, but we don't appear to like young people very much, and we don't seem very interested in respecting or appreciating these grass-roots conservatoires – or even seeing them.

It is always important for young people to have somewhere to go, where it's warm and (mostly) safe, and where there are welcoming adults or older peers who offer respect and encouragement. It was important for specific reasons in the mid-1980s. Teenagers were suffering time-specific stresses. Unemployment for men averaged at 15.7 per cent in 1984, affecting over three million working-age adults and therefore huge numbers of children in terms of how easily their parents could care for them, and of course negatively influencing their own prospects. The Miners' Strike permeated every aspect of life for entire communities and, in the interconnected way of things, the entire country, even if the main impact for families comfortably removed from coal seams was the presence of trade unionist Arthur Scargill on TV every night. Section 28 made it illegal for schools to 'promote' homosexuality.

Margaret Thatcher's government went to war with teachers over pay, and there were rolling three-day school strikes throughout the mid-1980s. In 1985 over 20,000 schools were affected by a day of industrial action, and between 1984 and 1986 the NUT and NASUWT unions expressed their resistance through the medium of working to rule. This meant teachers reluctantly removing their labour from anything not included in their contracts: for example, photocopying, running lunchtime chess club or organising after-school discos. Racism and discrimination impacted everyday life for many British citizens, nearly two million of whom were identified as Black or minority ethnic in 1981. For their children and teenagers, the statistical chances of being considered intelligent at school, of being considered for jobs or of being promoted within a job were considerably reduced. These young citizens frequently experienced a police force, not a police service, something which remains unchanged today.

While it's not comparable in terms of the effect on life chances, it feels relevant to mention the polluting effect of being racist on racists themselves, and the spreading nature of this pollution, which would also have affected their friends, family and children. I don't say this to encourage sympathy for racists. I say it to recognise that racism comes with a huge social cost that affects everybody. Perhaps the only people that escape this social cost are those in power, who are in charge of setting the national tone, curating national mythology and making decisions about the degree to which they'll encourage the human tendency to hatred.

Other generalised worries at the time included the ambient threat of nuclear annihilation, or of being bombed by the IRA, who continued their campaign on the mainland until the year before the Good Friday Agreement was signed in 1998. Teens in the 1980s needed space to decompress, and the youth club became a central decompression chamber. Diana Keppel, Countess of Albemarle, was the unlikely midwife of this mid-to-late-20th-century British institution. Her social conscience surfaced after taking a skiing trip to the Austrian Tyrol, just weeks before Hitler arrived in March 1938, and this set off a chain of events that led to her central role in the evolution of British youth clubs. Her *Times* obituary reported that she 'was appalled at what she saw during the Anschluss' and that she turned her horror into action. She sent her children and nanny home and went to Vienna 'so she could focus on helping "friends, Jews and others"'. I can't ask her what effect this experience had on her without engaging the services of a medium, but her subsequent actions suggest that it allowed her to understand, in her bones, how quickly fascism can descend and that society needs to mitigate against this risk. Back home, she used the considerable soft power granted to women of her social standing by joining committees, becoming the chair of the Women's Institute, and later joining various royal commissions. She became exceptionally skilled at the slow work of social change, and described chairing committees as an art form, like conducting an orchestra. In 1958 she became chair of a committee tasked by the education secretary to review the contribution that the national Youth Service could make in 'assisting young people to play their part in the life of the community' in the context of the new emerging teenage culture. Two years later her committee produced *The Albemarle Report* – a bold and visionary document, albeit one rooted in Britain's structurally classist assumptions and systems. Reading it, I can almost hear her clipped tones marshalling items off the agenda into facts on the ground. The report insisted on a near-doubling of investment in youth funding, along with a ten-year plan to refurbish and build youth clubs in towns across Britain. The country had suffered war and deprivation. Rationing had ended only six years earlier. Investing in young people – literally the future

– must have seemed like an incredible symbol of national rejuvenation. The report directly referenced dancing in a list of activities that were deemed 'valuable for their informality and the opportunity they give for social mixing' – and stated that specially designed youth centres should contain coffee bars and 'larger rooms for dancing and games'. Within hours of publication, the Conservative government accepted almost all the main recommendations, and broadly kept to its word.

Youth worker and historian Bernard Davies detailed the financial commitment required in his authoritative *History of the Youth Service*. The government allocated £23 million between April 1960 and March 1968, generating over 3,000 buildings and 160 youth sports projects. His interest in the subject stemmed from experience: he attended the Jewish Lads Brigade and Club in pre-*Albemarle* 1940s Manchester, stayed on as a voluntary worker and was inspired by the club's full-time youth worker to join the vocation after he finished university. His club produced their own cultural material – the pop group 10cc rehearsed at the club. 'I recall they went on to have quite a following,' he says with a smile that radiates down the phone line. In 1976 he published an influential pamphlet, 'Part-Time Youth Work in an Industrial Community', which detailed his experience of youth work in an anonymised town he described in the introduction as 'small, unfashionable and neglected'. By the end of his short and soulful publication, he comes to a conclusion that is as true now as it was in the mid-1970s: 'Youth work, like any form of people-work (or indeed any form of work) is inescapably a political act through which a political commitment to freedom, equality and justice is constantly expressed.' The

dancefloor was one of the places where this could be practised, on a weekly basis.

In an ongoing commitment to solidarity, Bernard sends me
paperwork from his personal archive, including a photocopied
article titled 'Buildings for Social Education'. It featured Maltby
Youth Centre, near Rotherham in South Yorkshire, which was
built in 1967 and had a sunken octagonal dance and drama
area with hardwood floors. It was soundproofed and also contained a girls' powder room – 'An early safe space,' says Davies
– as well as a gym, a games area, a craft room and an open-air
courtyard where motorcycle repair and other hobbies might be
pursued. He also sends an August 1963 article torn out from
the *Times Educational Supplement*, about the Withywood Centre
in Bristol. It contained a central area with 'a resilient floor and
a cheer-absorbent roof', its architects recognising that while
some people would want a quiet space, others were deemed to
be 'pop fans who like[d their] music good and loud'.

Between meetings, Lady Albemarle would lead her fellow
committee members into clubs, bars and cafés to witness 'original youth work', so there's little doubt she'd have approved
of the breakdancing happening in early-eighties Sheffield. I
imagine her telephoning around and insisting on a visit to witness kids popping and locking their bodies into robot shapes
and spinning on their heads to the sounds of hip hop and
electro.

Kids were able to dance, countrywide, in the 1980s because
there was plentiful space, and because there had been plentiful space for over a decade. Material held in the Sheffield City
Archives paints a colourful picture of youth-club life at the time
and features repeated and regular references to dancing. The

Greater Manchester Youth Association (GMYA) annual report from 1980 showed 250 affiliate clubs and included dancing as the first entry on the page outlining club activities. It read: 'In many youth clubs the "disco" is a popular attraction and has again proved to be an exciting theme for its supporters.' Other documents reinforce the idea that moving to music was important to young people. Cheshire and Wirral had 130 boys' clubs and youth clubs, noting in a report that 'disco dancing is a popular event'. The Lincolnshire Association of Youth Clubs reported in July 1981 the official opening of a new disco 'which is of a high standard and well worth a visit by any other club'. A report on youth clubs in Barnsley, Rotherham and Doncaster – an area of South Yorkshire containing over 160 clubs by 1982 – noted that 'meeting friends was the predominant factor in attendances, with males being more interested in the activities offered and females in the clubs' discos'. It also found that 77 per cent of respondents and 91 per cent of girls wanted to see more discos in their area.

In the late 1970s and early 1980s the National Association of Youth Clubs ran a disco-dancing competition, with sponsorship by Coca-Cola and arranged by Mecca Leisure. Greater Manchester entered 65 teams in 1978 and 1979, reporting that over 700 people attended the Steppin' Out final at the Ritz Ballroom in Manchester in 1980. 'As in previous years,' reported the GMYA, 'this competition attracted disco dancing teams from all over the country.'

Youth-club discos were pushed into existence by Lady Albemarle's brisk agenda and then prioritised, certainly by Sheffield City Council in the decades that followed. There were 33 local authority youth clubs in Sheffield by 1974, in addition to voluntarily run clubs, with 19 full-time council-employed youth workers and over 260 part-timers reaching an estimated 8,000 young people, along with another 72 registered voluntary youth organisations. Rowlinson Youth Club was attached to the school of the same name and was open six nights a week, attracting 500 young people every month. It benefited from a full-time youth worker and 24 part-time workers, and was used by senior citizens, under-14s and those with learning difficulties, as well as social services, various luncheon clubs and the probation services. The building's contract was signed, post-*Albemarle*, in 1969, and it was built alongside a school sports hall and swimming pool. DJ, promoter and producer Winston Hazel went there in the early 1980s and remembers the interior clearly. Up some stairs was a juice bar, where you could buy stamps (pen pals were a thing), and a disco room, which contained a DJ booth with twin turntables, blacked-out windows, a mirrorball, disco lights and a decent sound system.

The Sheffield city architect drawings for another local youth club, Hurlfield, show the degree of care and attention that went into making these spaces, and the way that architectural ideas were shared and replicated across the country. Hurlfield was a beautiful wooden building, with octagonal rooms that sat around a spacious central activity area, each one including another lovely way for youth to pass the time and learn more about themselves and their friends: a coffee bar, a quiet room, powder rooms, a garage workspace and, of course, a discotheque. Youthclub discos mimicked an ideal outside world, in miniature.

Winston Hazel's first creative excursion came in the shape of his breakdance crew SMAC 19, which came into existence at these two Sheffield youth clubs, Rowlinson and Hurlfield.

Today, there's an original t-shirt bearing the legend of his crew in the Manchester Hip Hop Archive, on the other side of the Pennines. Winston is a cultural instigator, locally famous for his role in building a distinct sound and dancefloor culture in Sheffield. He was one third of Forgemasters, whose 'Track with No Name' was the first release on the internationally famous Warp Records – 'And the reason to set up the label,' he says, when I ring him for a chat. Winston and DJ partner Parrot played the effervescent Jive Turkey parties with John Mattar and Mathew Swift, which spread brand-new electronic music throughout the city in the eighties and nineties. More recently, Winston co-ran a series of clandestine parties under the name Kabal with best mates Raif Collins and DJ Pipes. He's been on key Sheffield dancefloors for decades and therefore has a unique insight into what these spaces can teach and generate. 'The early days of going out clubbing were almost like our little nights in the youth club,' he says. 'The DJ over there, everybody dancing on the dancefloor. Youth club was a precursor to going out. It was a joined-up experience.'

Winston was one of the many people allowed to practise movement through these locally built systems, spending creatively productive teenage time at youth clubs across Sheffield. 'There was nowhere for us to hang out together other than the street, so the youth clubs brought us together . . . We knew that we had less opportunities than certain other types of privileged people, but what we had was unique to us and that empowered us. [Youth club] gave so many people a voice and a way to express themselves.' It allowed a sense of belonging, but it was also 'a breeding ground' for his creative life. It allowed him to develop important skills that weren't – and still aren't, often – on offer at school. 'It allowed me to be spontaneous,' he says. 'You responded to your environment, and the dancing was born out of that.'

Specifically, it offered a place to dance. Winston and his friends could roll up with some lino and a box of records and transform these 1960s buildings into an extension of a New York street corner. A local youth worker called Deborah Egan – now director of Sheffield Arts Centre – organised a tour for SMAC 19. They visited multiple youth clubs in South Yorkshire throughout the mid-eighties, running workshops, performing their moves and passing on the knowledge. 'That experience of going to youth clubs in Rotherham or the Sheffield city region had a massive impact in terms of the people that got fed into music culture and clubs in the years to come,' says Winston. 'Ten years down the line I'd get people coming up to me saying, "I remember when you came to our youth club when I were thirteen! You were breakdancing! You changed my life!"'

It's worth pausing here, briefly, just to remind ourselves again of the fundamental role of the dancer in music culture. To give just one example, consider the way hip hop developed in the late seventies after Jamaican-born DJ Kool Herc noticed that dancers responded particularly well to the instrumental sections of old soul records. The idea of mixing between two tracks on two turntables occurred in order to extend the break and to give the dancers more of what they were requesting with their feet and outstretched arms. The dancers provided the seed of a new idea, and that new idea became hip hop. On a more simple and general level, the dancer is quality control. If the music or the presentation of the music isn't good enough, the dancers will respond listlessly, informing the person responsible for the sounds that they'd better do better. They don't need to say a single word in order to communicate what is required.

Teenagers in Sheffield and around the country communicated at the youth-club disco. They brought their lives onto the dancefloor, along with new sounds and movement that the UK was absorbing from North America. This is how dancing works, I think. We bring our raw material onto the dancefloor and use it as the basis for any dancing we do, whether that's a low-key wiggle or spinning on your head like Winston. I believe that dancing improves more than just muscle control. I imagine it as tools you pick up in a video game: a good dance might allow a group of friends to pick up confidence points or mood stars. It might earn them cheat codes that allow access to an otherwise impenetrable cultural life. It might transform them, temporarily powered-up.

In the late 1990s and early 2000s there was a network of youth clubs in east London that had miraculously survived Thatcherism. They nurtured the early forward motion of grime, allowing young MCs and DJs to spit bars and spin tunes for people their own age. Dizzee Rascal once told me that he played his first set at his local youth club, under the name DJ Dizzy D. He wasn't alone: in 2013 nearly 29 per cent of the UK's 10-to-15-year-olds were still using a youth club at least once a week, according to youth-work historian Bernard Davies.

Lady Albemarle would not have been amused by a 2019 YMCA report showing that cuts to youth services instigated in 2010 by the then majority Conservative government's austerity policy had resulted in the closure of 750 youth centres and the loss of more than 4,500 youth workers. Fortunately, the youth of today are highly skilled autodidacts, learning much of what they need online and sharing their knowledge in a digital boomerang. Physical space, however, remains essential – a point that has been made repeatedly by experts in the context of serious youth violence.

The implicit encouragement of plentiful space pre-austerity helped create perpetual waves of everyday dancers who made their way into the specialist nightclubs that built the UK's broad, wide, deep and globally influential music culture. Youth clubs helped create a bedrock for this dance-related culture, which created a dance-related economy. In 2010 there were an estimated 2,150 nightclubs in the UK, with approximately 49 million admissions reaping £1.4 billion in revenue, according to Mintel – although one in five subsequently closed permanently during the pandemic. Youth clubs aren't a sub-sector of charity. They're culture machines.

———

I went to a couple of local youth clubs: very occasionally at our Catholic church (occasional because it was intermittent and not very exciting), and weekly to a brilliant parent-run Thursday session at the Methodist church, where I made loads of friends and had wholesome fun with my peers and a bunch of socially minded adults. The culturally powerful one, though, was a fortnightly under-18s event where brand-new hip hop, house and electro was played in a council-owned hall on the edges of the London borough of Bromley known as the Civic. It existed in a long tradition of passing on knowledge, and an even longer tradition of making money from music-mad teenagers.

Soul DJ Andy Ruw ran under-18s events at the Civic in the late 1970s and early 1980s, as well as hosting Saturday-afternoon sessions for teenagers at the Wag in pre-gentrification Soho. 'I was one of his DJs,' recalled Gene-R on the Soul Source forum in 2007. 'My main residency was at the Wag, keeping the underagers out of trouble, away from the peep shows and red light areas!'

I find more detail down the back of the internet, in a lovingly compiled recollection of late-1970s dancefloor life written by Peter Solar Angel, who was known as Peter Thomas when he was growing up in the Orpington children's home attached to the primary school I'd later attend. His blog post described the first night of a new soul and funk session at the Civic, which replaced a disco night, and outlined what he was wearing: 'I had an old pair of thick woolly pegs [trousers] I'd found in the airing cupboard upstairs in the children's home where I lived. I had a grey v-neck jumper with a white t-shirt and a pair of moccasins, and a white handkerchief in my back pocket.'

Suitably dressed, he could learn moves with his friends from the home and from school, practise them at the Civic and take them uptown to the now-legendary daytime session at Crackers. 'We danced together as "dancing spas" and when the Olympic Runners' song "Keep It Up" came on we did a Gene Kelly, Fred Astaire, Nicholas Brothers move where we switched feet from side to side, facing each other and one went one way and the other went the other way,' he wrote. 'It was something we learned at the Civic . . . we waved our white handkerchiefs around like morris dancers and the handkerchiefs doubled up to wipe the sweat off our brows.' He won a dance contest (to Stargard's disco track 'What You Waitin' For'), and lists the music that was played like a prayer: Herbie Hancock, Earth, Wind & Fire, Third World's 'Now That We Found Love'.

Third World's classic tune was still being played when I attended, although the track was now surrounded by new electro, hip hop and proto-house music. A number of people who went to the Civic ended up working in music, including Pete Reilly, a long-time stalwart of London record label Soul Jazz and the shop Sounds of the Universe. Pete recalls the resident DJ at this iteration of the Civic being Jim Colvin, who was affiliated to JFM, a pirate station which broadcast from Crystal Palace under the tagline 'broadcasting to London, funk capital of the world'. 'It was exciting and somewhat surprising that there was a proper pirate-radio, street-cred DJ playing at an under-18s disco in Orpington,' Pete tells me. 'This would have been end of 1984/into '85, after which me and my mates were 15 and sniffily thought we were too old for an under-18s disco. I was obsessed with hip hop so was always a bit disappointed that they really only played the big hip-hop hits like "White Lines" and "The Message", but [they were] top tunes, and this was still great as a 14-year-old living in the 'burbs. I liked soul, disco and a bit of jazz-funk, too, which is what they mainly played. We also discovered the delights of alcohol and were trying to talk to girls, so it was a heady mix of Liebfraumilch and embarrassment.'

Enquiries to JFM DJ Jim Colvin, Bromley Council and various other rabbit holes failed to confirm Pete's recollection. Eventually I decided to try BBC London DJ Robert Elms and his regular 'Notes & Queries' segment. No one replied – in fairness, it was a very niche enquiry – until the last five minutes of the show, when Andy from Sidcup called in to say that he'd attended the Civic and that he also remembered it being connected to Jim Colvin and JFM.

JFM had a big influence on this part of suburban south-east London, which edged into Kent, largely because one of its DJs was Froggy, who was a huge name in the loosely affiliated southern English crew of DJs and promoters known as the 'soul mafia'. Froggy and his suburban DJ pals oriented thousands of English kids – especially suburban white ones who didn't have access to much African-diasporic music through their families – towards soul and funk at weekenders, often in coastal holiday camps. Weekenders contributed and responded to a wave of home-grown funk and soul bands, including Light of the World, Hi-Tension and Incognito, which were also nourished by clubs and a vibrant and overlapping rollerskating scene. Unusually for the suburban soul pirates, JFM also offered community news, from Greater London Council bulletins to people organising charity events.

Located next to Orpington train station, the Civic was accessible to non-locals. Ross Allen, who'd later become a DJ, label-runner and A&R man, had attended, catching the bus from Erith to get there. The club had a reputation – Allen remembers a friend of his being hit over the head with nunchucks – but it remained very popular with the 13-to-15-year-old demographic. I queued up outside in 1986 or '87, aged around 14, eager to receive its musical offerings.

The DJs played old soul, funk and jazz-funk, alongside established hip-hop classics and brand-new music, often on promo copies before the actual release. This meant tunes that had entered the canon – like Grandmaster Flash and the Furious Five's 'The Message', Herbie Hancock's 'Rockit', Kraftwerk's 'Tour de France' or Shannon's 'Let the Music Play'. It also meant contemporary sounds from across soul, electro, hip hop and house, including the SOS Band's 'The Finest', Dynamix II's 'Just Give the DJ a Break', the Beastie Boys' 'Brass Monkey' or Timex Social Club's brilliant 'Rumors'. We responded with our moves. Boys would breakdance, rocking out a turtle or a windmill or simple bit of top-rocking, stepping one foot forward diagonally while the arms opened and crossed to the side and in front. Friends who went just after me remember dancing to live PAs, too, from early UK hip-hop artist Silver Bullet, whose '20 Seconds to Comply' remains a tuff gem, and a guest appearance by the cast of the original school-based TV show *Grange Hill*, whose musical output has aged less well.

I danced my way in. I learned to move one way to new hip-hop records and another way to late-1970s New York music that fed into it: hard disco like Candido's 'Jingo', which required us to switch up the styles again and step in lines moving sideways, with a clap-jump at the end, like an analogue typewriter's shift–return. I had to watch and learn because everyone else seemed to know the moves, although I now know that they'd have learned them too at some point.

All DJs know that the crowd sometimes likes to move to a familiar tune, like the way a wedding DJ will drop an inter-generational banger – Sweet Female Attitude's 'Flowers' or 'The Twist' by Chubby Checker – and that this can unleash a certain kind of happiness that comes from recognition and moving to music that contains layers of lived experience. Each tune would require a different specific set of movements: Sweet Female Attitude's garage classic requires a neat two-step, waist held up high; 'The Twist' rotates at the knee, which is bent forward – a pivot, better to push down into the floor.

At the Civic our dance-diversions included movements from the previous generation, like the Boat Dance, which would be instigated by a particular tune: the Gap Band's 'Oops Up Side Your Head'. Everyone would sit on the floor in a line as if we were in a long canoe, tap-tapping the floor one side, clapping above our heads and shimmying back and forth. Then there was Steve Walsh's version of the Fatback Band's 'I Found Lovin'', with its participatory terrace-goes-disco chorus, to which people would collectively raise an arm and poke the air, pointing as percussion and punctuation.

A few name dances crossed over to the UK in the decades that preceded the internet, and one of these was the Running Man. For this, you'd dance on the spot, sliding one foot back in order to give the impression of progress, knees up, arms pumping back as if making headway by pulling on a horizontal bar. It was a street-evolved bounce groove that had been transmitted to mainstream Western European playgrounds, bedrooms and nightclubs by dance-literate pop stars like Janet Jackson and MC Hammer – and Vanilla Ice.

All this dance-based transmission is made easier by the fact that we are a highly adaptive species. Anthropologist Joseph Henrich, in his 2016 book *The Secret of Our Success*, argues that evolution began to favour those who 'were good cultural learners'. He isn't talking about dancing, but he might as well be: humans are 'prolific, spontaneous and automatic imitators', he writes, 'even willing to copy seemingly unnecessary or purely stylistic steps'. I might add here that knowing how to dance to the tightly wrapped airhorns of Public Enemy was neither unnecessary nor purely stylistic. It showed fluency and cultural capital and could be the difference between being relatively safe and being hit on the head with nunchucks.

There was an undercurrent of violence that surrounded many aspects of suburban lives in the 1980s. It was in the Civic that I first came across the concept of being 'taxed' – that if you went to the toilets you might find your pocket money being redistributed without your consent – and heard stories of people being steamed on the train: some youths violently separating other youths from their belongings. This was just one of the reasons why so many of us headed for clubs uptown as soon as we could. It was better, but it was also safer.

Justin Boreland would travel on the train from Brixton to the Civic, a direct line that took about half an hour. He came from a musical family – his uncle, as we heard earlier, was fast-chat reggae MC and pop star Smiley Culture – and Justin began making music in his mid-teens. He was an early voice in UK hip hop, starting out with a crew called the Sly Faders and later appearing on Bomb Da Bass's 'Megablast Rap' as MC Merlin. 'I remember this place in Orpington,' he recalls, memory sliding back into his consciousness. 'We'd travel there – they had a disco.' He remembers it as the advent of hip hop and electronic music: 'We had a falling away of traditional ways of dancing and we had new, vibrant hip-hop moves. The fashion complemented it. It was a whole lifestyle, really. It was holistic, even down to your attitude. The music back then was much more empowering and generally happy, positive, progressive. It was very lively, very sociable – generally.'

Then a little chuckle. 'I loved it. I remember graffiti. A youth centre-type shape.' A little pause. 'I remember some of us mis-behaving because we had a group of us that was getting up to mischief. I really didn't like it, to be honest. They'd even rob boys, some of them. The robber ones weren't really us, but they'd latch onto us. It was kind of hard to tell them, "Step off with that rubbish." But that's exactly what we wanted to do.'

I start to imagine the teenage Merlin, locally famous and learning to manage all these competing aspects of a teenage disco: the pull of music; dressing up; girls; the compressing effects of being recognisable; the millimetres of wriggle room when robber ones latch onto you on the train between Brixton and Orpington. 'It would cause massive problems,' he says. 'They'd oftentimes come from Lewisham or New Cross; they were a harder strain of what we were – we went to chat to girls. They were about robbing and would use violence as their primary means of intimidation, ultimately for victim compli-ance. On rare occasions, they'd even stab people. You'd go up there the next week or the week after and you'd find your-self getting chased by a lot of grown men, after the pub, who wanted to kill you, literally. Because they thought you robbed one of their sons the week before. They were very organised then.' Justin is deep in remembering, and the feeling of long-forgotten fear transmits down the phone. 'To a certain extent I understand their grief. You can't do that, especially around their manor. You had to know where you were going, how you were moving.' We pause, recollect, collect. 'It's funny,' he says. 'To socialise, to communicate, to engage with other youth, you'd travel through hostile areas – just to hear a tune or watch someone dance.'

Across the country there were thousands of influential youth-club dances and under-18s nights run by people who didn't have to, catering for young teenagers who wanted to hear a tune or dance with their peers. For example, Kentish station Invicta Sound ran early-evening nightclub events for teenagers in Canterbury in a club by the station, and friends remember a long-lost event called Beefy's Mansion Jams in Putney. There were dedicated pop and disco nights for the underage at Bali Hai and Romeo and Juliet's in 1980s Hull. Daytimers were made by and for South Asian youth and created a rich cultural seam that would influence UK music and dancing at the time – the *Sun* newspaper was writing about 'acid bhangra' in 1988 – and in the decades to come. Underage events were nationwide and were organised locally by youth workers and savvy promoters. They offered fresh music played by DJs – many of whom would have benefited from their own teenage excursions – with specialist expertise in the contingent skills of music, dancing and managing youthful energy. The job required a mix of learned experience, improvisation and the ability to make space for the younger ones, readying the ground for the next wave.

6: SLOW DANCE AT THE SCHOOL DISCO

Learning to move in dinner halls, high-street
nightclubs and holiday camps, mid-1980s

Secondary schools in the 1980s often ran discos. For some
readers this will bring back mortifying memories. Others
might find a funny recollection bubbling up. Younger readers might just find the concept bizarre. Either way, this area
of extra-curricular life transformed school dinner halls and
assembly spaces into dancefloors across the country. I went to
St John Rigby, a Catholic school on the borough boundary of
Bromley and Croydon, on the far southern edges of Greater
London. It later fell into sink-school territory after the headteacher, an ex-nun, siphoned the school budget into Gucci
jewellery and trips to Malta with her favourite priests. She
went to prison, and the school slipped into a negative spiral
which ended in closure.

Many of my classmates had Irish or Italian parents or
grandparents, and we came from all across the borough, travelling five miles in my case to go to a school where I once saw
a teacher get into a fist fight with a child in the playground. It
was averagely crap for the 1980s, with a handful of genuinely
inspirational staff. The wash of hip hop's city-central explosion reached us through *Street Sounds* compilations, cassette
mixtapes and a short-lived, peer-to-peer breakdance club at
lunchtimes, where one breakdancing kid would try to teach
interested others, including me, how to do an arm wave. Boys

at my school had access to this music, carrying electro and rap in their Tacchini tracksuit pockets and easy manner. There was a tricky line here that related to my status as a girl, which was broadly based on whether boys fancied you or not, and which I recognised could be further disrupted by showing too much interest in or knowledge of music. Dancing was for everyone, but musical expertise existed in the realm that boys occupied. I knew that I loved music. I also knew that the easiest way for me to engage with it was by ordinary movement – and, perhaps subconsciously, by quietly sucking up the detail and stashing it away in my joints and muscles, ready to be released when I was in a more accepting environment.

Intermittent discos took place on a Friday evening, when older kids or a mobile DJ would roll into the dinner hall, turn the lights off and the music up. For many of us it was another part of the interlocking dancefloors that circled 'proper' city-centre nightclubs, of which we'd soon gain in-depth – if second-hand – knowledge by reading and memorising club listings in *i-D* or *Time Out*. The school disco was another easy-access, youth-friendly starter pack for club culture, for what a friend described as 'the *Grange Hill* generation'.

Geoff Barton is the General Secretary of ASCL, which is the main union for school and college leaders, meaning that he is regularly quoted in the media whenever it comes to education matters. In his youth he was an aspiring DJ, never quite operating under his chosen name of Geoffy B. When he was at school in the 1970s, Friday-night school discos were common and widespread, adding to a landscape of youth-club dancing and discos in local football clubs or community centres. 'I think this was because you had staff who saw their role not just as teaching in the classroom, but as having a strong community dimension,' he says, when we chat. Some teachers would have been embarrassed by dancing on school premises, he adds, but there were plenty who loved music and dancing and wanted to share and celebrate this aspect of their lives and culture: 'There was a sense that the adult generation was helping the younger generation to understand – this is what it means to go to a disco; this is how you behave.' Additionally, he points out, the pre-internet school disco was a rare place in which you could hear specialist music. 'It was an important moment because in the seventies and eighties you couldn't have music in your pocket, and you couldn't control a playlist. You were reliant on what Radio 1 was playing – except at the school disco, when suddenly you had this democratisation. The DJ would play the music that you in your school wanted to hear.' It was, he says, 'a proto-type' for club culture.

I have a fragment of memory from my own school discos: of dancing on the margins, by the canteen shutters, where I might have done some high kicks. A boy – let's call him Gerard – who was tall, and who later got suspended for setting the soles of his shoes on fire, pointed and laughed at me. I stopped doing high kicks, immediately and for ever. Dancing can release and repair, but it can also contain a person within the invisible walls of shame. I was ashamed at having danced wrong, for having confused my love of gymnastics with how to behave at a school disco. It's a reminder that almost anyone can be shamed into stillness and that a snide comment can put someone off for life.

It didn't entirely put me off, though, because in 1987 I organised a fifth-year (Year 10) disco with my friend Anna to raise money for a CAT scanner. I don't recall exactly why we were raising money for a CAT scanner, but maybe it was something to do with my dad, Rick, who was suffering the slow-motion loss of his muscle strength. He was trying, with incredible effort and occasional outbursts of rage, to keep going under very difficult circumstances. I think of the word 'degeneration' and how it relates to his role as father, and how disability can disrupt your place in the generational hierarchy. I learned that it's hard for a daughter to cut food up for their parent, although probably not as hard as it is for a parent to be fed cut-up food by their child. We were all de-generationed by incoming quadriplegia.

Two sixth-formers at John Rigby ran a mobile disco called R&B Groovin' and, in the time-honoured tradition, gave younger members of the school community the encourage-ment of example, alongside practical advice on DJing and the broader culture. Their protégés Raj and James were behind the turntables for our fundraising party, playing records like 'All and All' by Joyce Sims, absorbed from real London dance-floors, alongside chart songs that covered electro, house, soul, hip hop, pop and soft rock: Timex Social Club's 'Rumors', Whitney Houston, Wham! and Rick Astley. Some of the year group bobbed up and down slightly self-consciously, with others testing out moves half-learned off TV. There were unprepared, unformatted dances in which a friendship group formed a circle around which there would be basic dancing – no one entering the space in the middle. The dancing wasn't particularly good, but it was great fun.

One of my very first memories of secondary school is watching my friend Bernard Achampong taking on St John Rigby's top breakdancer in the first year of school, outside the languages block. He'd have won, too, had the headteacher not charged onto their tiny dancefloor of taped-up cardboard boxes and put an end to the uprocking, freezes and caterpillars. Bernard also found the ladder that linked school discos to proper nightclubs, and later helped set up BBC Radio 1Xtra, picking up eight Sony Radio Academy awards along the way. 'Dancing was a superpower,' he said, when I asked him about it, offering a magnanimous perspective on our shared school discos. 'There was honour reserved for those who could move. Not because they were technically superior but because they were liberated. It's less about control over your body and more about non-conforming to the limits of it.'

There were, he recognised, sexual politics in the school disco, which offered him a 'new lesson in identity, social hierarchy and gender preference'. He then told me a story about sitting next to a girl on the bus. This particular girl was considered to be undeniably fanciable across the whole school community, and their interaction, innocent as it was, bumped him up the hierarchy for the rest of the school year. 'However,' he said, 'because my place in the pecking order had been set from an earlier dancefloor sorting, she was out of my reach.' He also remembers seeing, for the first time, two girls dancing with each other. 'I would hazard a guess that for some, this dancefloor encounter was their first access to the kind of relationship they wanted to have.'

The slow dance offered the chance to learn what it felt like to be pressed up against another body: three or so minutes

of standing embrace in which you moved together, feet stepping a tiny circle so that you'd rotate, girl arms up around boy
shoulders, boy hands lower. Leon Dawkins asked me for a
slow dance at our school disco. He was one of the first genuinely charismatic people I'd ever met – a big character in the
small world of a secondary school. We danced close and warm
to perennial end-of-nighter 'Move Closer' by Phyllis Nelson,
and I discovered that the combination of physical proximity,
music and movement can dissolve time. Leon went on to
manage early hardcore crew Ratpack, and I bumped into him
at Ministry of Sound a decade or so later. We stayed in touch,
intermittently, until he died aged 29 of complications caused
by a car crash he'd barely survived a few years earlier, and
which happened on the way to a rave booking. RIP Leon, and
thank you for dancing with me.

The last two or three tunes at school discos, youth clubs
and high-street clubs all across the UK almost always involved
slow dances. They represented the tail end of partner-
dancing in everyday British society, and would soon shuffle
off the dancefloor entirely. We've already heard about national
dances, but we'll pause here for a basic and necessarily partial
tour of partner-dancing in this country to better understand
how Generation X grew up dancing slowies.

For much of history, and in many places around the world,
close partner-dancing was considered immodest and therefore
not to be enacted in public, especially by unmarried people,
let alone schoolkids. Early depictions of dance in Britain tend
to show round dances or circles where people hold hands and
move around, something we can still see in the Hokey Cokey.
Many popular pre-19th-century European dances required

partners to be respectably side by side or separated by arm's length, although I wonder if some people danced close anyway, perhaps during raucous seasonal celebrations away from self-appointed arbiters of decency.

Quadrilles were gentle, miniature square dances for a handful of couples, and they moved between European countries, absorbing and changing as they landed and bedded in. There are Caribbean quadrilles – camp and ballroom-style – which exist for obvious reasons. In the 19th century new variants of the polka and the waltz arrived in the UK from mainland Europe, transmitted by travelling orchestras playing new compositions in theatres. Both dances allowed for new levels of pre-marital proximity and, naturally, both were initially considered scandalous before becoming mainstream. In 1909 *Punch* satirised the newly popular Boston Waltz, in which 'the recommended upright posture of Victorian generations was flagrantly disregarded in favour of a lounging closeness between the sexes that challenged moral propriety', according to Emeritus Professor of Dance History and Ethnography Theresa Buckland in 'Dancing Out of Time: The Forgotten Boston of Edwardian England'. Buckland illuminates the difference between the old style, where high-status Victorians were expected to engage in light conversation while dancing, and the new style, in which it was 'treason to talk'. This is a dancefloor rule that will be familiar to music lovers across the space–time continuum, and I have a recent example. Decades into my dancefloor life I began attending the weekly Steam Down jazz jam in south London, where the host would sometimes shout a half-sentence into the microphone. 'If you wanna talk,' he'd say, pausing, so that the entire room could finish the sentence, '. . . go outside!'

Theresa Buckland's work brings the early 1900s to life, beautifully. Sprung dancefloors began emerging, including one at the Savoy built in 1911 to an 'entirely novel plan' and resting on 150 steel springs that 'ensured the desired amount of elasticity for dancing'. Light classical composers often doubled up as conductors of dance orchestras, using the response of the dancers to inform what they composed next. She quotes bandleader Felix Godin, who said, 'The first and really essential thing to know is what the dancers want.' Partner-dancing was a well-established part of the ordinary, everyday way British people danced at weddings, in fancy dancehalls and in momentary celebrations in front rooms and kitchens – whirling or being whirled around. Other dance configurations weaved in and out across the decades in response to the music of life and demographic circumstances, sometimes literally changing the landscape. Travis Elborough's *A Walk in the Park: The Life and Times of a People's Institution* describes a fad for dancing in parks in the 1920s. 'In public parks the craze for syncopation . . . began to affect the topography,' Elborough writes, explaining that bandstands became sunken and that seats were ripped out. From 1938 onwards Mecca Ballrooms created novelty dances like the Lambeth Walk and Knees Up, Mother Brown as marketing tools that allowed thousands of people the pleasure of doing very simple dances all together, without having to learn complex partnered steps.

One more example of partner-dancing: American GIs during World War II brought Harlem-built, African American pair-dancing in the form of the highly skilled Lindy Hop and the simplified Jitterbug, both of which were widely adopted into a version generally known in the UK as 'the Jive'. Couples would face each other – sometimes holding one hand for better leverage or to change the centre of gravity – before mirroring and refracting each other's steps and riffing on a movement theme. In the fifties and sixties a wave of pop productions arrived with simple, collective dance crazes baked in and which were distributed to mainstream US teenagers through TV show *American Bandstand*, then subsequently exported across the Atlantic. Dances still required other people – your best friend, your boy or girl, the other people squashed in around you – but they'd lost the formal, codified constraints of partnered dancing. The Twist coiled the dancers away from each other, and from the early 1960s onwards many dances in the UK and North America involved individual movement, done collectively. There were – and are – exceptions (for example, in many South American dance styles) that remained partnered.

School discos themselves were beginning a decade-long shuffle towards extinction. The details and context of everyday life were changing in the multiple ways they're always changing. In particular, music began heading towards acid house and rave, making it harder for schools to countenance having something so heavily drug-associated on their patch. ASCL's Geoff Barton, aka DJ Geoffy B, offers another part of the picture, which relates to concerns about the sexualisation of young people. People were getting squeamish about things like slow dances, he said, and were beginning to ask if it was appropriate on school premises, 'on our territory, on our watch'. Gradually, the school disco spilled down to primary schools, as an end-of-school ritual to mimic what the big kids did, even though the big kids weren't doing it any more. By the mid-to-late nineties secondary-school discos were anachronistic; by the turn of the millennium they'd been replaced by a new dancefloor: the Year 13 prom, which arrived in the UK from the US. Nostalgia for school discos became the basis for a popular event. *Time Out*'s listings for New Year's Eve 2001 included 'School Disco at the London Arena', catering for 10,000 twenty-somethings who'd dance to live PAs from Go West! and Ben from Curiosity Killed the Cat, alongside the house band the Sixth Formers, until 6 a.m.

Dance as part of the curriculum has been in significant decline in UK schools since 2010, according to One Dance UK. The act of moving to music releases endorphins into the bloodstream, which can be useful for children and young adults experiencing worries or challenges. It also improves thinking skills and creative problem-solving, which should be of interest to those who plan the education of our young. A few wonderful schools have embedded dance into the curriculum. I'd say it should be prioritised everywhere else, too.

———

In the final quarter of the 20th century most people who lived in towns could name a local nightclub that would send you free tickets for your 18th birthday and which was usually up or down some carpeted stairs off the high street. It was mildly multi-generational and mainstream, with chrome-and-mirror decor and very sticky carpets. You'd get underage school kids chancing it – high-street clubs were accessible to anyone who didn't look 12 – alongside people in their twenties and thirties who lacked the desire or means to go anywhere else.

Local spots near me included Langtry's by Beckenham Junction train station, the Blue Orchid in Croydon and Bonnie's in Downham. Whatever the club was named, it got an extra 's' on the end, like there really was a person called Bonnie in Downham who opened a club and invited us all round. At least some of them were owned by people, not corporations – my friends at Orpington College knew someone whose dad owned Zen's in Dartford, and so we traipsed down there, over the Kent border, to mimic jacking to house music by Marshall Jefferson, in the days before we had the capacity to get ourselves uptown. High-street clubs were another practice pen, where we could accumulate the forward motion we needed to leap to the next level. Many of these local nightclubs have now closed, but some of them still exist and some are even still owned by members of the local community. Timepiece in the south-west of England, for example, has been run by two music fans for 25 years, under a self-deprecating tagline: 'Exeter's Half-Decent Nightclub'.

I had Cornish cousins, which meant I also got to experience a local nightclub outside of my immediate environment. The Harbour Lights was on the Cornish side of the Tamar river in Torpoint, with big glass windows that looked out across the water, and I went with my cousins, aged 14 or so, when we visited one summer. To get there, you had to board the Torpoint Ferry, which moved up and down the river on a big iron cable. More importantly, you had to get the ferry back, otherwise you were stranded. Being able to see the water from inside the disco helped, if you counted success as having to run for the last ferry before throwing yourself onboard like a cartoon character. We walked up the stairs and quickly began dancing, all girls together, until the boys – a mix of local kids and teenage cadets known as 'matlows' from the nearby naval training centre at HMS *Raleigh* – were drunk enough to join in. The mixture of people on the dancefloor represented local tensions, creating rare opportunities for different parts of the community to engage in the same activity, in the same place. Sometimes, of course, hostilities broke out. There were also opportunities for reconciliation, with boys and girls slow dancing together to Serge Gainsbourg's 'Je t'aime . . .', which was always played at the end of the night.

I learned that I moved differently to my cousins, who comprised Saltash's tiny psychobilly scene (basically, them and their friends from up the road) and hence moved with more of a punky bounce than me. In Cornwall I looked more like a Londoner than I did in London, and that was at least in part due to the way I moved. I was at a suburban house party many years later, stepping side to side, shoulders sliding backwards in a slow groove. Someone came up to me, drunk, and said, 'Oh my god, you dance like all the hard girls at my school,' then stumbled off. I wasn't a hard girl, and this wasn't really a hard-girl dance, but I had clearly absorbed – borrowed, perhaps – moves that were culturally recognisable to someone who'd also grown up with people from a range of backgrounds.

And, finally, in this round-up of movable teenage discos, there were holiday camps. These contained purpose-built function rooms that were similar to the larger chain nightclubs, albeit attached to a caravan park or campsite. Butlin's in Filey, Yorkshire, had been built with two large dance spaces, each taking 3,000 dancers, with room for another 2,000 seated at tables. These spaces had been hosting off-season weekend-long celebrations of music and dancing for thousands of funk and soul-loving UK youth since 1979, when DJ Froggy held the first Caister Soul and Funk week-ender. The culture was documented at the time by Danny Baker in an episode of the London Weekend Television pro-gramme *Twentieth Century Box*, broadcast in 1980. Footage introduced us to four fans who were flicking through the vinyl in Solar Records, in the forecourt of Brixton tube sta-tion. They were members of one of the many soul and funk tribes – in this case the 'Brixton Frontline', a group of young people from the area with day jobs as van drivers, computer programmers and shop assistants. Footage showed them at a Caister reunion night in north London, where a few skilful dancers and energetic boppers were making the most of the space. A group made a human pyramid, with the top per-son presenting their bare bum to the room in the culturally specific tradition of the moonie. DJ Chris Hill introduced a song, 'We Are the Ovaltineys', which was the theme song to a popular Sunday-afternoon children's programme on proto-pirate Radio Luxembourg back in the 1940s. Two girls in sailor-neck t-shirts with the word 'Ovaltiney' sewn in fab-ric on the back executed their pre-prepared dance onstage, between the DJ and the crowd, which the DJ completed with an 'oi oi' powered through the mic. A conga made its way through the squash, underneath balconies that were draped with homemade banners proclaiming the presence of the various tribes in the house. 'Ain't no stopping us now,' said the DJ, lowering the volume on the tune of the same name. 'Who wants a national soul day in 1981?' The crowd roared in agreement.

During the summer season, holiday camps would host more mainstream weekend discos offering chart music and a level of anonymity not available at home. For the shy but curious individual this was a chance to explore the dancer you might be when removed from people who might otherwise destroy you with the body-stilling powers of public humiliation. For me, a caravan park in Saundersfoot, near Tenby on the south coast of Wales circa 1985 provided a space where I practised dancing to Madonna and Prince with my sister, both of us dolled up in fancy dress as punks, which meant wearing a black bin liner as a dress over fishnet tights and using black eye liner as lipstick. I could expand the edges of my dance-floor self there, hundreds of miles from controlling boys and hard girls with short haircuts and brutal takedowns. I learned that it was easier to connect to other people, anywhere, on any dancefloor, if you had some basic moves. Learning how to move signalled a confidence that I didn't really possess but which I learned how to approximate.

Johnno Burgess had a similar experience in a caravan park in Woolacombe, Devon. He and I later worked together, inventing our own jobs with mid-nineties music magazine *Jockey Slut*, which he followed with decades running a club, Bugged Out!, and multiple music festivals – including week-enders in holiday parks. His is a life lived in music, and it began for him at a campsite disco, aged 15. 'I was terrified of the idea of dancing. I was the last one to get up. I thought, "I'm too shy, I'll be rubbish at it." By the time I did get up, I wouldn't leave the dancefloor, to the point where everyone else was bored and wanted to go home and I was still dancing on my own. It's that connection – "Oh my god, all the music I love, I can move around to it!" Something dawned on me, and after that you couldn't stop me.' We have to find our dancing feet somewhere, and it's easier to find them away from the mocking gaze of peers who are acutely attuned to any external manifestation of internal weakness. 'I wasn't in an environment where everyone was a lot better than me,' said Johnno. 'I was surrounded by holidaymakers. "This is totally fine," I thought. "I can dance by myself."' He went home and within a year was running a mobile-disco set-up, providing the sounds and space for his peers to experience the same revelation.

Youth-oriented dancefloors offered the opportunity to learn that the music sounds better when it's danced to, and when it's communal. Listening is active, and there are elements of music that you can access only by moving to it. Moving together creates connection with the people around you. For better or worse, many people of my generation had the opportunity to learn this together, in schools, in high-street nightclubs and in holiday-camp discos.

7: JACKIN' IN THE GYMNASIUM

The 1980s Chicago high school that
helped build house music

The dinner hall of my secondary school where we danced at early-evening discos was over 6,000 kilometres away from Mendel Catholic High School, a popular boys-only fee-paying school located at 111th and King Drive, in the historically Black area of South Side Chicago. It was light years away culturally. Mendel was at the epicentre of an informal network of high-school dances that had a direct role in the evolution of Chicago house music and dancing – a combination of sound and movement which would have a huge influence on global culture.

I wasn't the only music-mad adolescent in the UK who felt a connection with the city of Chicago. In the late 1980s and early 1990s young people all over the country knew the names of the city's top DJs and producers because we saw house-music artists on the weekly BBC chart run-down *Top of the Pops*, heard them on mainstream and specialist radio and listened to them on the *Now That's What I Call Music!* compilations given as birthday and Christmas presents. Farley 'Jackmaster' Funk reached the top ten with 'Love Can't Turn Around' in 1986, while 'Jack Your Body' by Steve 'Silk' Hurley hit number one the following year.

The music hopped across the Atlantic through a variety of routes. Another of these involved Michael 'Jazzy M' Schiniou, who hosted a regular show on pirate station LWR from 1985 that featured house-music takeovers by Chicago station WNUR-FM and aired the latest tunes. WNUR was a college radio station with a powerful transmitter that could reach around four million people, with a focus on the northern and western suburbs. Rob Olson was responsible for dance programming and, in 1986, released a compilation, *Rob Olson's Chicago Jack Beat*, for UK label Rhythm King. The label organised a tour of London record stores, where Olson met Jazzy M, who invited him onto his show. 'Hanging out during his show we came up with the "link up",' says Olson, after I track him down on LinkedIn (he switched from house to houses, and is now in real estate). Recently he donated copies of his two compilations to the Modern Dance Music Research and Archiving Foundation at the DuSable Museum of African American History in Chicago. 'It was a bit of theatre of the mind, but we played it like we were linking up by satellite, and I would play the newest releases in Chicago house. In actual fact, I was recording the shows on cassette and mailing them to him.'

The show was renamed *The Jackin' Zone* – Jazzy M tells me it was the first house-music radio programme in Europe – and it became an important link in transmitting the sound from one set of dancefloors to another. We were dancing to the same beat, which created a powerful sense of togetherness. I found evidence of this when I watched a video of the parties that my friend Graham Styles ran in Chislehurst Caves in suburban south-east London between 1990 and 1991. The footage degraded badly before he transferred it to YouTube, but it still shows a lot: the promoters setting up, DJs playing hard funk and then house music, and a fleeting moment where I can see myself standing by the wall, smiling. At the very end, the cameraman – who has been on the dancefloor all night – films one of his friends, who is pretending to be a news journalist. 'Reporting from somewhere in Chislehurst Caves,' he begins, rapidly losing the ability to speak coherently, 'not too far from . . .' The cameraman finishes the sentence for him: 'On the Chicago borders.'

———

House music developed in Black and Latin queer spaces in Chicago in the late 1970s and early 1980s, most famously in an intensely rough-and-ready club called the Warehouse, which was run by Robert Williams, with Frankie Knuckles as the resident DJ. The music drew from disco and European electronic music, and turned those ingredients into bare-bones tracks designed for dancing, at an average of 128 beats per minute. House music began as a highly creative and ultra-local sub-genre that answered the needs of a marginalised community. It's now global, and big enough to be celebrated by the city authorities, with annual events alongside those focusing on gospel, jazz and the blues.

School dances, or 'sock hops' in the gradually disappearing terminology of the 1950s, were standard fare across the US at the time, although Mendel High students had access to unimaginable levels of musical excellence, the dance-music equivalent of having Jean-Michel Basquiat drop into after-school art club or Serena Williams cover Friday-afternoon PE. The city's best DJs played at the school's bi-level parties: Frankie Knuckles, and Ron Hardy – who took over at the Warehouse when Knuckles left – and the city-famous Hot Mix 5 DJs, who reached a million listeners a week. A flyer from September 1986 has the headline 'Ron Hardy Strikes Again at Mendel Bi-Level', plus a short note from the DJ himself ('I will be jacking you at Mendel') and the tagline 'Come ride the rhythm'.

Only 10 per cent of Black students in the US went to fee-paying schools when professors Diana T. Slaughter-Defoe and Deborah J. Johnson published *Visible Now: Blacks in Private Schools*, just two years after Ron Hardy got thousands of Mendel kids and their friends riding the rhythm in the school gymnasium. It was not perhaps what the middle-class families who could afford to pay for education had in mind when they sent their kids to Mendel. Parents forked out on average $1,624 a year, according to the National Catholic Association, who published 'Catholic Schools and Their Finances' in 1986 (and included Mendel in their sample of 208 schools).

Mendel was considered a Black school by the time of the Bi-Level parties, according to Kirkland Townsend, who started at the school in 1975. The student body was still 60 per cent white when he joined, with 1,900 students on the roll, he told a 2019 panel discussion for the Chicago Black Social Map. By the time he left in 1978 all the white students had left, leaving an all-Black graduating class of only 900. The cause was white flight, and the exit of so many students at once caused the school multiple headaches, not least that of running a large establishment at less than 50 per cent capacity. Luckily for the school bursar, Townsend was on the roll. He persuaded the Augustinian friars who ran the school to let him DJ and run dances, and for 12 years he packed the place out every Saturday night.

The scene had been set, and this dancefloor was primed for success. 'Early eighties, mid-eighties, I provided a platform for all the house artists,' Townsend said. 'I gave them a platform to perform in front of three or four thousand kids. It started out with the private schools and the Catholic schools in the South Side, but it grew.' The money he raised, he said, 'kept the doors of the school open from 1979 to 1988'.

The presence of house music's originators at Mendel's Bi-Level dances prepared large numbers of young Chicagoans from a range of backgrounds to amplify and strengthen the networks of juice bars, rollerdiscos and front-room house parties that built house music as a genre. They bumped it out of one locality and into a global genre that is still living and evolving decades later. Part of the reason house grew was the presence of the physical space in which thousands of very young people could experience and share the music in a safe facsimile of the adult environment. These circumstances gave young people ownership of the culture, not least because it was happening in their school. House music wasn't being presented to them as a finished entity for purchase and consumption. It was incomplete and therefore able to absorb whatever they wanted to bring to it: a new sound, dance or way of dressing – or just their complete attention, in the moment.

Ron Trent is a prominent DJ, producer and artful dancer who grew up a few blocks from Mendel High. By about 1986 his 14-year-old self was attending Bi-Level dances and soon graduated to DJing in the basement cafeteria. He's a very funny man, prone to looming towards the screen to lighten another insightful point with a facial expression or gesture and a baritone chuckle. 'The music of the day, for the cool kids, was the soundtrack being created by Frankie Knuckles and Ron Hardy,' he explains, adding that Mendel was known as 'top tier'. 'The culture, the kids that went to that school, it kind of spilled out.' This expansion from neccesarily niche beginnings to events catering to a wide range of teenagers represented what he describes as a 'coming of age' for house music. 'The culture was starting to spin out to the heterosexual community – [before] it had mainly been gay.'

A *Chicago Tribune* story from April 1986 explained an overtly educational slant to one Mendel school dance. DJ and community activist Kitty Neely had been playing on radio station WJPC for three years, with an estimated audience of 10,000 teenagers. Usually this would precipitate the formation of a Kitty Neely fan club – fan clubs being a 1980s version of a verified Instagram account in which you'd send off an application to join and then would get items back in the post: maybe a badge, a newsletter or a signed photograph. Kitty had an idea that merged house music's appeal to teenagers with the kind of pedagogical impulse that had James Brown recording his 1966 stay-in-school single 'Don't Be a Drop-Out'. She came up with 'Joining Academics with Music', or J.A.M., motivating listeners to get better grades by setting a C-average requirement for membership.

J.A.M.'s first dance party was at Mendel High, with a line-up that included Farley 'Jackmaster' Funk, who would very soon have a number-one UK hit with 'Love Can't Turn Around'. Sensibly from a promotions point of view, you didn't actually have to be a member to attend, but if you did join J.A.M., you'd also get access to group skating and bowling parties, discounts at On Records and, of course, that autographed picture of Kitty Neely. You would, though, have to suffer the indignity of showing a photostat of your most recent grades on the door to prove that your membership was still valid. 'The idea,' wrote the *Tribune*, 'is to get your grades UP and have a GOOD time.'

Regardless of the grades required to gain entry, the high-school dances offered a high-quality foundation degree in the music. Queer Chicago house historian Micah E. Salkind quotes DJ Celeste Alexander describing the networks of spaces that schooled young dancers as 'stair steps': 'At each step along the way senior dancers who hadn't yet graduated to the next level would socialize younger disciples, teaching them how one moved, dressed, or courted a partner before leaving to learn a similar set of social practices in the next institution up the chain.'

By 1987 local TV stations, including Channel 7's *Eyewitness News*, were reporting from the dancefloor at places like Charlie Club and the Power House, the latter being widely acknowledged in the house history books as the venue Frankie Knuckles went to after the Warehouse. Footage shows packed dancefloors, with dressed-up men and women moving their bodies in a range of ways: some are sliding their shoulders, many have their arms in the air; everyone looks in the zone.

Highly skilled dance crews were also part of the mix, although their era of dominance was fading by this point. There are whole other books to be written about this aspect of Chicago's cultural life, but for the purposes of this story it's just neccesary to know that they existed and were important. The rise and spread of house music – and the sheer numbers swept up in its addictive and sensual grooves – meant that people increasingly moved how they felt, within the basic movement language of the music, rather than following the choreographed brilliance of crews in matching t-shirts. House music suggested – requested, even – that you come as you are. This was also true for the crews as they adapted to the new sounds. Jose 'Gringo' Echevarria told the story of his Latin dance crew All Stars and their rivals Zoolitos and Tasteful Dancers in *The Real Dance Fever*. 'House music was doing well and underground music was everywhere,' he wrote. 'If you wanted to dance to good soulful house music you went to the Power Plant, Music Box, or Club La Rays. There were so many clubs, since the creators and inventors of underground house music, the music we loved, were in Chicago. It was raw, soulful and very expressive. You could say what you wanted to say and dance to what you wanted.'

'I belonged to one, voluntarily–involuntarily,' says Ron Trent of the dance crews, communicating the essence of the situation through the medium of raised eyebrows, 'because they inducted me. I will spare you the gory detail.' It was, he says, very eccentric. 'These dance crews had their own style that set them apart; their own dances that they did, that were kinda seminal to the underground ethic, which was more the idea that we get on the dancefloor and we express ourselves. There may have been some dances [like] jacking, but everything else was free-form. The idea and the concept was being developed.'

Despite the original span of movement styles, house music became intimately connected with jacking, and vice versa. It's a dance with a human name instead of the animal nouns that famous dances have sometimes adopted, like the Turkey Trot or the Funky Chicken. The artists in this emerging musical style absorbed the dance into their titles: Farley 'Jackmaster' Funk, Jack N. House and Jackmaster Dick. Multiple tracks contained the word 'jack', like 'Time to Jack', or its b-side 'Jack for Daze', released under the artist name Chip E. the Godfather of House. 'House is suited for the way people dance now, which is like being in bed but standing up,' said 20-year-old Chip E. to *Spin* magazine journalist Barry Walters in November 1986. '"Jacking" is to house what "boogying" was to disco. We gear our music for dancing, not radio.'

Jacking required further explanation to *Spin*'s readers, and the explanation was delivered in the context of peril: '. . . for Chicago's Black gays threatened by AIDS, jacking the night away at an afterhours club has become the most physically gratifying alternative to sex'. In 1986 a graph showing HIV diagnoses in the city was only a small way up a steep line. By 1988 3,748 Chicago men and women had an HIV diagnosis, a number that would continue to rise until 2012, when 36,064 people found their test came back positive. A comment by @DavidB underneath a crackly version of 'Jack the Dick' by Jackmaster Dick on YouTube evokes the broader dancefloor: 'I was a young teen when this was out. Whole time I remember watching the hood chicks jack to this. We'd jack our bodies til we were soaked with sweat.'

Informing the city's dancefloors was a social and cultural context that provided a particular flavour to what took place. 'Chicago, you have your historical Southern migration. You have the jazz era. You have the oppression, the segregation; so it's more of an aggressive, blue-collar approach to things,' says Ron Trent. He makes a bear-like roar: 'More "got to release a lot of stress!"-type thing.' Compared to the 'finesse' evident in New York, he says, illustrating the point by moving his arms around elegantly, everything in Chicago is 'more aggressive. That has a lot to do with the state of mind, the refinement, or lack thereof. There's beauty in rawness, too. That is expressed through the dancers, what they're living, what they're going through. It's the difference between a punk ethic and an Alvin Ailey show.'

What people were living through in early-1980s Chicago included urban decay, with all the subsequent effects on unemployment and failing infrastructure. For queer communities of colour there was the additional burden of serious homophobia. House music became a coping mechanism for some – which also meant that being into house music identified you as queer or queer-friendly. 'When you were called "house" it wasn't a term of endearment,' said Duane Powell, a DJ and house-music historian, during the Chicago Black Social Map panel. 'It was trying to say, "Look at them house fags."'

Let's visualise the jack as it's understood today. The lower half of the body is rooted, pushing into the floor in a bounce groove while the upper body is pulling up. Someone who can expand this description is artist–scholar Dr Meida McNeal, who has decades of involvement with house-music dance-floors. She's an academic at Columbia College in Chicago and a founding member of African-diasporic feminist dance collective Honey Pot. She first saw the jack as a pre-teen, when her older sister took her to house parties between 1986 and

1989, and again, later, when she and her friends reached high school and began going out to their own parties and basement jams. There were other dance styles present too, she says as we chat over Zoom. For example, a basic box step, where you'd start by stepping right foot over left, step one foot back, then the other, and then step it over to start again. This was the end of the era of dance crews, she says, although you'd still have some showing up with prepared choreography. The main move, though, was the jack.

Like all dance styles, it has deep roots. There's a story, says McNeal, about Black fraternities at university dancing to house music, and this being incorporated into the jack. 'You can see this kind of quote–unquote masculinity in the aggressiveness or the attack [movement quality] of the form,' adding another element that fed into the jack's lineage mix. 'Punk and slam dancing – definitely an influence,' she says. 'There were moments when the circle could get really rough. It would oftentimes be when boys, men, whatever, would take over the floor and push everybody else out. It was physical, really aggressive.' There was, she says, often a woman or two in the mix, but it was considered slightly dangerous.

The jack appears to be unpartnered, a 'stripped-down social dance', as McNeal says, but that's not the whole story. 'It's not a partner-dance,' she adds, 'but you might be connected with someone in an exchange. And so to that end it reminds me of forebears in Chicago, of [dance styles] bopping or stepping. It's not the same, it's not smooth like that, but there's an exchange between you and a partner that reminds me of those older forms.' Sometimes jacking dancers would move together, people jacking up and against each other, or jacking with the speakers in a man–machine movement duet. Jacking's deeper origins show up in the ways the hips are activated and the lower body is weighted, she says. 'It's that counter-pull; you're going up but you're going down. There's something really grounded about jacking. You're really push-ing into the floor as you're pushing up, and the root and the foundation of that is West Africa.'

It was McNeal's time living and studying in Trinidad – and attending the island-wide parties known as fêtes, which take place during the annual Trinidad & Tobago Carnival – that helped her see the connections in new ways. 'I began to feel, "Oh, there are some parallels here." Connections across the diaspora, in terms of the party as life-affirming celebration, and trance-inducing through endurance and the durational experience of folks being together, with bodies close together, and sweat, heat, bass and music. My experience of Carnival, of the fêtes, was: "This feels like a club, a house set."'

The jack might have been central but, as McNeal points out, there was a lot of varied dancing going on. The variation also extends to nomenclature: dances have multiple names across time and space, and jacking was – is – no excep-tion. Respected Chicago DJ John Simmons, whose father's Foxxplayer Sound ran the sound system at high-school dances throughout the 1980s, including at Mendel High, told me that jacking was also known as 'humping'. What is fair to say is that the jack is the dance style that was transported, in tandem with the music, to the UK, where house became known as 'acid house' after commingling with jazz-dance, electro, suburban soul and imported 12-inches. UK dancers retained the grounded aspect of the jack and added a new element: using the arms or hands to slice the air rhythmically in front of the body. The dance was evolving as it spread.

Mendel High and other educational establishments in the city allowed waves of local youth to transmute life experience into a shocked-out, repetitive, trance-inducing dance style. More broadly, they created additional space for teenagers to learn a palette of dance moves, to become educated in the culture and to school each other, and to use that knowledge to dance their way into new venues. The Bi-Level dances couldn't solve Mendel High's financial problems entirely, and the school closed in 1988, just as house music hit large sections of the UK.

8: SMOKE AND STROBES

Girlhood stresses ameliorated by acid house in
London, Leeds and Liverpool, 1988–1991

We've already heard about people needing to dance when
times were hard, whether they were rural kids squashed
together at a cheap dance in Ireland or teenage steppas at a
Jah Shaka dance. We'll spend a bit of time with the girls in the
dance – especially worried teenage ones – and I want to start
with a reminder that this remains a topical issue.

Anna Duberg works at the intersection of physiotherapy and child and adolescent psychiatry at the University of
Örebro in Sweden. In 2013 she published her own research,
looking at the effects of a twice-weekly collaborative dance
class on girls aged 13 to 18 who were experiencing anxiety-
related headaches, stomach aches or tiredness. She found that
relaxed, improvised dance sessions increased how well the
young women felt and decreased physical symptoms, emotional distress and daytime tiredness. Dance also decreased
the use of medication. Less easy to fit in a tick-box list was the
'blossoming' she saw in the young women she worked with,
or the happiness which spread over her face as she described
the project. 'Creative movement can be an avenue for self-
expression,' she explained over a video call, 'and it enables
dancers to explore emotions through movement.' Dancing,
she added, allows young women to begin a process of homecoming to their bodies. Teenage girls inhabit a new body, one

that will have changed drastically since they were children, and which will continue to change over the coming years. Perhaps they need to get to know their new shape – Duberg's 'homecoming' – and do so by moving it, owning it.

The research didn't just sit on a library shelf. It became Dans för Hälsa (Dance for Health), which now takes place in 150 cities across Sweden and which has expanded into Hungary and Finland. Her classes fostered a non-judgemental atmosphere and what she calls 'supportive togetherness', something I recognise from the acid-house dancefloors I attended as a teenage girl, carrying my own troubles. She also experienced the benefits of dance for young women, finding that it provided 'integrity', in the sense of stability. 'Dance made it easier for me to know who I was,' she said. 'And to find a value in who I was. It became like a wall, in a positive way. I know I have value because I have found it in my body.'

I asked her if there's any difference between moving to music in a dance studio or in a strobe-striated basement. 'The body doesn't know or care,' she replied. 'It's movement, and that's the secret. You can do it everywhere. The important thing is to do it your way.'

———

I was doing it my way in October 1988, when I attended the opening night of Rage at Heaven, a subterranean club between the River Thames and Trafalgar Square in London. Rage went on to become heavily influential and can legitimately claim to be the fire that sparked the music genre known as jungle – thanks to Fabio and Grooverider, who were resident

DJs, initially upstairs in the smaller Star Bar – but at the tail end of 1988 it was simply an exciting new weekly session at a famous venue. It was the first autumn of acid house – the UK iteration of Chicago house – which, in the locally specific version I landed in, also included strands of eclectic pop and electronic music from mainland Europe, transplanted by DJs from Ibiza and known as 'balearic'. House music had arrived. I fell in love with the genre and, in time-honoured fashion, diverted money meant for school dinners into 12-inch records and *Jack Trax* compilation albums.

Heaven was a 2,000-capacity club underneath the arches beneath Charing Cross railway terminus which had started life as a large wine cellar for the hotel above. On Valentine's Day 1973 it opened as Global Village, a multi-purpose venue with two dancefloors, restaurants and an upstairs auditorium showing art-house films. It was renamed Heaven in 1979, with a roller-rink in the main dance area, and was bought by entre-preneur Richard Branson two years later.

By the autumn of '88 there were two weekly acid-house nights at the club – an example of new culture benefiting from spaces that had been opened up by communities that experienced disproportionate levels of violence. Heaven was London's largest gay nightclub, and in April 1988 five Leeds United supporters appeared at Southwark Crown Court, having allegedly punched and kicked people in the queue, shouting, 'Kill the queers,' and attacking one club-goer until he was unconscious. The judge directed the jury to find them not guilty because he was 'not content with the identification evidence'.

The club night known as Rage took place on Thursdays, and on the opening night I arrived early with my friends. I was

16, and only managed to get myself in the queue through a combination of family complications which made my parents less attentive to my whereabouts and which made me more keen to dance my situation away. It also helped that school was on half-term that particular week. We slowly moved closer to the woman who took our £5 admission fee at a makeshift table at the door. Inside, the large corridor was flanked by arches, under which someone was selling vinyl records, and a hippy calling himself the Peace Prophet was walking about offering people flowers. We were drawn by the music to the back of the room, away from the stage and the DJs, even though most people were still arriving or milling about. The music was loud, powerful, and the dancefloor filled up around us. People appeared in the gaps between the spooked green lasers that punctuated the darkness and which invited touch, even though they were untouchable. I was dancing a very basic version of the Chicago house jack, pushing into the floor and slicing my arms through the air in a circle with my friends, and gradually we separated out as Heaven filled up.

Acid house, as I experienced it, was very mixed in terms of gender and ethnicity. There were, no doubt, middle-class and historically wealthy people in the place, but I'd say that most people on that dancefloor weren't middle class and didn't come from families with long lines of inherited wealth behind them. Older people were in the place, too. At some point in the late 1980s or early 1990s I read an interview with Mark Moore from S'Express, who had a big pop hit with 'Theme from S'Express' and who I'd see out in the clubs. I recalled him telling the story of taking avant-garde composer Philip Glass to Rage. So, in the spirit of the 10,000 rabbit holes on which this book is built, I emailed Moore. He replied within the hour. 'I arranged to take Philip,' he confirmed, 'so he could experience the music in a suitable environment. We warned Philip that we were going to be taking ecstasy, and I must say we weren't quite sure how he was going to react. "The thing about young people," he said wisely, "is that you think you're the only people who have taken drugs." In the club he didn't dance but listened intently to the music, nodding his head gently in time to the beats. After a while he looked up at me with a big smile and said, "I get it. And I also get why you think my music is connected to your music." I have to say, Philip Glass not only makes great music but he's also one of the most chilled and wonderful people to party with.'

Heaven was a queer club, but queerness wasn't particularly obvious at the acid-house nights it hosted, because there wasn't a lot of people getting off with each other – as far as I remember anyway. Simply being in a venue that was known as a gay club meant that I was exposed to new ideas, and I doubt I was the only one. I heard the phrase 'sexuality is a spectrum' for the first time on the train up to the club, and this was mind-blowing in the context of the Catholic binaries I'd grown up with.

Resident DJ Colin Faver knew how to draw everyone onto the dancefloor with songs we already knew from tapes and our townie forays – the Night Writers' 'Let the Music Use You' or Mr Fingers' sublime 'Can You Feel It' – along with songs I didn't know but quickly got to know: Richie Rich's 'Salsa House', Sandee's 'Notice Me' and Ralphi Rosario's 'You Used to Hold Me'. We were being pushed into action and feeling by the DJs, and at the same time we informed their decisions about what to play next through the way we responded to their selections. I don't remember hearing any Todd Terry tunes that first night, but they were almost certainly played, because his releases – which fused house music with a hip-hop kick – were massive, and because he was visiting London that week, playing at the Wag Club. He understood that the dancers had high expectations and that they desired intensity. 'They want action,' he later told me of his DJ sets. 'I've got to keep it harder, play all they want to hear: "Bango", "Can You Party". That's what they want. I try to kill people on the dancefloor.'

For the next two years, until we turned 18, when some of us peeled off to jobs or further study in other cities, we went back to Heaven as often as we could and adopted the stance of regulars. The repetition of returning as often as possible – even if, for me, that was mostly during the school holidays, and sometimes only for a couple of hours because I had to get the last train home – generated a layered experience. Having butterflies in my stomach in the queue in October or January, when it was cold, and then again, in the summer, wearing a t-shirt with a huge E in the middle and the words 'Can You Feel It?' printed underneath. Hearing the same big tunes on repeated visits and soaking them up slightly differently on each occasion. Hearing a new track for the first time, and someone leaning down to tell you that they know this one or that they heard someone else – Weatherall, Farley, Oakenfold – play it out, and occasionally being able to pass on key information yourself. I distinctly remember 'French Kiss' by Chicago DJ Lil Louis in 1989, certainly before it became a pop hit, reaching number two in the UK charts, because tunes could circulate on DJ-only promotional white labels for many months before they became available to buy. Most of us wore trainers or Kickers – I had a pair of much-cherished Reebok Classics – and this inevitably affected our moves, although there was little collective expectation around skill or technique and little judgement around dancing. I didn't feel like I had to learn any moves. I just had to dance in a way that made sense to the people around me.

As well as Rage on a Thursday, we went to Land of Oz on a Monday. Paul Oakenfold's Spectrum had been taking place at the club since April of that year but had been forced to briefly close and rename itself after the *Sun* newspaper ran an investigative story about acid house at Heaven, linking it with LSD use. One night at Land of Oz my friend Darren tapped me on the shoulder and motioned that I follow him. He'd created a space for himself in the culture by reading magazines, talking to people in record shops and selling jeans that he'd accessorised with hand-drawn smiley faces – and, of course, going to loads of clubs. He took me up some stairs that looked down onto the dancefloor and into a dark corner, right at the back of the club, so that I could see something that most people couldn't see: an actual doorway. He pushed the door, and it opened. There were no bouncers, just an entrance between Heaven and the stand-alone venue next door, the Soundshaft. He wanted to show me where a renowned and tiny club night called Future took place. I wouldn't have had the requisite stripes to make it to the front of the very long queue outside Future – I only barely made it past the bouncer eye-rolls at my teenage face and into Heaven. We stood on a balcony that looked down into the smaller club. A photograph by Dave Swindells from earlier in the year captured a moment between strobe flashes at this intense night: faces, hands, a blonde bubble perm, dreads, bandanas, t-shirts sticking to bodies that were dancing right up against each other. I realised that there were levels to the dance, and that there were ways of gaining access.

William Gibson famously once said that the future's already here, it's just unevenly distributed. The same could be said of the past. Echoes of London's recent past showed up in the bright newness of acid house. I remember seeing Matthew Glamorre enact a piece of performance art on a podium in the middle of the dancefloor at Rage. He was part of a clubbing DNA that included performance artist Leigh Bowery's infamous club Taboo and the New Romantics that came out of Taboo's cultural predecessor the Blitz. Glamorre's presence among the jacking Chicago house and European body-music 12-inches was a reminder of both Heaven as a queer space and of London's recent cultural past. The dancefloor is broader and wider than you might imagine, especially when you're looking back at it through the narrowing lens of time. The band St Etienne, who combined sixties pop music with dancefloor flavours they picked up through their own nightlife excursions, played their first-ever show at Rage, in autumn 1990. 'The subsonic bass was unbelievable,' says keyboardist and producer Bob Stanley, when I ask him to verify this half-remembered fact. 'Our singer was Donna Savage and we had a rapper called Spider. Our set was made up of a mid-tempo techno thing, "Stoned to Say the Least", and our two singles, "Kiss and Make Up" and "Only Love Can Break Your Heart". The tempo of our set was about 50bpm slower than anything else I heard that night. The bass was amazing, but it didn't help my nerves. We couldn't afford keyboard stands, so we used ironing boards.'

St Etienne playing keyboards on ironing boards doesn't fit exactly with our current perception of acid-house dancefloors. However, it illustrates an idea that I believe to be true: that each dancing space contains the leaf-litter of what went before and the seeds of what will follow. If you look closely, you'll find examples of both.

Author and DJ Brian Belle-Fortune, who also worked as an intensive-care nurse at the world-famous Great Ormond Street Hospital for Children, bridged another of the sub-cultural worlds that preceded acid house – that of jazz-dance. 'A lot of the skill of dancing went out when the rave scene came in,' he told me. 'It's not a criticism, because rave was about "just do your thing, shake it all about". Kemi [DJ Kemistry, who went on to have an influential role in the early days of jungle and drum 'n' bass] was going out before some of her friends, and she described the way people moved as "the dance with the arms".' London's acid-house dancefloors focused on the hands, the arms and the waist, he said. 'I started going to raves in 1988, didn't do any Es till about '94. It democratised the dancefloor. You could do anything. In the old dances – places like Crackers – you really had to bring your best bits. This, anyone could dance. Anyone could jack their body. It was "move how you want to move", and no one's going to laugh at you.'

Freedom, within the broad movement language of Chicago's jack, appealed to large numbers of people. An edition of *Time Out* from October 1988 included 70 nightclubs in the listings and showed house and acid house being played every night of the week. A handful of entries indicated the style's ubiquity by advertising themselves as 'aciiiid-free' or 'no house', while Dave Swindell's Clubs Editor column described acid house's 'incredible popularity'. The Astoria, just up Charing Cross Road, was turning away 'up to 1,000 ravers every Friday and Saturday night' for Nicky Holloway's Sin sessions, according to a Thames TV documentary from 1989.

There is also a story about drugs. Some might say that the popularity of dancing to house music in the late eighties was entirely to do with illegal drugs, predominantly ecstasy. Those people have clearly never experienced what happens to your body when you've been moving together in time with other people for hours and hours. The way your body overtakes your brain; when the music talks directly to your chest. Many people had, of course, discovered the kinetic glow initiated by MDMA, but it's not true to say that *everyone* was on drugs. Me and my best friends weren't. We were too young and too high on just being there, and would joke-chant to ourselves and anyone that would listen: 'We don't need drugs! We get high on the music!' So, yes, ecstasy was there if you wanted it, and a lot of people did, but it was also expensive. The standard £20 per pill was inaccessible to people on the receiving end of WH Smith Saturday-girl wages.

Drugs and dancing became conflated. While drugs might assist dancing, dancing is not required in order to take drugs. You can take drugs anywhere: in bedrooms, parks, bus stops, or in the toilets of an expensive restaurant. Actually, it's harder to take them in clubs because there's a man on the door whose exact job, theoretically at least, is to stop you bringing them inside. The importance of drugs within house music in the

UK lay in the interconnections between the chemicals, the way it gave some parts of the community permission to dance, and the dancing. I believe that a bedrock of dancing existed within families, and was built upon in the quantity of spaces available for dancing.

DJ and dancefloor aficionado Marsha 'Marshmello' Smith was on similar dancefloors to me, and she made an important point when we discussed the subject on a panel. She had been encultured into dancing within her Caribbean family, watching reggae dancers stepping at house parties when she was a small child, and later danced her way into clubs and raves, including those at the Astoria, where Thames TV cameras panned down Charing Cross Road to show the sheer numbers waiting to get in. 'The way I grew up and started raving, it was always about music and dance. Culturally, I didn't need drugs to dance,' she said. 'I was so happy to be in the dance or at a rave. I was just feeding off the energy of other people, not even knowing they were on drugs. People used to ask me what E I was on, and I didn't know what they meant.' MDMA was an additional doorway into dancing, which also explains why people who already had such doorways might not have needed it so much.

We – me and my friends – spent months basking in the ambient glow of culture happening within an accessible distance. We familiarised ourselves with the terminology of personnel and location, mentally placing the information on our expanding maps of the city and learning to navigate it like a Monopoly board. We replaced the game's landmarks with clubs, record shops and famous (to us) locations, like the stretch of road where acid-house night Trip had spilled out onto the street and dancers had jacked to the sound of police sirens and someone's car stereo. If you wanted it, it was there, even for a suburban girl like me who liked school and was expected to do well, whatever that meant. I was unaware at this point of the Bromley Contingent, the famous punk crew comprised of Siouxsie Sioux, Billy Idol, Soo Catwoman and their friends, but I imagine the glow extended outwards back then too, giving other local youth the peacock strut of being in proximity to cultural greatness, even when your actual back-drop was Bromley North station.

There was, eventually, a full-blown moral panic. TV and print media covered acid house extensively, usually in the form of undercover investigations involving the words 'evil dance craze'. One journalist reported seeing 'thousands of ecstasy wrappers', clearly not knowing that ecstasy never came in a wrapper – even I knew that it came in fat pills or capsules. I remember reading a report in which a policeman was asked for his perspective on having witnessed thousands of young people raving all night to amplified electronic music. His answer focused on the movement: that the youth were not even dancing with each other any more, they were dancing alone, atomised. He expressed shock at this, but we weren't separate and everyone was included, even those without a partner to dance with. We were together, like tiny dancing dots that – zoomed out – revealed a much bigger picture.

I knew how to dance to house music without going any-where near a club. Partly because the music contained instruction – the 4/4 beat scaffolding the simple movement of limbs, just as other time signatures or instrumental inflec-tions suggest hips or footwork – but also because there was plenty of it to see. The music and culture had straddled the underground and the mainstream from the start, with music videos that hit the charts, news reports and as freeze-frames in the photography that accompanied the increasing number of magazine and newspaper articles on house music's rapid expansion across the country. The video to D-Mob's poppy 'We Call It Acieed' showed dancers doing an anglicised version of the Chicago jack, with feet planted hip distance apart, torsos contracting back and forth from the core, and with arms flung up and down like an updated version of 1960s dances like the Jerk. The music and the dancing arrived together, were transmitted together, and continued to evolve together in the clubs.

London DJ and producer Frankie Valentine played widely throughout the early days of house music in the UK and across mainland Europe. He played with Chicago originator Frankie Knuckles and Ibizan instigator DJ Alfredo, and had residences across London – at the Park in Kensington for the promoters behind Sunrise; at Back to the Future at the Limelight on Shaftesbury Avenue; then later at the End, off New Oxford Street – and in Berlin at Tresor. He was the guy the Detroit techno originators Underground Resistance chose to support them when they toured Japan in 1995, which is like being asked to support Stravinsky. He's still going today.

Valentine's name was ubiquitous on the flyers I enthusiastically collected when the clubs closed at 2 a.m. Flyers were fast-turnover DIY artworks: red rectangular Rage flyers that toyed with early computer graphics; or club informationals that doubled up as a comic strip, as was the case with one for Labyrinth in Dalston, which contained a story about Captain Rave, who could rave for 96 hours straight. The flyers were like prescriptions, offering detailed information about what clubland's medicine cabinet contained. Today, Valentine carries with him four decades of dancefloor observations. He's also a thoughtful and exceptionally understated person, prefacing everything with 'I can only speak for myself' when we catch up in a late-night phone call.

'When people listen to music, they dance their story,' he says. 'Some people will only have five minutes of story in their feet. Others will have a way of expressing themselves for hours and hours.' He pauses. 'Most people dance to express themselves and how they're feeling at that given moment in time. They're dancing their own story, but they're also dancing the story of what's being played to them by the DJ. It's a combination of both things. Your way of expressing, of dancing your story, is unique to you.'

In many ways this is obvious. Body language betrays our feelings, because movement contains the emotional results of our story, even when we try to pretend otherwise. Perhaps we can work it out through movement just as effectively as we can through talking. This is true for everyday difficulties as much as it is for the most extreme trauma. I'm reminded of something I read once, about a Rwandan elder who explained the problems they had with Western volunteers after the genocide in 1994. The volunteer mental-health workers wanted to take people into dingy rooms, where they'd ask them to relive their horrific experiences verbally. What they needed, said the elder, was sunshine, dancing and drums.

———

The dance reflects and provides for the collective times, but it also reflects and provides for the individual. A number of things were happening when I first started going to clubs, which may have amplified my need for movement. My dad was becoming increasingly disabled. Tissue growing on his spine was shutting down the nerve pathways that convey information around the body, causing loss of strength and, therefore, movement. He'd have major spinal surgery on more than 20 occasions. The operations would provide a temporary pause in the losses, but they required lengthy recovery times and a long haul back to what was already a diminished position, strength-wise. This regular peril of surgery and the everyday slog of physical disappointment took a toll on him and the rest of the family. He was a remarkable person whose tenacity and generous encouragement was a refutation of the deficit model of disability. His physical weakness generated huge reserves of determination. However, anyone who has lived with a disabled parent will understand the cost of coping. Unwell adults can be understandably volatile, especially ones going through a marriage breakdown. Me and my siblings absorbed our family's reality in a variety of ways, sharing the idea that we were loved and that illness was part of life, but experiencing the ramifications in our own ways.

The realities of our family situation required a different stance depending on the location and context. Inside the family home, there's a need to see and not see: I see that I am cutting up your food, or helping you get dressed, or brushing your hair (badly), but I can't be entirely in myself when I'm doing it because these tasks require separation. A teenage daughter is not supposed to help a father pull on his trousers.

This teenage daughter has to help this father pull on his trousers, and to do so requires a certain kind of dissociation – probably on both sides. I stood in a certain way if we were out. Not just because my dad would probably tell me not to slouch, but as a kind of brace against looks and comments. Holding or tensing up body parts – armouring, as it would be described by therapeutic professionals – can be a useful way to contain emotions, striking new adaptive shapes in the face of difficult events. My need for movement increased in tandem with his decreasing strength.

Luckily this coincided with a cultural moment that took place in nightclubs, warehouses and (for some people) fields, and I danced my way through the trouble. This meant that I was at a few important beginnings and endings, including the last night of an already famous club called Shoom, by then taking place on a Wednesday night at the Park in Kensington. I'd applied for a membership card on a previous visit, which meant I was on the mailing list for the club newsletter. A letter announcing the final night came through the front door while I was getting ready for school one morning in early November 1989. I poured milk onto my Shreddies and waved the photocopied A4 sheet around the kitchen table. 'Well, you've got to go,' said my mum, Meg, attending to the tea and a stream of toast, as if I were talking about a school drama performance or a cross-country race. 'It's the last night.' My friend Angela had a different experience with her mother. She took her mid-teen self to an acid-house night at the Pleasuredrome in Birkenhead and had the sobering experience of seeing her mum appear through the dry ice, ready to march her daughter back out past the bouncers.

My mum's response was an unexpected turn of events. Firstly, she had always been pretty strict: I had to go to Mass every Sunday, plus Holy Days of Obligation, and to regular confession, at which I had to invent sins because I didn't have enough real ones. Secondly, my dad would have gone spare if he'd known, because there'd be no way he was letting his teenage eldest daughter go to a nightclub until all hours of the morning – are you kidding? – especially ones that were all over the news as being evil and drug-crazed. Although, honestly, he was so wrapped up in his own undoing at this point that his ability to know where his kids were was as diminished as his ability to pick up a fork. He might insist on a strict curfew, but he wasn't really in a position to enforce it. Meg crept out of bed, slammed the front door and ran the bathroom taps so it sounded like I was home. She made it possible for me to dance more, at a time when she danced less because her husband and dance partner was becoming physically incapacitated. This was how I went to the last night of Shoom.

The club had started in autumn 1987 and was the first place to affix the hippy-era smiley face to what would become acid house. The club's flyers stated 'No ruffians!' and advertised the music policy as 'Chicago House and Frankfurt Beat', aiming for a 'mixed/gay crowd', according to Matteo Sedazzari, who ran the *Positive Energy of Madness* fanzine and was a regular at the club. I was one of the last people into the last Shoom, a fact that I can't take too much pride in, partly because this involved ditching my friends. The club was an intense, musically and culturally powerful catalyst, but it also soaked up too much of the acid-house story and, later, I helped write that into stone. The story was that Shoom was at the centre of the universe, but, in reality, it was just one of the many nerve centres that existed in London, Leeds, Blackburn, Glasgow and other places. It provided an important spark, but it wasn't the only one.

That night at the last Shoom I skipped down the stairs into a sweatbox. There was air conditioning at the Park but it didn't make much difference, because it was like walking into a wall of heat and dance-generated humidity. The movement was intense, people rocking out and sending their gestural energy towards the DJ, Danny Rampling, who was behind the decks, eyes closed, arms marking out time above his head. His then partner Jenni was standing on top of a speaker, jacking and rocking, free and deep in the sound, in the moment. I remember seeing Boy George and a girl from my primary school. There were chants that fell off the football terraces, transformed, into the club – '*Shoom, shoom, shoom*' or '*Happy, happy, joy, joy*' – and Boy George's band Jesus Loves You performed 'After the Love'. I danced my feet around Frankie Knuckles's mesmeric 'Your Love' and mirrored my friend, who had his tag name 'Razor' on a bespoke lettered belt, twirling his finger upwards in its own tiny dance. The night finished at 2 a.m., and I don't know how I got home, but I do remember crunching quietly on the gravel in the driveway and carefully opening the back door, slipping into bed for a few dreamy hours. My mum might have let me go out midweek, but there was no way she'd let me take any time off school the next day. I sat in maths, happy.

Jolyon's feet would tell a different story to mine. He started going to clubs in Leeds at the same time I was going out in

London. His place was the Warehouse. It was a 1,100-capacity venue that opened in 1979, with a heavyweight sound system installed by American DJ Greg James, who had opened London's first New York-style club, the Embassy. He held a residency at the Warehouse for the first six months of its life, teaching the other DJs the freshly imported skill of mixing so that Yorkshire dancers could experience this new way of hearing music before most other people in the country.

Jolyon and I met on a Manchester dancefloor, and we went to the Warehouse together in early 1991. We share some spatial memories: a large dark building with plenty of space to roam around; a DJ booth where the resident DJs Nightmares on Wax held the crowd and responded to them; packed dancefloors; sweaty stairs; and the amplifying qualities of the heat, dry ice and strobe machines. I sent Jolyon a message one evening, asking about his early experiences dancing to house music at the Warehouse. 'It was all about what was happening on the dancefloor,' he wrote back, DMs spilling through in a wave of recollection. 'In 1989 that often meant watching some of the amazing Black kids and mostly white ballet-school kids doing spins and jazz dancing. There were times when a circle would form and we would watch these boys – rarely girls – showing off. This gave the dancefloor extra energy.' This was not the case in the London clubs I went to, although I later saw similar circles at New York clubs like Timmy Regisford's Shelter.

The story of the virtuosic northern jazz dancers is an important one. It's yet another example of the unacknowledged ways people who can trace their ancestry back to Britain's former colonies built not just the post-war state but also much post-war culture. The dancers Jolyon saw at the Warehouse were part of a countrywide community of talented physical creatives who'd been blessing dancefloors at all-dayers, soul weekenders and on the jazz-dance scene since the late 1970s.

Mark 'Snowboy' Cotgrove's deliciously detailed history of the UK jazz-dance scene *From Jazz Funk & Fusion to Acid Jazz* defers to the dancers. He spent nearly a decade interviewing people across the country, including a section on Leeds dancers with names like Mad Max and crews named the Elite and the Tuxedos. One interviewee, Miller the Driller, benefited from a state school that included dance on the curriculum, and described deepening his education by watching crews like the Firm, who would practise at the local community centre, the Mandela. This is the equation in action: encouragement + space = movement. Another Leeds dancer, Ian Hylton, described going to the Warehouse and, in a five-word phrase – 'when they'd let me in!' – encapsulated the everyday humiliation and disappointment of racist door policies, wherever and whenever they happen.

There was a tacit agreement at the time (which persists in some places), applied by club owners through the medium of bouncers and door pickers, whereby dancers with Fred Astaire levels of skill could be denied entry. Hardly anyone got turned away for being too young, but loads of people were turned away for being too Black, despite the undeniably Black roots of house music. Young men especially were routinely turned away from all kinds of clubs due to racist door policies. A small number of Black British citizens were allowed in so that club owners wouldn't fall foul of the Race Relations Act, but the rest would be barred. Door policies of this kind are individually painful and nationally embarrassing.

As I've mentioned already, I started going out aged 16, with my friend who was 15. We went with her brother and his friends, who were also underage. I don't remember anyone in my immediate or extended group of friends being refused entry to a club on the basis of age (although one of my underage friends was arrested for foolishly rolling up a joint in the queue – then came back to the club a few hours later after he'd been released). Some bouncers and door people let underage people in through this nationwide loophole because they didn't care, or knew the owners didn't care – or because they understood how much the younger ones wanted to gain entry. In the early days of acid house I heard of a small contingent known as 'Shoom Babies', who were 13 or 14. You didn't need ID – frankly, ID didn't really exist then – and the idea of taking a passport to a club was as ludicrous as being asked to bring a letter of recommendation from your headteacher or parish priest. I benefited from this applied nuance in ways I couldn't imagine at the time.

Door supervisors, or bouncers, remained unregulated throughout the 1980s and 1990s, until a Security Industry Authority licence was introduced in 2001. Underage clubbing became harder still when clubs began demanding passports or photo ID, usually as part of licensing demands handed out by local authorities and the police. I'd hazard a guess that at least some of the young men and women who made acid house such a vibe, and who evolved and mutated the music into the next phase of hardcore and, subsequently, jungle and drum 'n' bass, didn't have passports, regardless of whether or not they'd reached their 18th birthday. Passports are expensive. And that's not to mention the exclusion experienced by people who don't have settled residency for one reason or another – including approximately 120,000 young people living in Britain without full citizenship or secured status, 65,000 of whom were born in Britain. How do they get into the dance? I consider it very weird and scary that nightclubs have become an extension of border patrol.

Clubs in the late eighties and into the nineties regularly went well over capacity. The words 'health' and 'safety' didn't have an ampersand linking the two, and the magnetic bringing together of the words 'safe' and 'guarding' was decades away. Nights might not have seemed safe to an outside observer, but the era did bring a certain quality to our movement. Clubs were packed and there wasn't room for detailed footwork. Dance styles changed, and as the music became harder there was less performance on the dancefloor. Things became more uniform: a kind of basic voguing, with lots of arms. The constraints of space and the democratically low bar for dancers, many of whom arrived straight from youth clubs and school discos, caused the emergence of a new and idiosyncratically British style of rave dancing where kids would supplant technique with stamina. You'd see dancing on the spot with hands flexed and swooping or jabbing, creating fast shapes around the head and torso, or arms in the air, transmitting and receiving at the same time. The moves emerged because of the music, but also because of the spaces into which we were packed like slippery sardines.

My generation's interpretation of Chicago's jack-central dancefloors contained the potential to change the way young men and women related to each other. I got chatting to a guy in Liverpool, after an event where I'd been talking about clubs and community centres. This was decades later, so we were both looking backwards, collecting what we could from muscle memory and fragments of recollection. He was telling me about Voodoo, an influential techno club that created a centre-of-the-universe moment in the city in the early 1990s. 'It taught men a lot,' he said, his feet slipping back towards that dark, sweaty cellar. 'We all looked the same. Girls dressed the same as us. It made you feel different about copping off.' He was saying, I think, that clubs like Voodoo taught him that young men and women had plenty in common, were equals, and that this revelation caused him to rethink his approach to finding love or sex.

I might have been one of those girls. I was in jeans and a t-shirt, recognising how my body liked to move, how it could stretch and contract on its own terms, without having to consider how this affected my status as it related to being fanciable, as it had at school. I was there to dance, and I would dance for hours and hours. Anna Wood's poem 'Lines Written a Few Miles Outside Blackburn, on Revisiting the Site of the Sett End Pub, April 10, 2021' contains embodied recollections that send me back in time: '*An unspoken, predicted life melted . . . I moved out of control, into softness.*'

My predicted suburban life melted away under huge speaker stacks and on wooden dancefloors. I dropped the tension life had provided and I too moved into softness.

———

There is a clip on the internet that lasts under a minute and was filmed at a club called Quadrant Park in Bootle, Merseyside. The dancers are drowning out the opening bars of N-Joi's 'Anthem' with the shouting and the whistles and the noise dancers make when they're in full collective conversation with the DJ. Arms are raised, dancers are picking notes out of the hot air with their hands, heads bent back like baby birds. There's a pause in the music as the tune prepares to rebuild around its own bare bones. Collective music created by the thousands of dancing bodies punctuating the tunes powering out of the sound system. And then an eruption as the tune drops, dancers generating a mass rhythmic spasm that causes an outburst of involuntary laughter in me as I absorb the scene through the remove of my laptop.

Quadrant Park opened in 1985, playing commercial dance music, and was popular enough to attract *The Hitman and Her*, a roving TV show hosted by Michaela Strachan (now better known for her role on BBC's *Springwatch*) and pop producer Pete Waterman from within a commercial nightclub. By December 1989 attendances had dropped to a few hundred. The owner, Jim Spencer, recognised that house music was the place to be and hired Mike Knowler as the new resident DJ. He had his own experiences in the dance, alongside a professional life as a college lecturer and professional audio engineer. He knew what was required sound-wise, and ensured the club brought in a three-way, 20-kilowatt rig, similar to one you'd use for a rock concert. Within six months people were travelling to the club from all over the UK and attendances regularly reached over 2,000 each week. In December 1990 it was voted the number-one club by the

UK's best-selling DJ magazine, *Jocks*, which would soon be retitled *DJ Magazine*.

The club was well known across the dancefloor community and had a reputation for being intense, even by early-nineties standards. It was considered to be more part of rave's lineage than club culture, which is to say that it sat on the working-class side of dancing's class divide, even though the soundtrack was almost identical to more middle-class places. Acid house and rave slung together large numbers of young people from different backgrounds, in a highly social situation. Most of those caught up in the first few years of acid house would have gone to socially mixed schools in and around cities, with classmates whose parents were council tenants or homeowners, employed (or not) at different levels in a variety of industries. England's class structures sorted classmates into different spaces after school – unless they met on equal terms on the dancefloor.

The story of Quadrant Park provides an excellent example of the layered links between early-nineties dancefloors and those populated by working-class youth a generation before, specifically those of northern soul. Mike Knowler had grown up in the late 1960s, dancing all night at the Twisted Wheel, on Whitworth Street in Manchester, a famous and influential soul night that schooled a local generation in the rejuvenating powers of all-night dancing. It took place in a venue in which I'd step and shuffle to house and techno more than two decades later. Knowler was a gifted dancer and could do the acrobatic moves associated with northern soul. 'I'd take pride in the fact that I could do the splits and spin like a top,' he says, when we delve into the past on the phone. 'As well as the Twisted Wheel, I used to go to the Highland Room at the Blackpool

Mecca and, much later, Wigan Casino. I would dance non-stop, for up to eight hours, fuelled by amphetamine sulphate. I did this between 1969 and 1977. I could lose a stone and a half in a night's dancing. I loved the disco era and learned how to do the Bump and the Hustle. My best friend from the Twisted Wheel went on to study dance at the London Contemporary Dance School. In another life, I would have loved to have been a professional dancer.' Instead, he unleashed the dance in others. They might not have been able to do the splits or a tight turn on the balls of their feet, but they danced how they felt. They matched what they had in their bodies with what the music required, and they danced for hours.

Now, with the passage of time, I realise that nightclubs and dancefloor-focused venues are cultural institutions that contain multitudes. They're valuable like the Royal Opera House or the National Gallery. Berlin recognised this when it gave famous club Berghain 'High Culture Status', which brings with it a lower tax rate. I wish we would do the same in this country.

9: NORTHERN DANCEFLOORS

Detroit techno, Daft Punk and the Chemical Brothers
in the first half of the 1990s

We are a dancing nation because of the youth. It wasn't middle-aged people throwing themselves into the polka in Victorian times, and it isn't predominantly old folk generating new dances on the internet today. The world is always changing, and those in charge of the future – young people – will generate culture that reflects their reality. And so, in the final decade of the last millennium, it was people in their mid-teens to early twenties who used their feet to expand and create new culture in repurposed dance spaces. We were adding a new verse to an old song, and we did so at scale.

The collective way in which communities dance moves in waves across time and space. Sometimes that crests generationally, like at the infamous dance marathons of Depression-era North America, when couples would dance for hundreds of hours for cash, or at the high point of a cultural moment at, say, Quadrant Park or the Haçienda or a packed venue that only you and your friends remember. Sometimes the collective dance is atomised, in retreat, as it has been in the UK since 2010, as venues continue to be picked off by property developers courtesy of profit-facing planning laws; and sometimes it's stilled, at the lowest of low tides, during illness, anxiety or bereavement or under repressive regimes, when we retreat indoors, dancing out of sight, solo, or only in our imagination.

Professor Theresa Buckland, at the University of Roe-hampton, described dancing done for pleasure rather than performance, aka social dance, as 'the Cinderella' of academic dance studies. Her phrase suggests to me that everyday dancers and ordinary dancefloors are beautiful and yet have been sidelined, made invisible. If social dancing is Cinderella, then the steppers, stompers and red-light ravers dancing in clubs and raving in warehouses could be seen collectively as a character from another fairy story: the troll under the bridge, hidden away from sight and feared by the mainstream.

There was a lot of dancing in the 1990s. A survey by research company Leisure Consultants showed attendance (a word I read in two parts: atten-*dance*) to be large-scale, with over 200 million admissions to nightclubs in the UK in 1994. They compared dancing to other entertainments and found it outstripped admissions to sports, film and the remaining 'live arts'. Another piece of research by economists at the Henley Centre for Forecasting claimed over 50 million attendances a year at 'rave events' in the UK in 1993. Another way of getting hold of what these 50 million admissions means is to understand that there were only 35.7 million people aged between 16 and 64, according to the 1991 census.

People like me were dancing to house and its sibling genre techno, which had emerged in Detroit, multiple times each week, in clubs, at 'All back to mine!' house parties and in semi-derelict flats and warehouses, without consciously learning dance steps and without considering ourselves dancers – although I recognise the limits of my perspective. In comedian Gina Yashere's autobiography *Cack-Handed* she describes going out at the same moment in time as Soul II

191

Soul's Friday-night residency at the Fridge in Brixton. She'd spend hours there doing the Running Man or the Wop. She also brought 'every move we'd spent the previous week copying from *Yo! MTV Raps* and practising in front of our mirrors'.

The dancers of this decade expanded the dancing estate. The sheer volume of young people wanting to go out in Stoke-on-Trent, Plymouth or Middlesbrough forced new dancefloors into existence. The dancers queued their way into pub backrooms, high-street discotheques and purpose-built nightclubs created in the shells of old factories and bus garages. Many venues no longer exist, and with their absence comes a forgetting. Places like Stoke-on-Trent had a powerful dancefloor culture that influenced the rest of the country through clubs like Shelley's or the Void. Culture matters when everything else falls away. You can't eat culture and it doesn't pay the rent, but it does provide pride and history, which are useful starting points for recovery.

———

I enrolled at Manchester Polytechnic at the opening of the nineties and had a few weeks of dilettante ridiculousness, in which I decided I was into indie and the blues, despite knowing zero blues records. I quickly came to my senses and found the dancefloors I needed. The movement information around me was different to the London clubs I'd been attending, however, and I needed to tune in again, absorb some new information, lose some accent, add some accent. This wasn't a phenomenon that was specific to me, or to then. We all do it, all the time. We modify our moves in response to what's around us, or we don't, better to revel in our differences. I realise now, in a way that was invisible to me at the time, that dancers stamp out local detail in the moveable architecture of the dance. People in Manchester danced differently to me, coming as I did from the suburbs of south-east London, influenced by soul weekenders I'd never been to. We danced to local weather, even within a city: born-and-bred Mancunians moving to brilliant DJs like Jam MCs or Hewan Clarke, and doing so differently to students like me who'd washed in from across the country.

I began with what was closest: the Friday-night Poly Bop, which was a student-union night with cheap pints and an indie disco. I joined in as my fellow 18-year-old arrivals danced to the B-52's with a boingy surf pogo or to Happy Mondays' records that caused the room to shift into mass mimickry, doing the bow-legged freaky dancing that Shaun Ryder and his pals developed by their favoured booth at the Haçienda. I expanded outwards, joining the exoskeleton of the queue at a student night at the newly opened Academy. This 1,500-capacity club and concert venue had been built by Manchester University Students' Union. They had followed the lead of Sheffield University, which had provided dancing spaces and restaurants for students – a strategy that responded to what students wanted – and also recycled student loans back into finances depleted by funding cuts. DJ Dave Booth dosed the Academy dancefloor with supersized versions of Chicago house that had increasingly whomping hoover basslines and tracks like Xpansions' 'Move Your Body'. When I think about the Academy I see everyday dancers on podiums, in permanent motion, dancing on the spot. I see movement that retains some of the jacking style that travelled across from Chicago, with more arms, more elbows, less crunch at the core, and more movement of the head from left to right, as if dancing a version of a road-safety video, checking the vicinity for traffic. Some of the podium kings and queens might have been of interest to Visual Contact, 'Britain's first rave dance agency', which *i-D* magazine covered in 1992. 'Some of the dancers are not professionally trained,' said club promoter Lou Clouter. 'They are the people who used to stand by the wall before acid house, then dropped an E and their inhibitions, and now provide a visual representation of the way the music sounds . . . they give off an energy that makes everyone else buzz.'

Our gestural polyphony changed the temperature, too, heating venues up with human-generated humidity. I recall the muscular relaxation that happens when waves of heat hit you along with waves of bass, and I knew how to cool down: you'd hold your wrist under cold water to reduce your body temperature, unless the venue had turned the taps off in order to send us to the bar. Sometimes Greater Manchester Police would come and join us at clubs like the Haçienda, Home or the Boardwalk. In my memory it would go like this: a line of maybe 15 riot-ready police with hard hats and shields would enter the dance in a strict line – a queue on the move. They processed through the dancefloor, drawing a black line across the room until they reached the other side, whereupon they circled back through the dancefloor and out through the exit in a stiff kind of groove. It was a show of strength that, to me, made them look strange, even comic. This was a time of heightened tension between competing gangs in the city, so maybe the copper conga was for them. At the time I assumed it was aimed at us: the dancers.

I may have been at least partially right. In 1990 *i-D* magazine reported that Greater Manchester Police were taking the Haçienda, Konspiracy, Precinct 13 and a number of other clubs ('i.e., any that play house music') to court in an attempt to get their licences revoked on the grounds of alleged drug use. 'This has to be the most concerted attack on youth culture in years,' wrote Clubs Editor Matthew Collin. 'Let's just hope the magistrates see the police action for what it is – ridiculous.' The chief constable at the time was James Anderton, memorialised in 'God's Cop' by the Happy Mondays. He was fond of moral pronouncements, was pro-capital punishment and used his Christian faith as justification for extreme homophobic views. Greater Manchester Police's arrival threaded a contrail of tension through the room, which dissipated through dancing bodies in the minutes after they left. I remember seeing an overexcited raver tap the policeman at the rear of the conga on the back of his hard hat – rude percussion.

I am set firmly against anything which veers into 'it was better in the olden days' territory and, generally, I'm with Gil Scott-Heron, who enunciated the 'no' at the start of 'nostalgia'. I believe in the archive as encouragement and permission, but I don't believe in parading generational gains in front of those who lack the physical space we had. However, we're all allowed to break our own rules every now and again, and this is one area where it's probably not possible to avoid it. Clubs in the olden days were properly loud, with speakers either purpose-built in the style of New York's finest underground clubs or borrowed from reggae sound systems. This meant feeling the music as much as hearing it, with all the benefits that sound brings to the body (less so the ears).

Paulette Constable knows all about this. She was a resident DJ at Flesh, the first queer night at Manchester's famous
Haçienda. It was a hugely popular night, at a time when it was
broadly unpopular to be queer, and at which I can attest there
was unusual dedication to dancing. People were dancing on
the dancefloor, on the stairs and on stages, and on top of the
banquette behind Paulette's DJ set-up downstairs in the Gay
Traitor bar. Sometimes this led an enthusiastic individual to
slip down the leather sofa and into Paulette's records. She had
grown up in Manchester clubs like Pips, where there were five
rooms, each catering to different dance styles, from punk pogo
to Bowie-inspired miming 'like a sea of Marcel Marceaus'. She
has a lifetime's experience of moving to music. 'Clubs don't
vibrate like they used to,' she says, when we talk on the phone
one summer afternoon. 'I mean, you can't hear the emergency
doors rattling when you're in the queue.' I like door-rattling
intensity. I want to be expanded by sound that you can feel
in your stomach and under your breastbone. Paulette knows
what I mean: 'Dancing with people, being in the bass – you
can't do that at home. You can't experience the molecular
rearrangement you get when you're listening to music in a
nightclub, particularly a big one like Heaven or the Haçienda.'

My friends and I experienced molecular rearrangement
on a range of dancefloors in 1990s Manchester. There was
the 600-capacity basement under Jilly's Rockworld called
the Banshee, where they played new hardcore records like
4 Hero's 'Mr Kirk's Nightmare' and LFO's 'LFO'. It was a
place where some dancers' prolific use of amphetamine sulphate caused their dancing to morph into contorted marching
as it amped up their central nervous system. Speed or whizz,

as it was often described, was cheap and easy to obtain. 'Amphetamine,' said the *Independent* newspaper in 1992, 'was now an integral part of rave culture.' It reported that dealers often sold out of this drug before they'd run low on other items, like LSD or ecstasy. Police seizures of the drug doubled between 1988 and 1991, the paper said, adding that the total number of amphetamine seizures in 1992 had increased by 60 per cent, according to the 'UK Drug Trends Report'. If I imagine myself back in early-nineties Manchester clubs and look around, I see a lot more people dancing hyperactively on speed than the softer-edged movement ecstasy induced. Speed was so commonplace that a promoter I once knew would sometimes pay DJs in the drug – until DJs moved to London and acquired more expensive tastes.

Over in Hulme older men sipped overproof rum upstairs at the PSV, a venue which deserves a whole book of its own. It was a squat rectangular building in the middle of Hulme, a sprawling 1960s estate which, until demolition began in 1991, was a kind of *Mad Max* free-for-all. It was amazing if you were young and wanted chaos and culture all day every day; less so if you were stuck there with three little kids, trying to navigate multiple lifestorms – or, indeed, if you were one of those little kids.

The PSV had a pre-history in the shape of the Russell Club, which had operated as a cinema and music hall, with the Hughie Gibb Orchestra as the house band. Hughie's sons, later known as the Bee Gees, sometimes sang with the musicians. The original building was demolished during an attempt at urban renewal in the late 1960s, and was rebuilt half a mile away. Factory Records instigators Tony Wilson and Alan Erasmus ran gigs at the new club on Friday nights between 1978 and May 1982, when the Haçienda opened. Young Mancunians shifted their weight from one foot to another during sets by Durutti Column, Cabaret Voltaire and Joy Division. Echo and the Bunnymen, Gang of Four, Public Image Ltd, Iggy Pop, The Undertones, The Cure and Buzzcocks also played the packed, hot venue to jumping waves of stomping bodies. In 1980 the Russell Club was bought by a collective of bus drivers headed by brothers Pinch and Sonny Burton, and they painted the words 'Caribbean Club' above the venue's signage. They brought Gregory Isaacs, Alton Ellis and Dennis Brown to the venue, the latter playing in May 1984 to dancers who'd skank their way through the show. The Russell Cricket Club used the upstairs room for meetings, while, downstairs, 1980s dancers like Foot Patrol brought high levels of technique to the dancefloor. There's a video of the crew at the PSV in 1986. They were dancing to house music, but they weren't jacking like the dancers in Chicago or bobbing left to right like ravers. They'd adapted their jazz moves, carving out lines on the floor in their spats to Adonis's 'No Way Back', generating whistles and shouts in response to their moves, just as a new tune or an especially juicy part of a tune will generate whistles and shouts. 'Manchester's very own Foot Patrol,' shouted the MC. 'Massive and large!'

By the early 1990s the smoky upstairs bar at the PSV had scratchy fabric tiles on the floor, a glass window that looked out onto the dancers below, and top-quality soul and reggae played by DJ Buggs or Madhatter. Downstairs hosted a range of nights, including regular sessions with Moss Side-based Frontline Radio (tagline: 'It's Where the Action's At').

There was Slack on a Saturday night, with DJs Chris Crookes, Devious Devon and MC Cocksy playing soul, R&B and hip hop, and Manchester University's student-run Freedom to Party nights. The PSV was packed and hot, with one commentator describing the smell of the place as 'sweaty-sensi', the latter part of the term referring to the strong and popular weed strain known as sensimilla. A friend recalls that if you were nice enough to the man in the burger van outside, you could get details of how to get to the nearby shebeen known as Beanies, along with the password required to gain entrance.

I also attended a weekly night in the city centre called Most Excellent. It appealed to a different demographic: middle-class students from across the country, alongside Mancunians with a taste for the balearic music that drew from Ibizan clubs like Ku and Amnesia; DJs like Alfredo; Londoners like the Boy's Own crew, and especially their most innovative member, Andrew Weatherall. It was run by Justin Robertson, who earned his DJ stripes at the Jam MCs' seminal Konspiracy night and ran Most Excellent at various clubs, initially at the State (which in a previous life was northern soul mecca the Twisted Wheel, where Quadrant Park DJ Mike Knowler had spun and shuffled for hours in his youth). The club doubled up as the after-party for a Happy Mondays show. 'That was a tremendous mistake,' recalled Robertson when I asked him to step back in time with me. 'We had police helicopters over the venue, and someone walked out with the cigarette machine. It was total mayhem, although it was good-natured mayhem. There was no trouble, apart from massive pilfering. It was a baptism of fire.' In keeping with the times, off-licences in the city – at least the ones I visited – separated the customer from the staff and shelves through the medium of bullet-proof glass.

Most Excellent had moved to a nightclub known by two names – Millionaires and the Wiggly Worm – when it was ram-raided. A small group of young men had been refused entry and drove right into the place. I was standing at the bottom of the stairs when Elton, who worked the door, came scuttering downstairs. A stolen Ford Fiesta had driven through the doors, reversed out and driven off. The dancefloor was behind double doors, and the DJ carried on playing, mostly because this particular fracas remained out of view.

Around this time, co-promoter Ross Mackenzie bumped into someone who had been refused entry to the club. The latter held the former up against a wall and threatened to shoot him if he was denied entry again. Both incidents show something else about places in which a collision of logic took place, especially when it comes to logic that is built on life experience plus personality. For the person who was refused entry the logic was simple: use the threat of violence to ensure you get what you want. For the people who tried to put on club nights in the city at this time – a task which involved at least occasional interactions with various hoodlum elements – the logic was also obvious: don't let people who threaten to shoot people into your club because at the very least it's going to kill the vibe.

John Cage once said that utopia was a multiplicity of individuals who have the habit of respecting one another. In mid-nineties Manchester individuals were mostly in the habit of doing so, and consequently there was a rich eco-system and opportunities for expansion and mutation. One such mutation was a short-lived night called Naked Under Leather, put together by Phil South and Alex Kohler and their friends Tom and Ed in 1992. The four of them interpreted their time on the dancefloor as both permission and an instruction to send the pulse onwards by doing something themselves. What I recall about the various Naked Under Leather nights is heavy beats, pulsing my raised arm in the air like an arm-based jackhammer, dry ice, large amounts of rum, dancing in a way that allowed me to hold onto a pillar (partly because this was a rare phase when I was dancing in high heels), techno with depth-charged beats, and instrumental, airhorn-powered breakbeats. Records like Capricorn's panel-beating '20Hz', Renegade Soundwave's 'Thunder' and Todd Terry's 'Jazz Anthem', alongside what were known as 'balearic scream-ups', like La Banderita's 'Mediterranea'. I also remember a new tune that two of the DJs had made as a DIY summation of their favourite sounds, created to play at their club night and designed to instigate maximum dancefloor mayhem. It balanced a haunting and heavily processed female voice with juggernaut beats. 'Song to the Siren' was the entry point for Tom and Ed's evolution into a known musical entity. They began by naming themselves after Beastie Boys producers the Dust Brothers, and changed to the Chemical Brothers after the existing Dust Brothers expressed an opinion by sending a cease and desist letter.

We all knew each other. One night around 1993 everyone was back at someone's house, and I was talking to Ed, who back then was just Ed Simons but was soon to become 'Ed from the Chemical Brothers'. We were talking about nightclubs and the difference between being on the dancefloor week in, week out and just dropping in. 'Thing is,' he said, 'the clue is in the name. A nightclub is something you're part of. It's a club. You're a member. Members attend, regularly.'

It's about the layers of the relationships you build up when you go out dancing: recognising and being recognised by the doorman or the person taking your money on the door; people you begin to nod to; resident DJs whom you see play month in, month out; and the musical evolution you witness and support through your collective presence. Dancing with other people isn't passive, it is active, and it can create action: buying records or making music for fellow dancers; or creating a space where people can dance for the allotted five hours, before tumbling out of the exit and looking for more. This was as true in Manchester decades ago as it was when I attended a party run by the Touching Bass collective in a Peckham bakery in the late 2010s, or at Total Refreshment Centre, which helped curate a wave of new London musicians, like Nubya Garcia or Moses Boyd, who were deeply connected to the dancefloor. A large percentage of people at Naked Under Leather or Touching Bass or Total Refreshment Centre or any similar places across the country at any point in the last 30 years would have given something back – not just caught a vibe but made a vibe. Many of the people who attended made something in response to the dance, whether it was clothing or music or artwork or the fleeting but fundamental contribution of moving your shoulders to the beat.

Somehow, the dancers who conduct and instruct the music-makers are invisible. The largest and most powerful part of the machinery that makes music is hidden in plain sight. I wonder if everyday dancers are invisible because dancing is linked to the female, even on boy-heavy, broadly heterosexual dancefloors. Many of the qualities associated with dancing are also linked with femininity – intimacy, emotion, softness – and there remains a perception that women dance to attract men. Gender is expressed in how we adorn our bodies – and how we move them.

There were plenty of women and girls in Manchester clubs in the nineties, some of whom decided to write about the culture. I was one of a number of dancefloor-regulars-turned-journalists in the city who also happened to be female. There was Sarah Champion, *City Life*'s Nayaba Aghedo, my *Jockey Slut* co-writer Joanne Wain and Rachel Newsome, who went on to edit *Dazed & Confused*. Mandi James was a well-known music journalist when I was starting out, a big name in our small world. We shared informal encouragement when we were out and about in clubs: I was standing by the mirrors in the toilets at the Boardwalk when she approached me and said, 'I like your writing, you could do this if you wanted,' which was all the encouragement I needed. Our numbers diffused the attention and altered the tension. Onlookers might easily dismiss or overlook one individual woman writing about dance music, but there were a few of us. We were on the dancefloor, and this gave us implicit authority. We had opinions based on receiving the music as it was meant to be received: in clubs. We wrote from our perspective.

Our existence as young women documenting the culture around us didn't feel anomalous within our community. It was unusual, though, if you look at the broader picture. Most music writers were men, and there is still a whole heap of gender disparities – among other inequities – that exist in the industries that sit around club culture. A male journalist who is a few years younger than me was once talking to a female writer friend, who is younger still. 'Men are just better at writing about music than women,' he told her, pulling the shrugging gesture in which the speaker's body moves back and their arms and shoulders rise, palms forward. It is a gesture that operates as a physical quotation mark, better to distance the speaker from their words.

———

The context within which people experienced this music was changing. Clubs had always had the occasional live PA, but the mid-to-late 1990s marked the beginning of dance-music producers developing a touring stage show, with DJs in a supporting role. Initially this didn't affect the dancing much, partly because of the way that clubbers and ravers understood dance spaces, but also because live sets at this time often involved lightshows that obscured the performers almost entirely. Dancers could get lost in the sound and the lights without having to watch anything, which is less true for subsequent stage shows that centred and illuminated the artists.

Daft Punk provide another example. *Jockey Slut* co-editor Paul Benney wrote the first feature about the pair in 1993, and for the next few years they'd regularly play the clubs my friends and I were connected to. I saw them take their version of filtered Chicago house music to the next level at the Trans Musicales Festival in Rennes, France, in December 1995, soon after 'Da Funk/Rollin' & Scratchin'' came out on Soma records. This music previously existed in packed specialist-music clubs up and down the country, but now it had been transported to a cold, massive aircraft hangar. I mostly remember this early iteration of club-as-festival being freezing cold, a little empty at the back and somewhat lacking in atmosphere, bar Daft Punk's electric set.

By the time I interviewed them for a *Muzik* front cover they were pop-star famous. Towards the end of the interview Armand Van Helden's 'You Don't Know Me' came on the hotel stereo, and Thomas Bangalter got up and did a little dance. The other half of Daft Punk, Guy-Manuel de Homem-Christo, used words instead of moves when I asked about their relationship with the dancefloor: 'We don't think about which records are crazy and which records are cool. It's just about dancers and dancing, and playing good music.'

That night, they played a heaving DJ set at Mass in Brixton, where the dancefloor was peppered with people on shoulders and dancers doing a fist-pumping jerky body dance. Thomas and Guy-Man were playing Robot Man's 'Do Da Doo (Plastikman's "Acid House" Remix)' and Danny Tenaglia's 'Music Is the Answer' alongside their own tunes, augmented with the bank of kit they brought to their hybrid live shows. The changing context first expressed at Trans Musicales had become embedded. Acid house turned stages into an extension of the main dancefloor. Live performance returned this space to paid performers. A new generation of clubbers became used to artists performing with samplers, laptops and drum machines. The gestural tendency changed: look at the stage, like at a rock gig, and dance while watching, instead of turning off your eyes and tuning into the sounds through your ears and the rest of your body, something

Chicago DJ Ron Trent described to me as 'a whole third-ear kind of experience'.

An increasing number of artists in the mid-1990s were expanding their DJ sets into live re-creations of the music, and the extension of the craft brought growing pains for the artists and for the dancers. In 1995 I saw Matthew Herbert perform a live set as Wishmountain at Bugged Out! (at Sankey's Soap, a nightclub built within a Grade II-listed former cotton mill and soap factory in Ancoats, in the east of Manchester), during which he opened a crisp packet, sampling and looping the sound into a tune which he then tap-danced to. It was inventive, memorable and extremely brave, because Bugged Out!, like most clubs at the time, was predicated on non-stop dancing for five hours at a time. Live sets were an interruption to the flow. I remember Herbert's set being met with a vague undercurrent of mutiny. Iconic Chicago producer and DJ Larry Heard, aka Mr Fingers, travelled from Chicago to perform a live set, also at Sankey's. Unfortunately, he arrived at a lull point where his originator brand of house music was too recent to have attracted legendary status outside of niche music heads and simultaneously old enough to be invisible. I was one of approximately 20 people in attendance. He stood on the stage in a bow-tie with his synthesisers, as we crowded round his side of the stage, puffing ourselves out in an attempt to appear more than we were out of love and respect for him and out of sympathy for the youthful promoter.

In the mid-1990s Ancoats contained only the bare bones of city life. Once you crossed the busy main road that flanked the eastern edge of Oldham Street onto Jersey Street, parallel with the Rochdale Canal, you stopped encountering shops and instead just walked past derelict cotton mills. Ten minutes down the road was Sankey's Soap and the adjoining building, Beehive Mill, which housed office space. *Jockey Slut* magazine, where I worked, was based there, as was A Guy Called Gerald's record label Juice Box and studios used by drum 'n' bass DJ Marcus Intalex and Happy Mondays offshoot Black Grape. There was a cab company whose instructions to drivers leaked through our office speakers, a corner pub and a hole-in-the-wall caff that sold thick tea from an urn and fried items. This was an industrially degraded area which had been emptied out, as if the mills had been lifted up and shaken out at some point during the years when the industrial era became post-industrial.

Every week dancers filled the room at Sankey's Soap for Bugged Out! People would lay claim to their favourite part of the dancefloor or raised stage and stay there, digging into the techno and the harder end of house music for a solid four hours, sometimes longer. My fellow *Jockey Slut* writer Joanne Wain had good moves, honed in the northern soul youth clubs of her teen years; her sliding footwork demonstrated her movement heritage. Others bounced and bopped, stepping and swaying and swatting the air with clenched fists. There were arms in the air, conducting the beat. We danced to the resident DJs James Holroyd and Rob Bright, and to the greats of techno and house at a time when their greatness was only a handful of releases deep. Dave was one of my dancefloor buddies at the time, and he can still remember the intensity. 'I can vividly recall dancing with you to three tunes that James Holroyd was spinning and the delirium in your face,' he tells me, when I track him down by email. 'It

207

was one of the few times he DJed the last set of the night. You felt the music as much as me. Mad times indeed. I still dance crazy and, as the missus notes, without always keeping the beat with my hips.'

I danced at Bugged Out! to Detroit techno legend Carl Craig and then watched an end-of-night negotiation as one of the club's sweaty, trenchant regulars attempted to swap t-shirts with him, like they were footballers at the end of a match. Other legends of house and techno came too: Jeff Mills battered us with relentlessly inventive iterations of 'The Bells' and unreleased Underground Resistance records; Richie Hawtin brought skinny Canadian energy and hypnotic techno; Robert Hood, in a fedora hat, played deep, minimal body music; and I dance-watched DJ Claude Young power through his set on three turntables, scratching with his elbow. The Detroit DJs came in waves, and the city, this club and our delirious stomping welcomed them in.

Our appreciation was amplified by the architecture. The landscape in Ancoats was so similar to parts of Detroit as to be uncanny, something I saw for myself when I eventually visited the city. I was driving around the Milwaukee Junction area of Detroit with my friend Amy when we passed the old Ford Piquette Avenue building. I asked her to stop – it was the double of the disused mills in Ancoats that surrounded Sankey's Soap: red bricks, hard edges, large windows lined up close to each other on every floor. The Ford Piquette Avenue plant was modelled by architects Field, Hinchman and Smith on New England textile mills – which were themselves modelled on Manchester's industrial architecture. The footnotes to Les Back and Vron Ware's brilliant book *Out of Whiteness* show that dance was of concern to Henry Ford Sr himself. Much like Cecil Sharp and the Irish priests and politicians, Ford was against new urban dancing and aggressively in favour of what he believed to be white American dance and folk culture. He denounced jazz in his newspaper, the *Dearborn Independent*, in anti-Semitic terms – 'Popular music is a Jewish monopoly. Jazz is a Jewish creation' – and described it as 'the drivel of morons'. 'In 1925 Ford, himself an accomplished dancer, began a campaign to revive – or more accurately reinvent – rural folk dancing,' wrote Back and Ware, explaining that Ford invited 200 Michigan and Ohio dance instructors to his plant to learn old-time steps that they, in turn, could pass on.

The industrialist also published a series of articles in the *Dearborn Independent* titled 'A Dance a Week' that explained steps and contained sheet music so that readers might commit to learning dances which were 'part of the life of the pioneers . . . People who are not acquainted cannot dance the quadrille or the circle two-step or the Virginia reel without quickly becoming acquainted. People on unfriendly terms cannot dance these at all and remain so. These dances are social in the sense that they inevitably make for sociability among all who dance them. Thus they are pre-eminently the home, neighborhood and community dances, in the sense that other dances cannot be.'

Ford recognised that dance has the capacity to create togetherness, and he attempted to harness this power in service of division. Back and Ware show precisely how dangerous these ideas can be: 'Ford's failed attempt to invent and popularize a nascent version of white American folk culture in many ways anticipated what the Nazis implemented in Germany ten years later. It is no surprise, then, that Henry Ford Senior was the only American to be mentioned in Adolf Hitler's *Mein Kampf*.'

Fascists have instrumentalised human movement in the past, through marching or the prioritisation of sports, and this makes me wonder what fascists here would try to dig up to get British people dancing to a nationalistic drum. The Morris Federation protected their dance form against right-wing appropriation when they made a statement in July 2020 calling on all of the UK's morris organisations to eliminate the use of blackface, formalising the motion at their AGM later that year. I can't imagine modernist blackshirts getting on the floor to the soul boy Boat Dance, so maybe they'd drag back the waltz instead, and get thousands of us dancing round in circles, following preordained steps.

———

I wasn't on a Manchester dancefloor when I had a seizure. I was hanging out in my friend Dan's bedroom in the south of the city with a handful of friends. We were listening to brand-new Detroit techno that had arrived via labels like Transmat and Metroplex and which we heard on the dancefloor, week in, week out. One minute I was standing by the door, the next I was coming round next to a wardrobe. A short period of disconnected frames: not on the floor, sitting on the bed; not sitting on the bed, slipping into staccato movement – a dance of bad electricity. My friends were mute and didn't know what to do. 'I'm fine,' I said, not really knowing what had happened. 'Let's just go home.' Someone drove me back, and I went to bed.

The after-effects spilled out gradually. I placed an invisible wall around myself in regard to the subject and spoke about it as little as possible. I wanted it to un-happen. To rewind back, make a different decision, somehow steel my body better, or at least get myself somewhere I could have lost control of my limbs privately. I experienced this as a contraction of self where I moved inwards, no longer able to trust how my body would move.

Eventually I went to the GP. He prescribed medication, and this brought additional misery. The pills created unpleasant feelings of waves across the surface of my brain, and I continued to feel like it was going to happen again, a welling-up from my stomach, a dangerous heat radiating up and out. I carried small white dots of valium in my purse, just in case. I continued to go out, fully wrapped up in my Do Not Discuss polytunnel, and held onto the bar or stuck my nails into my palms if I felt myself go. It worked, pretty much. It's a weird thing to keep a fact that everyone knows secret, and it eats up large amounts of energy. You become two people: the person who you have convinced yourself appears in the world, and the person who really appears in the world. Self-war is trouble, and fighting yourself is a fight you are 100 per cent going to lose.

The dancefloor provided a release from this self-imposed isolation. I was standing by the bar at Electric Chair, a brilliantly energetic monthly night run by Luke Cowdrey and Justin Crawford that took place at the Roadhouse in Manchester, a basement club next to the Van Dang Martial Arts Centre. I was feeling on edge, as I often felt at that time. A guy I knew from the dancefloor at Bugged Out! and after-hour parties in Hulme bobbed past me. Mike was skinny, kind and deep, frequently high, and prone to discussing all manner of cosmic profundity in the dance when not hammering his arms and legs outwards to whichever visiting American DJ was on the decks. He knew all about loss. His dad had died from a heart attack directly after a family argument which included Mike kicking the TV in. He knew what it was like to have a fact hanging over you. He handled his life circumstances much better than I did. He talked about his dad. People knew about it. I knew, because he'd told me in a late-night conversation in a flat once the dancing had petered out and there was just slumping.

Mike stopped: 'How you doing?' We chatted, talking about tunes or the DJ – generalised music chatter. Then he breached the stance I was holding and spoke directly into my ear. 'If you're ever feeling like you're going to have a fit, just tell me. I'll come and stand outside with you. I'll get you home.'

I knew his story, and I saw him dancing his story week in and week out, and I accepted his help. I let his words in and let them expand and shift my feelings. I couldn't control my body, but I could control how I felt about it. There was something about his kindness, his posture and his ability to name what had been happening to me, and to name it so normally, that was transformative. Things changed for me in that minute. I realised: people know, and they don't mind. People know, and they still care. I can't un-happen it and I can't un-happen people knowing about it, but Mike – endless gratitude to him – cut through my defences. Something changed in my body, and my mind followed. The environment helped, too. Luke Una, who co-ran the club, now quotes a release by house DJ Kerri Chandler to sum up the archetypal perfection he sought: 'A Basement, A Red Light & A Feelin'.' I was in a room that was unfinished and basic, transformed into a club by camo netting that lowered the ceiling and a banner behind the DJ booth. I didn't have to pretend to be anything I wasn't. The space invited communication and contribution.

I was lucky. The seizure arrived in my early twenties and it washed away over the following years. I came close more than once but found I could concentrate the feeling away by digging my nails into the palms of my hands. I changed GPs – my new one realised I'd never had any proper investigations; she sent me for MRIs and took me off the medication. I exited that process with no diagnosis of epilepsy, just new respect for the family tendency: that I could force a seizure if I tried hard enough by overworking, overindulging, not sleeping enough and consuming a diet made up largely of tea and toast. 'We're all allowed one,' said the consultant, when he handed me my ECG results and a clean bill of health. 'Off you go, enjoy your life.'

The experience, even as a one-off, created necessary change. Dancing was still good for me. Large speakers and walls of compressed air bellowing out as basslines still made me feel calm, connected, grounded. It was difficult learning how to navigate the dancefloor again, particularly dancefloors with strobe lighting, which was most of them. Blue lights were also tricky. The frequencies in blue light, and sometimes red, can trigger seizures in people with photosensitive epilepsy just as strobes can, which explains why I spent most of a wedding-disco rave in the Welsh hills in the car park instead of on the dancefloor, which had been transformed by ultra-violet lights into a deep-sea neon bath. I created darkness by covering my eyes, digging my nails into my hands and fighting the feelings. It worked, just.

I must say that even writing these lines is stressful. I am tentative, looking to the side of the page in the hope that avoiding eye contact with the subject will save me from further disgrace. I wonder if you can evoke illness by recognising it and naming it. I wonder if by naming it and moving with it, you can integrate it, expand your awareness of who you are, and I send these lines to any of you whose physical form has ever let you down.

Our bodies are more than just a carriage. We can't separate ourselves from them, like I attempted to do. The idea of a mind–body split is weird, when you think about it. Where is your mind, if not in your body? People talk about mindfulness, but I want an embodied life, in which the self sits in the soft inside of an elbow or in our muscles, not just in our brains. We can access the brain through the body, and our bodies contain ideas and experience. It's not all about the mind, wherever that is. I didn't know this when I was young, but I do now.

10: PHENOMENAL BASSLINES

Banging the walls to drum 'n' bass, 1996

There are always multiple origin stories of a cultural moment. Each contains some truth, and each omits elements relating to people, place or thing. It is broadly fair to say that the music known variously as jungle and drum 'n' bass began emerging in the early 1990s and directly connected electronic dance music to sound-system culture, Jamaican dancehall and what is increasingly referred to as 'Great Black American' music – including sampled breakbeats from the soul records that informed hip hop, specifically a short drum loop from 'Amen, Brother' by The Winstons. These sampled loops generated a strong response in dancers in the early days of both hip hop and drum 'n' bass, and in the latter caused producers to speed them up and place them on top of ultra-heavy basslines. In doing so, the DJ and the dancers created something new.

There's more dancing in the art form's genesis than is generally recognised. Key instigators of the genre had expert moves, like east Londoners Shut Up and Dance, a couple of professional contemporary dancers who, according to author Brian Belle-Fortune, 'couldn't find music fast, driving and hard enough to dance to'. Sonic innovator Gerald Simpson, aka A Guy Called Gerald, had professional training in contemporary, jazz and classical dance and made music with dance crews in mind. High-ranking DJ Fabio was a dancer before he started playing records, contributing his teenage moves at jazz events with his dance partner Colin Dale, who became a notable techno producer and DJ.

Devious Devon was known in Manchester for being a brilliant jazz-funk dancer. He'd honed his moves at Baguley Hall in Wythenshawe and at Birley High youth club in Hulme – which he described to me as 'an absolute sweatbox' – and was selected to dance with 'Mickey' star Toni Basil on an early-eighties BBC TV show called *Get Set for Summer*. By around 1994 he was bringing golden-era jungle to his residencies at the PSV and the Kitchen in Hulme, which was a studio in the daytime and a popular gathering spot at night. When the flat next door became available, the crew hired some pneumatic drills and made 'a nice big archway' into the now-extended space. He was also DJing at the Haçienda's city centre Dry Bar, playing just-released records from Goldie's new Metalheadz label. The logical next step was to take the music and the culture to the world-famous club itself.

The first Phenomenon One took place at the Haçienda in May 1995, followed by a second and final edition just over a year later. I spent five hours on the sweltering dancefloor at the latter, letting the powerful basslines dictate my moves. There are recordings of the DJ sets online, and so I know that Devon began his set with a now classic tune, 'The Chopper', by The Terrorist, aka Ray Keith, which is as lean, tense and brilliantly brutal as the name suggests. The rest of the DJs were locally and nationally all-star, too: Bristolian Roni Size, who later won a Mercury Music Prize for his Reprazent collective; and London originators Bryan Gee, Jumpin Jack Frost and Nicky Blackmarket, who ran the Black Market Records shop in Soho and whose mum went out dancing with 'the jazz lot', including Ronnie Scott 'before he had the club'. There were MCs, too: Trigga and Crystalize from Manchester, Spyda from Nottingham and Birmingham's Bassman. One of the fragments I remembered from the night was an off-the-cuff MC moment which was hardcore even at the time: *'Ladies! Keep your legs together! We are known as the ferocious ones!'* This was jungle, nineties-Manchester-style.

Phenomenon One was steaming hot, equatorial, and not just because aerosol cans were being turned into portable flamethrowers when Prizna's tune 'Fire' dropped. The heat was tropical, luxuriant, and it moved across the club in varying intensities, hotter in the centre, cooler by the entrance and coolest in the toilets, which were still like saunas. Women in Lycra shorts and men in sweaters and puffa jackets danced through the moisture-haze as molten new music erupted out of the system, like Dillinja's 'Acid Track' or Gang Related and Mask's 'Concentration'. I have muscle memory of it, too. Onto the dancefloor, right-hand edge, tessellated by people-proximity so that dancing becomes adapted to the circumstances, hemmed in, taking up space only where it appears. I remember the stance required to get you off the dancefloor and the body language required to get back on: something in the centre of the body that had to tighten up – core control, tensile, an assertive body language combined with awareness. It was only good manners to treat the environment with respect: this was not a beginners' club-culture situation – I'm sure that most people in the room had spent serious time on powerful dancefloors – but also because this was a majority Black, Brown and working-class space. My whiteness and suburban upbringing weren't a barrier to entry, a courtesy not always applied when the demographic tables were turned. Someone would flick a small flame out of their Clipper lighter or Zippo and hold it up in the air. Bassbins were amplified by whistles, foghorns, the percussive sound of feet stamping and the way a hyped-up crowd will add to the music with bellowed notes. The smoke would lift momentarily before the next band of apricot-scented dry ice rolled in, revealing the dancefloor variation: pockets of hyped-up whistle posses peppered throughout the floor like lights on a pinball machine; girls dancing together with varying levels of skill and technique, from exceptional to basic; lone men in leather waistcoats with incredible skill in their legs; steppas, droppers, skankers, ravers, boppers – all finding their dance in and around the heavyweight bass and the razor-cut breakbeats.

Rebecca Haslam was a young mother when she contributed to the dancefloor variation of mid-nineties jungle and drum 'n' bass nights in the north of England, initially in Manchester, where she grew up. Now she's a youth worker. She describes herself back then as moving like 'a giddy spider . . . I'd be all arms and legs, a bit like Animal from *The Muppets* meets a skinny spider, skanking my back out.' Around her, people moved differently. 'People would judder,' she says. 'They'd drop down low, like they were holding the bass in their hands, knees dropped as if the force of the beat was taking our legs from under us, making our knees buckle. It was ace.'

Manchester's sometimes 'moody' situations meant that she and her friends would later leave the city to go to Niche, the Sheffield club that created the sub-genre bassline house, even though her dance style marked her out as being from elsewhere. 'Mancs have got our own style of dancing, like Scousers or Londoners. People would only need to look over and they'd go, "Oh, they're Mancs." Because of the way we danced. Like in the Haçienda, the Salford [gang] would rock backwards and forwards, like they were pulling a steering wheel. You'd go, "That's Salford." It was an unspoken language that was conveyed in dance.'

Musicologist Dr Edith Van Dyck of Ghent University found evidence to explain the dancefloor variation. Her 2013 doctoral thesis described the spontaneous reactions that typically happen when a person listens to music: tapping their feet, nodding their head or wiggling their fingers. 'Dance,' she wrote, 'can be conceived as a creative act of expression, communication, imitation and reflection.'

In order to understand the relationship between music, perception, movement and emotion, she created a proxy nightclub in a laboratory. One hundred people in their early twenties were asked to dance in groups of five to specially designed 120bpm dance music that contained varying levels of bass-drum sound pressure. Motion-sensor tracking found that the groups tended to move in ways that correlated more strongly with each other than with the participants of other groups. She used a small-scale everyday example to explain this socially generated 'joint action': the way that friends walking together will walk in step with each other. Joint action can be seen on a larger scale, she explains, during pop concerts or in drum circles 'in order to form a group consciousness'.

Van Dyck also measured how people responded to the bass drum. The phrase 'tempo entrainment' describes the degree to which the human system locks into and responds to external rhythm, and she found that her dancefloor partici-pants moved more, especially in the hips, when the bass drum became louder. '[They] danced more actively and displayed a higher degree of tempo entrainment as the sound pressure of the bass drum increased.' There is, she wrote, a strong causal link between bass loudness and movement: 'The bass drum has a strong impact on dancing itself.' In loud, bass-heavy environments you can't help but move – and that's official.

I remember another MC improvising in response to the heaving mass of people on the dancefloor:

Oh my golly golly gosh
I can feel it
You can feel it
Can you feel the rush?

Nicky Blackmarket remembers the rush. 'You were there?' he asks, right at the start of our phone call. 'That night was iconic.' Phenomenon One oscillated at a notably energetic fre-quency, even by Blackmarket's standards, and this is someone who knew the temperature across the whole country, because he was DJing 'maybe five, six gigs in one weekend in England . . . First time I played those parties in the Haçienda, it was mad,' he says. 'It was the first time I saw real gunshot.' He laughs. 'You see it on the television or whatever, it's different from real life. The DJ booth was up the top, so I'm hearing this noise and I'm thinking, "What's that?" Next thing I'm seeing sparks. People were letting off rounds into the ceiling. How you got in with a gun? But that's just how it was, and everyone was like, "*Wheeeeyyyyyy . . .*" People were having fun and enjoying themselves.'

I ask him if the feeling was very different to what he was seeing in London at that time. 'Ummm,' he says, 'you wouldn't really see gunshot going off in London. I loved playing up north. It just had a completely different vibe. Energy was wicked.' I have to say that I don't remember noticing anyone firing into the ceiling but, then again, there were loads of gunshot sounds on the records, so perhaps it all just melded into one.

———

In summer 2022 I hosted a panel on music, dancing and mental health in Frankfurt, Germany. The panellists included a psychologist who specialised in using the body to deal with emotional distress and a professionally trained contemporary dancer who was bringing the Israeli 'Gaga' movement language into Berlin's queer clubs. The other speaker was Damon Frost, a US-born dancer, music producer and educator who came through the West Coast's first flush of hip-hop dancing before moving to Sweden in 1985 and helping to popularise the movement in Europe. Between the three of them, they offered warm and fascinating observations that touched on anxiety, the transformative power of dancing with other people, and the idea of a 'trauma-informed' dancefloor whereby clubs could become oases of care and safety – a kind of uber-safe space.

Afterwards, Damon and I sat on the edge of the stage, chatting. 'You know what?' he said, leaning forward. 'You sometimes *need* an unsafe situation. You have to go through the fire, like in an initiation – go out into the wilds, come back with the knowledge you need.' The fear factor, he said, heightens your senses with the mix of adrenaline and dopamine, in a way that wouldn't be possible in a more protected environment. 'Therapy is partly about getting acquainted with your fears, so that you can live a life without being impeded by them. The dancefloor is a training ground where you're allowed, on your own clock, to get used to fear.' He looked up, towards the doorway, where people were exiting into the sun-baked afternoon. 'On the roughest, rawest dancefloors you can find tools that you can superimpose onto your life.'

Underground inna Moss Side is an eight-minute documentary produced in 1996. It features Phenomenon One promoter Devious Devon and producer Johnny J. 'It's working-class, it's Black, it's underground,' says Johnny J to camera. 'If you're over 22 you just will not get it, which is great, because that's how it should be. It should be handled by the kids. They're setting up labels, they're setting up their own jams. They're exporting it. They don't give a damn about what was happening in the sixties or the seventies or the goddamn eighties . . . I wish everything in England was like jungle music is at the moment.' He was describing a microcosm of the country in which things worked; in which effort equalled success.

The next interviewee is Zipparah Tafari, now better known as Mr Zip, whose 'Where Me Keys, Where Me Phone?' found him success on *Britain's Got Talent* in 2012. Back in the mid-nineties he was perched on his bike and flanked by MC Trigga. Zip has cultural history: a decade earlier he was a dancer with prestigious jazz-fusion dance crew Foot Patrol. He has authority, and addresses the interviewer directly.

'Don't fear jungle and it won't fear you,' he says firmly, hand marking time between phrases. 'Jungle's for the people. It's a national riddim, an international riddim. But we got to tell you where it's coming from, G. It's coming from the hood. All the hoods! All the hoods in England.'

The music and dancing was a response to the pressure cooker of Zipparah Tafari's 'hoods in England'. It reflected and refracted the harsh realities of the mid-1990s UK. I remember flicking through the jobs pages of the *Manchester Evening News* at the time and seeing very little, except for opportunities for butchers that paid £80 a week. The community on the dance-floor was absolutely multicultural, as were the people who inhabited and operated the surrounding culture, with white middle-class people taking a minority role. However, it was inarguably built on Black British and working-class expression, in particular the ongoing iterations of sound-system culture. The music and the dancing existed in response to life experience, just as the reggae dancehalls had done decades earlier.

Pulitzer Prize-winning writer and activist Alice Walker called her 2010 collection of poetry *Hard Times Require Furious Dancing*. In the introduction, she wrote about the role of dance in the healing of families, communities and nations, through the lens of her experience as a Black woman in the US. Newly bereaved, she hired a local hall and a local band and invited friends and family to 'dance our sorrows away, or at least to integrate them more smoothly into our daily existence'. Pressurised times in late-nineties Britain required furious dancing, especially for communities of colour – and furious it was. Over in Hulme the storied PSV hosted nights; the venue was now known as the Lighthouse, although that name was flipped to 'the Darkhouse' to better reflect the rocketing levels of energy that life instilled in Mancunian dancers.

A Guy Called Gerald had moved from Manchester to London by the mid-1990s and was therefore mostly absent from the dancefloors I've been describing. His music and influence, though, were ever-present. He is another of the musician-dancers who've been influential in more than one cultural moment. He created the spooked acid-house classic 'Voodoo Ray' (and has been engaged in a long-term legal battle to retrieve the royalties) and, as writer, had a major role in 808 State's top-ten hit 'Pacific State'. In 1991 Gerald started his Juice Box label, releasing an album, *28 Gun Bad Boy*, the following year. It is widely credited as one of the very first full-length drum 'n' bass albums and is considered a classic, as is his 1995 album *Black Secret Technology*.

Gerald was steeped in dance, stretching back to the late-1970s youth-club sessions he'd attended with his brother. 'The dancing thing is really personal,' he tells me. 'It brought me out of my shell. I found a way to communicate within the community. You could communicate with people in that space in so many different ways, just through movement.' After youth club, Gerald graduated to the cellar of a house known as Dungeons, where he joined an informal community of jazz and funk dancers known for their exceptional improvised moves. This was before electro and breakdance; there would be dance battles to Chick Corea's 'The Slide' or something more obvious like James Brown. By the end of a battle the DJ would drop the temperature through the medium of, say, 'Southern Freeez' by Freeez. 'You could look across the dancefloor and you'd see somebody and you could communicate

with them without talking or anything, just free movement,'
continues Gerald. 'You could show your familiarity with a tune
by picking out an instrument and doing your movement, your
gestures towards that saxophone or keyboard.'

Gerald and his brother took it to another level, training at
the Manchester Dance Centre, receiving extra lessons from a
teacher from the Northern Ballet company. 'We really wanted
to be professional dancers. We were in this kids' home, so we
had to have after-school activity where you did football or
boxing or whatever. We chose to do dance.' Plenty of story
to dance out there, I note. 'Oh, yeah,' he laughs. 'There was.'
Then he tells me something that surprises the hell out of me,
because my assumption was that a dancer with Gerald's level
of skilful footwork would find dance class easy. Turns out he
found choreographed steps difficult to remember: 'At dance
school we had to do routines, and I could never remember
anything. We'd do these really complex pieces where you had
to be in a certain position on the stage . . . The teacher mentioned Laban's theory [Labanotation – a system for recording
and analysing human movement, like a musical score but for
dance], and I went and got a book out of the library. You can
actually record where you are in space and time! That took it
to another level.' Dance school became an important part of
his life. 'It became like a drug,' he says. 'I'd always leave on a
high. The first half an hour warming up, you're on that high.
We had to go back to this kids' home, and I'd leave [the class],
and I'd be flying. Didn't want to get the bus, just wanted to
walk, listen to music.'

Gerald transformed the raw material of his life into dancefloor gold, spinning the richness off the dancefloor and into his

music. It's a big question, I say to Gerald, but what did danc-ing do for you? 'It gave me discipline and pride,' he replies. 'It introduced me to music. It's like when you're a writer and then you discover that the library's always open. Dancing became that for me.

'I think people need to be educated more about dance and movement and its relationship to music,' he adds. 'I can feel that it's going to be something that people want more of. There's the enjoyment of nodding your head, but you can get past that stage. It's just shyness, really.'

Earlier in this book I wrote about hesitant dancers and the barriers that life experience or cultural expectations can bring down, along with the ways that thoughtless or mean comments can switch the body off. The shyness that Gerald mentions strikes me as similar but different. While the hesi-tant dancer might lack confidence in their abilities and their role on a dancefloor, a shy one lacks confidence in themselves. There's a visibility, a 'you-ness' that is inevitably transmitted when you dance, and shyness – and its greedy little sister, social anxiety – worries about humiliation or rejection. Hiding yourself can seem like a reasonable response to fear, but shy-ness transmuted into action can be beautiful and humbling to witness, and can be personally powerful. The act of moving to music with other people is a process that can alchemise the weight of life experience into wealth, as Gerald and his brother found in dance studios and basement dancefloors throughout their youth.

———

The music and dancing that took place in drum 'n' bass club nights across the country had been sculpted and expanded on the dancefloor of Rage in London, when the dancers tuned in to DJs Fabio and Grooverider. Even when the pair were playing in the upstairs Star Bar, before making the move to the main room in the early 1990s, they would play back to back, 15 minutes each, feeding off each other's energy and generating a powerful response on the dancefloor. They did so away from the appreciative gaze of the mainstream. I'd moved to Manchester at this point and I remember hearing that Rage had been 'taken over' by 'cheesy quavers' – a disparaging bit of rhyming slang for broadly working-class people who listened to hardcore and went to raves. A culture lag existed between the dancers and the mainstream: the former appreciated what was happening, while it took the latter decades to realise the importance.

Fabio and Grooverider brought their formative experiences in reggae sound-system culture into dance music, and they also transmitted their love of hip-hop breakbeats, speeding them up and mixing them into techno records. The dancers loved it. 'We noticed when we did that, we got a vibe,' said Fabio to camera in the mini-documentary *Rage: The Club That Inspired a Generation*. 'People were dancing in a different way to the normal four-to-the-floor house.' Once again, it was a feedback loop between the person presenting the music and the dancers commentating on it with knees and elbows. The dancers gave the producers a powerful command: play music like this, and we will reward you with whistles, shouts and the percussion-instruction of thousands of amped-up feet, and our bodies will tell you if you've got it right. Producer Lennie

De Ice left a comment on a YouTube video of his 1991 tune 'We Are I.E.' which reinforces the point. He described playing a live improvised set at a Bank Holiday all-dayer at a venue called Dungeons, on the Lea Bridge Road in east London. 'The whole of the room kicked off. There was a moment when the penny dropped. Watching the crowd, we were one, on a mission. While still buzzing from the rave I encapsulated that moment in "We Are I.E." That moment? We had it together.'

Drum 'n' bass music was usually made by DJs for the dance-floor. It's almost impossible to know exactly how much music was created because releases were often fast-moving and informal, but there are ways to approximate. DJ and author Uncle Dugs has the longest-running 'old skool' show on Rinse FM and has just under 1,000 tunes in the 1995 folder on DJ software RekordBox: 'Probably 50 per cent of those would have been classed as hit records of the time, tunes that people would know. That goes to show the volume and turnover and the interest in the scene at that time. That's how healthy the music releases were back then.' Record marketplace site Discogs has 3,840 drum 'n' bass records listed as released in the same year, although not every record would have been archived on the site. Over 3,000 of these came from the UK. Staff at specialist music distributor ST Holdings remember releasing about 'ten drum 'n' bass tracks a week by 1998, with a larger distributor like SRD releasing around 50 a week'.

There were large numbers of people dancing to the vast quantity of jungle and drum 'n' bass that was being made. *Knowledge Magazine*, a leading publication that championed the music, began running club listings in November 1996, featuring jungle nights happening across the country, from

Plymouth to Cambridge and Sheffield – and London, of course, with its accessible satellites like Milton Keynes and Croydon. An event at Pawlett Manor, halfway between Bristol and Exeter, on Boxing Day 1996 had Andy C and DJ Rap headlining alongside Rat Pack and Jason from Top Buzz. 'Oh my gosh!' read the listing. 'The atmosphere should be special in all three arenas with room for 13,500 revellers.' The London-based promoters AWOL were taking their events on tour at this time, and a listing for 17 January 1997 shows that their Cardiff all-nighter offered space for 7,000 dancers over four arenas. The numbers give a sense of the popularity. They also show how far the music and dancing had spread beyond their roots.

I spent a Saturday night in autumn 1996 with DJ and producer LTJ Bukem and his MC partner Conrad, for a feature in *Jockey Slut*. Bukem had released a number of huge records over the previous years, as well as running a powerhouse label called Good Looking Records and co-running a notable club night called Speed. I sat in his car (the first time I'd encountered heated seats) as he and Conrad drove north from his label offices in Elstree to the massive On It at Middlesbrough Arena, then down to Leeds to Back to Basics, a club better known for house and techno. In both clubs the effect was the same: mayhem. 'You see someone standing in front of the decks in sheer amazement,' said Conrad, explaining the regular conversions he'd witness as they were travelling up and down the country. 'Then they come up to you at the end of the night and say they've never heard drum 'n' bass before, someone had dragged them along, and it was like a religious experience, or something.' At Basics, the downstairs basement

– previously a techno lair – had been transformed into a cavernous sauna of bass where mashed-up househeads and drum 'n' bass devotees skanked giddily and sweatily together. In both venues – as had happened during the rave era – the dancers were spilling off the demarcated area of the dancefloor and making space in club thoroughfares, up and down the stairs, on actual podiums and even, occasionally, on the bar.

Some of the ravers that night found it relatively easy to move to this music, perhaps because they were familiar with it – the scene was, after all, a few years old. Others just moved to whichever bits of the tune they were hearing. The two clubs I visited with Bukem and Conrad were whiter spaces than, say, Phenomenon One, and some of the club community were finding their way into a new movement language.

For this crew, moving to drum 'n' bass was a somatic experience that required learning through doing, testing out which part of the music to tune in to and realising in your body that you could drop away from the hi-hats and move instead to the bassline. Dancers of all stripes could find their feet, whatever their starting point. 'I went to Jungle Fever, to Mannheim, in the depths of Germany,' says *All Crews: Journeys Through Jungle* author Brian Belle-Fortune when we chat. 'Some people had difficulty co-ordinating their enthusiasm with the music. Germans were coming up to the Jungle Fever crew and saying, "How do you dance to this?" And some of the Jungle Fever crew were showing the German crowd how to dance. They wanted to connect and interact and dance properly with the music.'

Underage nights catered to the next wave of dancers. East London-based drum 'n' bass duo Subject 13 made music and

DJed at clubs. They also ran the monthly Sub Bass club nights for 12-to-18-year-olds at Kingston Football Club in Surrey for two years between 1996 and 1997. They booked popular DJs and MCs from the main circuit, including Jumpin Jack Frost, DJ Rap, Storm and Grooverider – the 'exact same format' as a top club night, just in the back room of a non-league football club.

As well as booking the top DJs, Subject 13 also offered their own version of a drug-awareness programme. They didn't work with any official organisations, but instead brought a range of drugs in plastic bags to show the kids what each narcotic looked like and to provide information, with someone on hand to ensure the plastic bags stayed put. 'What we'd do was we'd lay out everything, every drug known to man,' says David Stewart from Subject 13 over the phone. 'We told them the implications, what these things can do. We were saying, "We're going to get in all those DJs you hear about," and we're also saying, "You don't need drugs." We weren't into taking drugs . . . other people were, good luck to them. We got off on the music; we thought we could influence others, try and influence the kids to love the music in a drug-free environment.'

Drum 'n' bass dancefloors for under-18s offered community education as well as a safe environment in which the young dancers could get lost in the music. 'They were doing exactly what they felt, what was coming to them through the music. As children, they were being even more creative than the adults, without even knowing they were being creative,' Stewart adds. There was some replication of existing drum 'n' bass moves, he says, along with a lot of 'free-flowing liquid moving, a lot more swirling around, usages of the hands in

231

different gestures'. He pauses and recalls, remembering the gender roles that were associated with movement at that point in history. 'With the boys, they'd got to keep it cool, step hard, look a bit mean. Not so much swirling going on, because your peers were not going to be happy seeing female swirling going on . . . In most clubs, females are going to hit the dancefloor first. We're encouraged when we see women going there first. Men can learn to free themselves of inhibitions and let go. That's why music is such a sacred thing.'

It became harder to keep the Kingston event going. Subject 13 were playing Japan, being booked worldwide, and eventually they removed themselves, leaving it to local guys to continue for a while. 'We couldn't carry on,' Stewart says. 'It's a pity that these kinds of things aren't happening now, because people need them.'

Metalheadz DJ and producer DJ Flight is one of the people who came through the network of under-18s nights. She is a leading light of the scene, DJing widely, making radio documentaries for the BBC and co-running 'equality network' EQ50, which works towards fairer representation within drum 'n' bass. Her entry point to the music was Club 2000, an underage night at the Ritzy on Streatham Hill, in around 1992. The flyer promised a PA from SL2, performing their top-ten hit 'On a Ragga Tip', along with 'projections, roboscans, spectacular lights and a bone-shakin sound system' between 5 p.m. and 9 p.m. It was, she remembers, 'an amazing gig'. From Club 2000 she went on to house parties and then her first illegal rave, at Priddy's Yard in Croydon, followed by Elevation at Crystal Palace sports centre in 1994. She still has the flyer. 'This is where the diversity in the crowd really struck home,' she tells me. 'I was really taken by the power of the scene, everyone coming together and loving it as one. I was already sort of obsessed with the music, but being in a rave that size made it feel more real and exciting.' She made her way through big raves and events and graduated to the energetic intimacy of Metalheadz Sunday Sessions at the Blue Note in Hoxton, east London.

Dancing isn't the only way to contribute, of course, and Flight was on her way to joining the ranks of the selectors, choosing and mixing the music that would move the dancefloor. Metalheadz was the place where she began that transition. 'The energy between DJs and ravers during that time of mad progression and friendly rivalry was incredibly exhilarating – and it's when I stopped dancing as much. I tried to get up close to watch DJs' hands instead.' It is also probably relevant to mention that being small and female in a ram-jam basement isn't always easy. 'It used to get so packed,' she says. 'People would be flinging their limbs everywhere. Being so short I definitely got elbowed in the head a few times.'

Mid-nineties pressure created deep seams of music, which continue to offer high-quality mining. Hundreds of drum 'n' bass records are still made and released worldwide every year – digital-music site Juno listed 64 tunes released between March and April 2022 – powering tens of thousands of dancers who still attend drum 'n' bass-focused club nights and festivals worldwide. Cheeky Monday at the Melkweg in Amsterdam started in 2005, making it Continental Europe's longest-running drum 'n' bass club night, while Rupture at London's Corsica Studios is just a year behind in the longevity stakes. The longest-running event worldwide, though, is DnB Tuesdays in Seattle, which has been dosing the city's bassheads since 1998. And on social media, dancing to drum 'n' bass has been having a moment on TikTok, with over 825 million views of videos tagged 'drum and bass dance' in summer 2022.

———

Brian Belle-Fortune has a lifetime's experience in music, dance and medicine, with his dual professional career as a nurse – later specialising in intensive care – and as a DJ, music writer and acclaimed author. He grew up in a strict family in Hackney, east London, with parents who were part of the Guyanese *Windrush* generation. He remembers being a young child in pyjamas in the mid-to-late 1960s and looking down into family house parties through the bannister, 'clocking the way people moved'. He started clubbing in the early 1980s, initially on the 'insanely skilful' Black British, Caribbean-influenced jazz-dance scene. Scene-famous DJ–dancers included Paul 'Trouble' Anderson, Dez Parkes and Trevor Shakes, who would show off their moves upstairs at Ronnie Scott's and at a club called Spats. Some of his peers would bunk off school to go to Friday-lunchtime jazz-funk sessions at Crackers, which took place in a Soho basement at 203 Wardour Street, although he never attended that famous spot: 'I was never the kind of kid who'd play truant. Not with my parents! Jesus!'

In 1989 he added to his dancefloor education when he took up a place at Sussex University as a mature student. He'd decided on a career change (he went back into nursing eventually) and gained a degree in International Relations and German. Alongside the academic studies came valuable experience in the form of DJing in the common room and in Brighton clubs. He wrote and directed plays, met his wife and learned how to make radio shows. All of which led to him contributing dancefloor material to BBC Radio 1, Channel 4 and MTV. Not that the gatekeepers always listened to his expertise. His brilliant history of jungle and drum 'n' bass, *All Crews*, exists because of a blinkered knockback he received when suggesting female DJ Wildchild for a slot on a specialist music programme. Instead of pitching the idea elsewhere, Brian began interviewing all the major players and interspersed their words with his own careful observations. He typed it up, printed it out and took it to record shops, whereupon it sold out and was picked up by the appropriately named Vision Publishing.

In the book, Brian talks about dancing: 'The key to jungle is that you can choose your beat, dance at a pace to suit yourself, follow the bass, the drums or a combination of both and ride the riddim . . . there's flexibility, everything runs from crazy legs to breakdancing, rave-yer-hands-in-the-air stomp and rub-up-inna-Reggae stylee.' He quotes MC Det, who differentiated for a multicultural dancefloor with the words, '*If you can't dance, just nod your head.*' Dancing was for everybody, or if you separate out the word, for every body.

Brian had been schooled in the particulars of the early-1990s dancefloor by MC Det, DJ Brockie and 'the Kool FM, Jungle Fever lot'. 'They are Black, Hackney and working-class,' he told me. 'I was out with Brockie and Det, dancing. My head was going to the rhythm of the hi-hat, and they'd say, "Nah, bruv, you do it like this." They slowed me right down. You might start with the snare, quite fast, but there's another groove where you step right down and get into that.' After his induction you'd always find him in the same spot at the back of the club, banging on the walls when the moment demanded it, which was frequently.

After we spoke, Brian sent me a list of reminiscences that act as a whistle-stop tour around various dancefloor moments: VHS copies of the Michael Jackson 'Thriller' video; having to take another set of clothes to go home in because you would be drenched with sweat; the welcome arrival of hand dryers in bathrooms; Jazzie B and the Africa Centre and his phrase 'If you're not dancing, fuck off'; rollerskating and dancing and 'people recognising us from the way we moved on skates'; penny loafer shoes with white socks that would accentuate how your feet were moving. His list included one more entry, which we'll explore in a little more detail: bass face. The phrase 'bass face' describes the way facial expression responds to a dirty-enough bassline – chin back and down, face scrunched up. This appears to be an automatic response, judging by the videos posted online of babies, often in the backs of cars, pulling bass face when a tune drops. Something happens to the human face when the body responds to music; nature's screwface.

The widespread, energetic dancefloors described in Brian's book offered the chance to process life's pressures through the medium of movement. Some clubbers and ravers would have been as carefree going into the dance as they were leaving. Others would have been winding out everyday stresses of money, family or relationships. Others still were dancing out heavy loads. The promoter Sting, who ran events under the Telepathy banner (and, later, the grime-influencing pirate radio station Deja Vu), is quoted in Brian's book: 'We've seen man heavy with the weight of the world come into our raves. Boy, he's gonna be trouble, we think. See the same man at the end of the rave, skipping.'

There were also young men on drum 'n' bass dancefloors who didn't want to dance exuberantly or expressively. Still, they were able to find the part of the dancefloor they needed, which often involved standing against a wall somewhere. Leaning against a supporting structure, often flanked by friends, this part of the dancefloor demographic could receive and respond to the signal sent out by the music and the movement taking place around them. They were taking part in the dance – even if they did so by standing at the back, puffa jacket on whatever the temperature, nodding their heads and occasionally raising a hand up towards the ceiling. That is dancing, of a very minimal, stoned and masculine kind – but it's still dancing. Relinquishing control isn't easy, although the payoff, as all everyday dancers know, is communion – and I'm not talking about the wafer the priest dispensed at 9.15 a.m. Mass.

Brian never really left the dancefloor, despite the work pressures that come with being a nurse, bringing up a family, and the progressive effects of multiple sclerosis that have left him wheelchair-bound. He remembers watching cult 1994 documentary *All Junglists: A London Someting Dis* and noticing a scene towards the end that included a guy in a wheelchair on the dancefloor, soaking up the vibes and bringing the movement he had. 'I honed in on him,' he says, 'and I knew that if something horrible happened to me, I'd be on the dancefloor too.'

The Dance

Friends and family responded in all kinds of ways to the news of Brian's diagnosis: 'My best mate Daniel lives in Berlin. We were having a beer and talking about it, and the different changes I might have to make. We've always been able to talk about anything, but the thing we both found really hard was when he said, "What about dancing?" It was the only time we were both like, "Let's move swiftly on." Neither of us could answer that question.'

Brian has remained on the dancefloor. As well as DJing, he's a regular at Sun and Bass in Sardinia, and his *All Crews* book has been updated and is being republished as a vital contemporaneous document of a great British music genre. In 2021 he and Daniel celebrated 25 years of raving together. 'I've noticed that a lot of people on our scene have this different energy about them,' he says. 'I'm sure that's connected to your body and how you inhabit it.'

11: HOUSEHOLD BOPPING

Mother-dancing and sleeping children
at the Loft in 1990s New York

Dancing relates to family in ways that are as layered and varied as families themselves. I was heavily pregnant in December 1997, when I attended a midweek drum 'n' bass club called PM Scientist. It was held at a long-gone venue called Smithfields, down the road from a building site that would soon become famous London nightclub Fabric, and I'd been commissioned to write a magazine article about the night. I was gently stepping on the sidelines for a few hours, soaking up the endings and the imminent beginnings. The bass and the breaks carried me home, where my boyfriend and I nestled in to welcome this new person into the world in quieter surroundings, attached to our home by what felt like an ever-shortening elastic band.

My pregnancy made me an anomaly in clubs, not least because mothers-to-be – even young ones working in music – are often expected to be sedate. Dance educator and lecturer Beatrix Bánkyné Perjés offers another perspective. She's based at the University of Pécs, in the south-west of Hungary, managing their oversubscribed 'dancing university'. It's a year-round programme of high-quality classes that are offered to all staff and students, from which they gain the pleasure and benefits of moving to music, along with course credits. It acts as social glue across the institutional family, bringing

239

staff and learners from different departments and disciplines together on the dancefloor.

In 2020 Beatrix published research titled *Effects of Prenatal Dance Intervention on Fetal Neurodevelopment*. It included a tiny and fascinating study that looked at the effect of dancing on foetal development and on maternal well-being, analysing 16 pregnant women who took her twice-weekly dance class, which combined ballet, salsa and other styles with improvised moves. She then looked at motor skills and cognitive, communicative and emotional responses once the infants were five weeks old. She found all these functions were improved, compared to the babies in the control group, whose mothers didn't take Beatrix's class. One dancing participant who already had three kids reported that her new addition started talking much earlier than the others. Beatrix's hypothesis is that movement co-ordinated to music provides additional stimuli to the baby and helps the nervous system develop faster and further. By the age of three the children in the test group showed cognitive, communication and motor skills that were on average six months ahead of their peers, and achieved particularly good results in what Beatrix calls 'expressive communication'.

Dancing was good for the mothers, too. 'I tried to measure their physical, psychological, cognitive abilities and social wellbeing,' she told me. 'There wasn't much difference in their physical abilities towards the end of pregnancy than before commencing the intervention, but, in terms of all the other areas, they improved. Their social support systems developed, and so did their body awareness. There was cohesion; they could talk together and share their positive and negative experiences with their peers.' The best outcome, she said, was cognitive: 'Memory and creativity developed, both compared to their pre-activity abilities and to the control group.'

I asked her why creativity is useful for a new mother. 'We meet very unexpected happenings that we have to react to very quickly,' she replied, which caused me to recall the daily avalanche of terrifying and amazing Unexpected Happenings that occur when you're sent home with a brand-new person in your arms.

Dancing appears to be an excellent way to support pregnant women, to give babies the best chance of thriving once they've arrived, and to help new mothers make useful connections with other women in the same situation. It seems like a no-brainer, but I couldn't find any other research on prenatal dance, and nor has Beatrix. We're a long way from women being prescribed dance classes along with folic acid when they find that double stripe on their pregnancy test. Beatrix's research points to globally useful material: after all, everyone was *in utero* at some point, and at least some of us will have children ourselves.

You might be wondering at this point whether or not it's sensible to dance while pregnant. Dance USA's Task Force on Dancer Health is comprised of medical professionals who work with dancers and dance companies across the US and Canada. They released an informational paper on the subject, aimed at pro dancers. The list of things to avoid – big jumps, stretching the inner thighs in a straddle position, overstretching foot ligaments by spending long hours barefoot – shine a light on the myriad aspects of ordinary dancing that are considered reasonable by virtue of their absence from a list of risky practices. Exercise while pregnant, including dance, is considered broadly safe and beneficial, as long, of course, as your medical professional agrees. It is advisable to avoid very loud environments, something my younger self failed to do.

There's also emerging research into dancing and childbirth, prompted in part by women posting videos of themselves dancing in late pregnancy and early labour. A 2020 paper, 'Dancing During Labor: Social Media Trend or Future Practice?' found that moving to music during the first stage of labour may decrease the duration and intensity of pain. It's no surprise that the group of dances known as *raqs sharqi* in Arabic, or *oryantal dans* in Turkish – 'belly dancing' in the reductive vernacular – is frequently referenced in this context.

Dancer, researcher and writer Morocco, also known as Aunt Rocky, was born Carolina Varga Dinicu. She has been practising and documenting *raqs sharqi* for five decades and is a member of the Congress of Research in Dance, the Society of Dance History Scholars and the International Council on Dance. The connection between *raqs sharqi* and childbirth first came to her attention in 1961, when she met Farab Firdoz, a dancer from Saudi Arabia, who told her that *raqs sharqi* had been danced with and for women in labour in some rural areas of her country until the 1950s. Intrigued, she kept her ears open for more information, and eventually, in 1967, she travelled to rural Morocco to witness it for herself. She tells the story in her book, *You Asked Aunt Rocky*, describing women forming a series of circles around the labouring mother-to-be, who was squatting in the middle of a special tent. 'All the women were singing softly and undulating their abdomens, sharply pulling them in several times,' she wrote, describing slow and strong movements, which the women repeated while gradually moving the circle clockwise. The babies – twins – were born, and the women continued singing and dancing in the hours afterwards. It was, she says, a profoundly moving experience. Dances that imitate the motions required for doing a job strengthen the very muscles necessary for doing that job, she concluded. 'The birth "dance" I saw was not really a dance in the way we understand it, even though it used rhythmical motion and chanting. It was more a medium to induce semi-hypnosis in the woman in labour, who was also doing those movements.'

I told a newly pregnant friend about Aunt Rocky and *raqs sharqi* when she asked me to be her birth partner. We joked about a comic scene in the birthing room, where the midwives would walk in to find me belly-dancing at her. By the time she was admitted into hospital for induction we'd both forgotten about dancing through labour and were just doing all the compressed hanging around that early labour involves. A midwife suggested using the birthing ball to bring on contractions, so we went into the day room and my friend sat on the ball. I googled for some guidance on how to use it and found three movements, one of which involved rotating the hips in a similar movement to that known as winding your waist, or 'wining', in Jamaican dancehalls and which is familiar to my friend through her Caribbean heritage. It is sometimes done with your partner close behind you, connecting and pulsing on the beat. We wined opposite each other, her on the ball, me standing up on the other side of the room, laughing and joking about a Brixton dancefloor we'd been on together and miming imaginary partners behind us. Her contractions began coming harder and stronger, and eventually a baby boy arrived. In this small way we danced him into the world.

The first time my boyfriend or I held a baby as adults was when we held our newborn and brought him home. We realised that you don't just sing a lullaby – you dance it, too. You dance a lullaby with your baby in your arms as you move in circles around a small bedroom in the dark. I felt new parenthood through a dancefloor lens. It wasn't that dissimilar, in the sense of staying up all night and having a familiarity with the dawn hours. We bounced with this small person held tight to the shoulder. We rocked, swayed, shuffled, having switched amplified music for the song of newborn demands.

As he grew, we danced him around on our feet, like we'd been danced round on adult feet. New toddler friends did a demi-dance, shifting from one foot to the other with their arms open, and their adults danced it back; a mirror. On Saturday mornings there would be loud music and bursts of hyperactive dancing, between us adults and with him, something North American writer and sociology professor Maxine Leeds Craig calls 'household bopping'. Sometimes, we'd put him to bed and turn the front room into a dancefloor so that we could do what we needed, which was to move to music with each other and with our friends. Motherhood was not an exit from the dancefloor. It was a period in which dancing shifted from dark nightclubs to lullaby bedrooms and kitchen parties. It was a joyful and tiring pause and reset.

My friend Annette once told me that her mum would roll up the carpets of her suburban home and have house dances in the late 1940s and early 1950s, as would her friends. They were young brides and they needed to step out, even if they could only step out at home. This sounds so sensible and fun, and a logical response to the pressures that post-war suburban life put on social bonds. I tend to think of house parties as the preserve of teenagers, where friends bundle through the front door of a student house or a family home, then spiral out the back to be sick in a bush or just to get a breath after all the comedy that house parties inevitably bring – but they make sense for young families, too. Now, though, house parties seem to be the preserve of the past, what with noise-phobic neighbours and crappy new-builds with tiny rooms and tissue paper for walls. That's a whole other subject, but I'll just say this: new parents need the bonding powers of movement in a different way to children or teenagers, but they need it, too.

The artist Björk took a similar approach to Annette's mum. Living in New York in the mid-2000s she and her friends would take over the downtown Housing Works Bookstore and start DJing in the afternoon. 'We would start with symphonies and cello concertos and just sit there in the daylight with our kids and drink coffees,' she told me during an interview for the Red Bull Music Academy. Then, when the sun went down, the energy would shift. 'That sounds like a lovely grown-folks way to rave up,' I said. 'I've always liked this whole all-generations-hang-out-together thing,' she replied. 'I've got six younger brothers and sisters. In Iceland a small birthday party with only the closest relatives is about a hundred people. We're still in that 18th-century idea where there isn't this generational gap. So I've always liked this healthy partying together.'

In January 2020 I gave a talk at Berlin's CTM music festival. By this time I was not a young mother; I was in my forties. A writer, Maya-Róisín Slater, approached me and asked if she could interview me for a radio show. We sat in a small back-room office in the Haus der Kulturen der Welt, which is located in the Tiergarten park, shifting brooms and folders out of the way so we could sit and talk. Towards the end of our conversation, I made a passing comment about being careful how I approached dancing spaces because of being anomalous, age-wise. She pulled me up: 'That's exactly what society doesn't want, and that's why we need it.' Her comments reminded me of an ambient discomfort around the notion of mothers who continue to take their place on the dancefloor. In my experience this was sometimes expressed through admiration – 'I think it's amazing that you're still doing this!' – where surprise revealed the preconception. I wonder if maternal status collapses age, such that the constraints accorded to middle-aged women apply to mothers, regardless of their birth date.

'Everyone we think shouldn't be on the dancefloor, should be on the dancefloor,' said Maya-Róisín. 'Society has a tendency to throw people away if they're female-identifying or non-binary, and that's to do with women as products. A mixing of people with different life experiences is a better thing to want for a dancefloor.'

Maya-Róisín's a dancefloor thinker. 'The dancefloor is never just a dancefloor,' she said at one point, and I knew exactly what she meant. The dancefloor in its most positive and nutritious form can be a meeting point, a village green, an information exchange and much else besides. A cross-generational aspect can contribute, in the mix. 'It was impactful to see [Berlin] clubs could be these intergenerational spaces, and that when they are, it opens up the potential in raving or clubbing as a community-building, life-giving space,' she said. People with more life experience, she believed, can be 'keepers of history'.

Maya-Róisín's not a hugely comfortable dancer, hyper-aware of moving in public and of the repercussions of being in a young female body moving on the dancefloor. So much so that she'd usually take a notebook with her, so she'd have something to do. 'There was one party when I was dancing and having so much fun. But before I'd got on the dancefloor I'd been sitting with my friends, who are all in their forties, talking about their experiences of clubbing. I felt it like a familial vibe: these people are my non-binary parents. These experiences are a chance for chosen family and mentorship.'

She also has first-hand experience of mothers and dancing. She grew up in Vancouver in the 2000s and early 2010s with a single parent who trenchantly failed to adhere to the unwritten rules and regulations which dictate where mothers can go, and with whom. 'My mom took me to gigs and raves and parties in warehouses,' she said. 'She was ridiculed by a lot of people because I was out until one o'clock in the morning with her at these shows. I remember her being judged quite heavily on this.' The judgement arrived from all directions. 'Her boy-friend took her to Burning Man, and I remember thinking, "I hate this, it's so embarrassing, this is not what women of her age do." Then I got older and came to Berlin and realised all the ways you're taught to hate women and how that manifests in your mom.'

———

'I do kind of feel like I'm turning into a disco mum, looking after everyone.' Lucy Fizz is a model and dancer with Ibiza party Glitterbox and the subject of Melinte Reitzema's 2016 documentary *Lucy*, which explores her story as a trans woman. We're talking in a Dalston pub, sitting at a table. Usually she's on a podium or platform, waving her hands in the air and conducting the crowd as she surfs the peak of lost-in-music moves for hours at a time. 'I'm giving out my energy and welcoming the energy of people back in,' she says. 'Revving people up and transferring that energy back out.'

London clubs like Nag Nag Nag, Trailer Trash and Boom-Box helped Lucy build her everyday movement repertoire in the late 1990s and early 2000s, and also allowed her to build her identity and family. 'My chosen family are all the people I met on the dancefloor, and it's such an important part of having shaped the person I am today, putting me where I am,' she says. 'Most of who I am has come from being out on dance-floors.' While Lucy doesn't have the trained technique or skill of some of her fellow dancers, she brings her own style and flavour, which itself is an important part of the mix, as it's relatable and encouraging. 'Someone's gone down the runway and done all this amazing voguing, jumping into the splits at the end. And I have to go up next, and I'm like, "*Aarrrrgggghhhhhh.*" Then it comes back to the energy and carefree attitude I bring,' she says. 'I'm the same as everyone else on the dance-floor. They can see that they don't have to have all these fancy dance moves. They can flail their arms around wildly, like I do, and have a wonderful time.' She's building bridges in other ways too: 'Performing at festivals and clubs with drag queens and queer people who are visibly out, I see so much acceptance when people meet us on the dancefloor. I've heard stories about people changing their views on queer people.' She believes that moving to music can create a space in which an individual can recognise the need for a new stance, a new way of holding themselves – or to reject the pose they've been given by society. 'Nightlife allowed me to explore my gender identity,' she says. 'It's where I could explore dressing more femininely and passing as female when I went out in my late teens. But then I found the queer scene in London. That was a whole other awakening for me, and being part of that allowed me to develop another stage of my identity.'

It's really amazing to be part of creating these spaces, she adds, where people are able to question or explore themselves and learn about their gender or sexual identity. 'To be able to create spaces where people feel safe to come and express themselves is really rewarding.' It's a reminder: you don't have to have birthed a child to be a parent. Lucy Fizz is not a mother but she has many children. She is a disco mum, and her kids are lucky to have her.

I wasn't feeling too lucky when I was going through the bereavement caused by my dad's death in 2001. Our small family began breaking up soon after, and we reorganised ourselves around new realities. Ordinary, everyday dancing helped me adapt. These weren't influential dancefloors where new genres of music emerged. These were the front rooms of south-east London Victorian terraces where friends danced together, and where those of us with children tucked them in carefully upstairs. We expressed ourselves with lyric dances to Beyoncé or OutKast in one house, and bounced about to The Ramones and The Smiths in another. Local dancefloors were personally powerful. I could dance my way home, which, luckily for all of us, was just over the road.

———

Baltimore, August 2017. I was working on a project that supported US-based grass-roots social innovators, whether they were using the city's dirt-bike culture to teach science, maths and engineering, or running an integrated dance company that put wheelchair users at the centre of proceedings. It was an intense and sociable fortnight that included a night out at the iconic Shake & Bake roller-rink in West Baltimore and a club night at the Crown, a brilliantly no-frills music venue above a restaurant. I saw dancers using intricate footwork and squat-kicks that evoked jigs, reels and the kind of moves I associate with Eastern European sailors. This might not be entirely fanciful: Baltimore is a port city, with all the migratory detail that port cities contain. It's a dancing city, with dancers making the most of the rich culture and ruined economics – in doorways, on street corners and alleyways, and in the remaining community centres.

Baltimore is a highly segregated city where there is extreme poverty and gun violence – with the second-highest murder rate in the US – and where residents came up with an incredibly creative response to their situation. I began noticing stickers bearing the phrase 'Nobody Kill Anybody', along with information about something called the Baltimore Ceasefire Weekend. The grass-roots movement, instigated by activist Erricka Bridgeford and launched in May 2017, illuminates the war-zone realities. There are now four Ceasefire

Weekends a year, one of which is centred around Mother's Day. Baltimoreans are encouraged to run purposefully peaceful events over Ceasefire weekend, including block parties, where neighbours close off a street and turn it into a road-based dancefloor.

East Baltimore poet Kondwani Fidel expressed these realities in the documentary *Dark City Beneath the Beat*, when he said, 'Our dance steps are just our tears in portable form.' It was music producer Rod Lee, though, who provided the ultimate summation of the city's relationship to movement in his sparse yet weighty 2006 track, which appeared on *The Wire*'s soundtrack. It's called 'Dance My Pain Away'.

Photographer, educator and freedom fighter Shan Wallace was working on the same project that took me to Baltimore, and we reconnected over the phone to talk about movement and music. She grew up in the city's Baptist church in the early 2000s and absorbed the deep influence of praise dance, later going out to venues playing the localised and distinctly secular genre of Baltimore Club, which fuses raw house music with breakbeats. As a scene, Baltimore Club comes with its own movement language, including a springy, alternating jump-spread of the legs called the Spongebob, named after the cartoon.

Between 2015 and 2020 Shan photographed the neighbourhood dancefloor that emerged on Saturday lunchtimes at the downtown Lexington Market. A handful of folk would gather in a space between the shops to hear bands with names like Blackblues Magic or the RoseGold Experience on the Arcade stage in the east building of the market, and they'd be energised into movement by the locally famous Mr Wiggle (also known as Mr Wiggles), a dancefloor instigator who'd bring the dance with him wherever he went. The vibe was lively and the music was irresistible, and this combination would sometimes tempt a lady with two children and more than two shopping bags to join the dancers for a ten-second two-step before she rejoined the stream of shoppers. 'I had my camera with me and I started to dance,' says Shan. 'I couldn't help but dance because the music was so goddamn good.' Dancing built trust, as did the fact that Shan gave people copies of their portraits.

Saturdays at Lexington Market extended the dancefloor out to weekend shoppers. 'It was one of my favourite times of the week, dancing in a space where I felt safe. No one knew me, there was no one my age to really judge me,' says Shan. 'It's one thing to be on the art scene and to be kicking it with your friends, but it's something else to kick it with people you've grown to know, on a dancefloor that brought us together.' The space carved out for daytime dancing became a place of accumulation, where life experience could be felt, condensed and expressed in Mr Wiggle's wide hip-rolls or a little two-step, or an older gentleman finding his way back into the movement of his youth. The truth is that the street isn't an extension of the dancefloor, it's the other way round. The dancefloor is an extension of the street corner, of the marketplace, of the crossroads. It's all of those communal places, condensed and amplified.

Lexington Market has since been demolished, although the new building now contains a specially commissioned, large-scale photographic collage installation by Shan which captures market life and features Mr Wiggle. The loss of

252

dance spots, whether they're formal or informal, makes me think of environmentalist Rob Nixon's phrase 'slow violence', and it seems that this wrecking ball doesn't just stop at the dancehall doorway. It affects all kinds of dancefloors, including shopping centres.

Another of Shan's archives comprises a series of phenomenal portraits from within the local vogue community, the vast majority of whom would use one or more identifiers: queer, trans or non-binary. Her participation on the dancefloor collapsed the distance between her lens and the people visible through it: 'I remember going to some balls and some of the girls knowing that I used to vogue. They'd say, "Cmon, Shan, give us a spin." I would sometimes hit a drop or a duck walk, and they'd get really pumped. I'm doing these moves with my camera in my hand. We'd laugh about it. It was a way to see that we come from the same place.' Vogue, she says, is intricately connected to breaking (as breakdance is now known) – as they're both ways for communities to show off, show out and show up an opponent without resorting to violence. It is a language used between queer, trans and gay people with high levels of dance skills, and it's also allowed Shan to recognise and name elements of her own self, too. 'A way for me to understand my own queerness, my own identity, was voguing. It was something we all did without even knowing about ballroom or categories or getting famous. It was just something we did on the Baltimore streets.' As a teen in the mid-2000s her Baltimore-standard 4XL white t-shirt made her look boyish, but she responded non-boyishly when she vogued. 'I took note,' she says, recognising the broadening palette of identity and expression that movement allowed. 'I started to see examples. I was seeing gay men move their bodies like Alvin Ailey dancers. I was seeing butch women move their bodies like fucking Misty Copeland. It made me realise: it doesn't matter how you identify, it's about energetically what's moving through your body.

'There are so many ways I started to find [out] who I was through dance,' she continues. 'I didn't even think about any of that shit before you asked, but it's the real truth. I spent so much time dancing, being shy about dancing, finding myself through dance . . . I think people don't value it. Body movement and dance is survival.'

———

The concept of family shows up in multiple community-based dance forms. Hip-hop styles like popping or breaking are organised around the concept of crews – the handful people you dance with at competitions or performances – and 'fams', which act as an umbrella for a number of crews. The LA-born style of krump also has crews and fams, and senior dancers within a crew are known as 'Big Homies'. They act as older siblings to less experienced dancers, who are known as 'Lil' Homies'. In morris dancing, groups are known as 'sides', in which roles parody class-based work structures rather than family – each side has a 'squire' and a 'foreman' to teach new dancers the moves.

In vogue, though, ideas of dance and family are explicit. Many of the people who became involved in New York's early-eighties ballroom scene needed to find new families, given the high incidence of parental rejection, violence and homelessness many trans and queer people suffered, and continue to suffer. The dancefloor – or 'ballroom', as it was known – provided a space in which at least one creative solution emerged. Individuals would join one of many houses – the House of Xtravaganza, say, or the House of Ninja, and take the house name as their new surname. Houses were led by a mother, often a trans woman, and sometimes included a house father, too. These DIY families moved together, practising for balls on New York's piers and in parks and the clubs. Brilliant dancers came out of these close-bonded groups, but they were just doing the same thing as ordinary dancers. They were dancing their story, and using the dancefloor as a place where they could express and release some of life's troubles.

Sixty-one-year-old Archie Burnett was the first father of the vogue-famous House of Ninja and is the oldest surviving member. He was brought up in a strict Seventh-Day Adventist family in Brooklyn, New York, and was, he tells me in a long late-night call, 'forbidden to dance'. The restrictions – and the moves he secretly learned by watching TV – coiled movement deep into his body and set him up for a long and enduring association with the dancefloor: 'A personal relationship I've had for over 40 years,' he says.

It began for him at a New York members-only club called the Loft, which started in 1970 and took place in founder David Mancuso's home. It is another culturally famous locale that has been thoroughly documented (NPR called it 'the most influential party in history'), and which lives on, despite the death of Mancuso in 2016. For Archie, the Loft community offered an acceptance that was absent in his religious upbringing. 'All of us that are in this thing, we're misfits, we don't fit into society. Or society would say there's something wrong with us because we're not going with the status quo. When you find people of like mind, in a like journey, they become your family. There's people I've danced with for 20 years and I don't even know their last names. You know that every Saturday they'll be there, and you share this time . . . Family is not necessarily related to blood, especially when it comes to this.'

This was household bopping on a whole other level, because Mancuso hosted his Loft parties in his own home, decorating his spacious apartment with balloons and decorations that hinted at the kids' birthday parties he'd experienced growing up in a Catholic children's home. A spectacular, crystalline sound system was in place, through which Mancuso powered his exquisite disco and funk selections, like Sun Palace's 'Rude Movements' or Dexter Wansel's 'Life on Mars'. There was enough wonderful dancing for the event to confer its name upon a particular movement style – 'lofting'. A similar process caused house music to be named after Frankie Knuckles's Warehouse club, although the currently popular form of 'house dancing', which combines a fluid jack with shuffling footwork, owes as much to New York nightclubs of the 1990s as it does to raw 1980s Chicago.

It is important to clarify that lofting isn't a codified style with specific moves. 'It is an approach to dance movement,' says Archie. 'Because wherever you came from you were influenced by everybody else.' The end result was a room in which people moved together: 'Similar to contemporary dance, smoothly done, where you'd use bits and pieces of authentic or acrobatic moves, mixed with intertwining bodies.'

Ballerinas adapted their conservatoire-honed techniques to dance music, he says, alongside local kids, whose hard-rock, proto-hip-hop styles would be softened by the open-minded environment and the ban on cameras.

'That's what was special,' he says. 'These were "come as you are" parties. A kid from the hood, being planted in a scene where you don't have to look over your back to see if someone's going to shoot you – and where you see everybody moving a little bit smoother than you – you're not going to abandon your hard-rock style, but you're going to be influenced.' This was particularly important for the young men who attended, he says. 'If you move a certain way, that automatically gives another man information about how you're living: if you're soft or weak or strong. Men do that all the time. We size each other up. It's information to help you navigate.' In short, Archie knows a lot about the way that a person's movement style leaks information. 'Child,' he says, with a dramatic and just-long-enough pause. 'Your feet tell me everything I need to know.'

Colleen 'Cosmo' Murphy played music alongside David Mancuso at the 1990s iteration of the Loft. She remembers that adult clubbers were invited to a night of dancing and music that attended to needs often relinquished in childhood – to dance freely, to be accepted – and which could also wrap around parental realities. 'Someone, maybe it was a single dad,' she tells me, 'brought their kid. It was David's house; he had a bed and sofas, and the kid just went to sleep.'

Would that have been possible at any of the other clubs Cosmo was going to in New York at that time? I ask, knowing the answer but asking it anyway. 'No,' she says emphatically.

'No way. Gosh. No way!' her voice amplifying as she absorbed the memories the question pulled up. 'I would not take my daughter to those places now! Save the Robots [in an East Village storefront and basement], where they had a gun check? Where they had ammonia to wash down the floor? Quite a different scenario.'

The party has been going on so long at the Loft, she says, that it's created an intergenerational community of its own. Half a century of history means the club has one of the widest age ranges of any contemporary disco- or sound-system-related spot: today, the oldest member is in his late seventies or early eighties, and the youngest is a twenty-something.

Cosmo was pregnant within a year of launching the London-based, founder-blessed iteration of the Loft – Lucky Cloud – in 2003. Based at the Rose Lipman community centre in Hackney – as well as at a few other remaining community centres that haven't been destroyed by austerity and gentrification – the Lucky Cloud nights are run by a collective of around 30 volunteers, who own their own sound system. Not reliant on venues with high overheads and crippling business rates, Lucky Cloud is well placed to continue. 'It doesn't look slick,' Cosmo says. 'It looks homemade.' Her daughter was born three weeks before one of their parties, so she came along too, newborn and swaddled in cloth and music for a tiny moment of introduction to her extended sonic family.

Lucky Cloud continues the Loft's sympathetic approach to parental realities. There is an informal arrangement allowing the parents among their community to turn up with their children for the first two hours of the event, which starts at

5 p.m. 'It's a way of keeping people in touch with the party,' says Cosmo. 'It keeps the community together – instead of saying, "You can't come back unless you get a babysitter" or "You can't come back till your kids are grown up."' Children are given sweets on the door, there's food up on the stage, the music is turned down to a gentle 90 decibels and the crew of volunteers blow up extra balloons so that kids can each take one home.

Cosmo describes one of the unexpected benefits of allowing parents to bring their children for part of the evening. 'You get all these twenty-somethings who don't have kids,' she says. 'Probably the last thing they want to see is a child on the dancefloor. But [then] they all start to relax and, a lot of the time, they'll interact, throw the balloons around for the kids, and you can see something being brought out of them.' It's an opportunity, like a wedding, for neat footwork, friendly bopping and family moves to be passed down, with small children seeing adults moving to music and absorbing the information for later use. And, like a post-marriage disco, the Hackney Loft brings together a newly constituted extended family. 'There are a lot of people in our community that have felt the need to build their own family,' says Cosmo. 'Maybe they moved to another country like I did, or maybe they moved to the big city from their small town and didn't feel like they fitted in at home. Music and dancing should be a healing force. That's the real goal.'

Where, though, do you go for some musical healing when you've grown out of the dancefloors around you? Some people give up; others find a place where they're welcomed regardless of age. Bob Hill went for the latter. He's in his mid-fifties and is part of a cultural family that met at jazz-funk rollerdiscos and on soul-weekender dancefloors. His dance instruction goes back further, of course – he remembers his mum stopping him at a family house party and telling him to dance to the bassline, not the drums. Now he's a regular at Patrick Forge and Gilles Peterson's reprised Dingwalls sessions in London, where there's a shared understanding of spatial awareness and dancefloor etiquette. 'It's like when you watch starlings or a school of fish,' he says. 'We're all together, but we don't interfere with each other. We move as one.'

Dancing allows Bob to enjoy this phase of his life in unexpected ways. 'I'm having a good mid-life crisis because I'm not having a crisis at all,' he says. 'I'm really enjoying myself. I know my knees are going to be screaming like sirens the next morning, but the older I've got, the better I've got at living in the now, and dancing to music, old and new, is part of living in the now . . . I think dancing is vaccination against getting stuck in that "things were better in my day" mind-set, which is bullshit.' He continues, 'It reminds me that even though I'm getting older, I'm not getting old, and that's lovely for me. A lot of people my age seem really bloody miserable. They've turned right wing and nasty. I'm not trying to chase any lost youth, but I think that being involved with music and dancing has stopped me turning into some kind of horrible Generation X Brexit wanker.'

The dancing body can become a vessel through which it's possible to shift your reality to match what's actually around you rather than some stuck and staid interpretation of the past. Such an imagined past is tempting, not least because in the past you're always young. But dancing has a tidal effect, bringing you in line with the world and offering new, physical ways to think and exist. Dancing shifts and changes like a wave. Like water, it has a reflective surface, as do the dancers.

———

The writer Rachael Smart shone a light on the profound relationship between dancing and a life well lived when she posted on Twitter about her beloved grandparent's death: 'Thinking about my grandad. In hospital, age 94, and he said: "When you see my light start to go out, will you dance for me?" So I did, and I did it with commitment. And he said to the nurses, "Don't mind her, she's just my whole world, and I've asked her to see me on my way."'

12: SEARCHING FOR THE PERFECT NIGHTCLUB

A layered history of Plastic People, 1994–2015

The dancefloor can support a community. It can also generate new communities, as occurred in a small basement club called Plastic People. The story begins, however, with a music-mad teenager in the city of Ibadan, in the south-west of Nigeria, in the 1980s.

Ade Fakile was always tracking down new music, although his only outlet was to play new imported 12-inches by Cameo, Full Force or Timex Social Club at his school discos. He attended Loyola College, a boys-only school established by missionaries in 1953 as a Catholic grammar school, which was taken back into government control in 1977. A website dedicated to the graduating class of 1980 describes the school motto (*veritas*, or 'truth') and quotes a line from the school song to elaborate the institutional vision: 'We all strive for perfection or excellence here, in everything we do.' So far, so Plastic People.

The school ran regular parties in conjunction with affiliated establishments: the literature society at Loyola would send an invitation to the literature society at another school – say, St Anne's – and students would meet for a social. 'Lit Day' was theoretically about reading, but it was really an opportunity for music and dancing, and Ade DJed at them all. This unexpected subplot of Catholic spaces doubling up as clubs offered a solid foundation.

Ade moved to London aged 19 to study economics and quickly found his route into the clubs. He'd be at the Wag on Wardour Street, or in a 'horrible venue' deep underneath the YMCA building behind Tottenham Court Road, where jazz dancers gathered despite the presence of carpet rather than a slidy wooden floor. Mostly, though, he'd go to Fish, a small, rectangular basement club behind the door at 37–39 Oxford Street. The building had been constructed in 1912 to a design by architect Delissa Joseph, whose wife Lily was a campaigning suffragette and was detained at Holloway Prison because of her activism. She was 'well-known for her musical voice in the communal singing at the Brook Green synagogue in Hammersmith', according to local historian Lucy Handscomb, on her Riverview Gardens History blog. I think that our musically inclined suffragette would have approved of what followed. Ade didn't know any of this, of course. Nor did he know that he was taking part in a formation dance across decades. To understand how, we need to visit this basement venue in the early 1980s.

Enter Trevor Shakes – a storied character, and not just because he had a dual role of sublime DJ and phenomenal dancer, like a turntable-based James Brown. He was renowned for his virtuoso moves – chosen to support pop megastars Wham! when they went to China in 1985 as the first Western act to play the country – and a groundbreaking parallel career in fashion. He worked at Vivienne Westwood's SEX shop on the King's Road and became a successful international model and catwalk choreographer.

Shakes grew up in east London in the late 1950s, in a complicated household where shebeens took place in the cellar and people would travel from miles around to attend. He and his siblings lived there until he was six years old, and he would tiptoe around the house, looking through keyholes and hiding in corners to see what was going on. He began hanging out at reggae dances as a young teenager, then, inevitably, got involved with what came next. At the Lacy Lady in Ilford, around 1973 or 1974, listening to funk and soul, he saw a handsome, acrobatic dancer called Travis Edwards (who later had a second creative life making rave records under the name Satin Storm). Shakes decided there and then that he wanted to dance like that, and dance he did. Within a couple of years he, too, was known as a top dancer across the country.

In 1982 Sylma Laviniere and her brother-in-law Lee Wickins started running a club night called Spats at 37–39 Oxford Street. Shakes and his fellow DJ–dancer Dez Parkes played the music and held court on the dancefloor. 'When we first started,' Shakes told fellow dancer Fitzroy Facey of *Soul Survivors* magazine in an extremely rare interview, 'it was a hard slog and it took ages to get going but we persevered and I used it as a form of escapism.' In the early days, he added, the atmosphere was 'on another level, electric'.

Shakes's DJing style was to put on a tune like Sylvester's 'Here Is My Love', slip out of the DJ booth so he could dance to it, and then casually head back to put on the next selection. 'He was graceful,' said DJ Frankie Valentine, whom we met earlier describing how people 'dance their story', and who attended Spats. 'He would dance the way the records are made, portraying those emotions in every single breath.'

'You have to understand all I was doing was just dancing and I got lost in the music,' Shakes told *Soul Survivors*. 'If I wanted to dance *West Side Story*-style or dance like [iconic tap heroes] the Nicholas Brothers I would just do it. I got to a level where I could do anything I wanted to, as I had no fear. I've jumped up and spun three times in the air of a packed club. Could you imagine that?'

Cultural benefits were spinning out of Spats: resident DJ Dez Parkes went on to compile the monumental Rare Groove compilations for RCA/BMG. 'You had K-Tel, then Street Sounds. This was the next generation of must-have compilations,' said Fitzroy Facey, when I rang the DJ and dancer to dig deeper into this particular dancefloor, adding that Parkes went on to work on the equally notable Mastercuts compilations.

Dance groups frequenting Spats found that the club could be a launchpad. Unknown Kwantity (managed by Parkes) appeared in Diana Ross's video for her number-one hit 'Chain Reaction', playing backup singers, and Finesse changed their name to The Pasadenas, becoming huge mid-eighties pop stars. 'These were first and second *Windrush* generation, born in and growing up in the UK, and this is when we started to make headway, breaking into the entertainment industry as DJs, dancers and choreographers,' says Facey. 'This was practically unheard of for Black guys.'

Dancers broke ground because there was space for them to practise and develop as part of a community. Spats and a network of similar spaces also supported a new generation, who would gather to absorb some of the best moves on the planet and use the information to power their own creative lives. Norman Jay, Paul 'Trouble' Anderson and a very young Fabio, who went on to instigate the genre of jungle with Grooverider, all attended. 'Spats is the place where I saw the best dancers in my life,' said Frankie Valentine. 'I've been places and seen dancers, been to New York, Chicago and Japan. But for a place where the whole floor was filled with dancers – rather than dancers and an audience – it has to be Spats, when Trevor Shakes was playing.'

By 1986 hip-hop breakers were using the space, congregating on Saturday afternoons after breakdance sessions in nearby Covent Garden. B-boys paid £1.50 to get in, while fly girls got in for a reduced rate of a quid. Sessions featured a cash-prize dancing competition and were hosted by DJs Fingers, MC Family Quest and Tim Westwood. 'If Spats was the hip-hop Hadron Collider,' wrote blogger B-Boy Slippers back in 2011, 'the breakers were its particles, pushing the laws of physics . . . all of which created a big bang in the UK, paving the way for UK hip hop as it is now.'

One Monday lunchtime in 1994 Ade was walking down Oxford Street, heading to Mr Bongo's record shop in Soho. Someone was taking down the signage outside Fish, the club he regularly frequented and which previously housed the b-boys and jazz dancers at the club known as Spats. He stopped and asked what was happening. The landlord had taken it back from the guy who was running it, said the workman. A thought popped into Ade's head from nowhere, and a question came out of his mouth. 'Can I run it?'

'It was the maddest, stupidest question I ever asked anyone,' he tells me on a WhatsApp call from Lagos. 'Five minutes before, even two seconds before, I wouldn't have thought of it. An hour before, I was not thinking of running a dancefloor.' Once in, he had a couple of straightforward ideas. One was simply to play the music he loved – jazz, funk, soul, hip hop, house – as if the club were a massive home stereo. Another was to create a dancefloor on which dancers could move together in unison. 'I loved it when you entered a room and everyone was on the same vibe,' he says. 'There might be a ten-minute period when the whole room is making the same movement. I thought that was amazing. It was democracy. Everyone at the same time, making the same wave. If you could cut through the energy, you could use it to power a house.'

He installed two turntables, balanced on washing machines, and set about creating a club in which niche, tuck-it-away-on-a-Monday events were scheduled for the weekend – when nightclub promoters usually programme the most commercial music in order to entice people who spend good money at the bar rather than specialist music obsessives who have spent all their money on records, and dancers who only drink tap water.

'I didn't understand: "Yo, you're going to lose a lot of money because people aren't going to drink,"' Ade says. '[But] that was my saving grace. Sometimes when you know too much, all you see are the challenges. The minute I started doing it, people were like, "Wow! You're doing this on a Saturday – oh wow, it's amazing." But the money side of it was *terrrrr-rrrrrible*. The first six months of it . . . all the jazz records I'd collected in the previous ten years – I had to sell everything.'

Buying rare jazz records in the 1990s and early 2000s required relationship-building, obsessive trainspotting and money, meaning that this was a big deal. Talking about it today, traces of pain are still discernible in his voice. 'This was pre-internet. If you found a rare jazz record, you'd pay £150 for it and you were very happy. In those six months I lost everything. I didn't know what I was doing but I knew what I wanted to do, which was play my music on the weekend, so that this continuous movement on the dancefloor didn't just last for ten minutes. This continuous movement lasted for hours.' Fortunately, he had just enough records left to keep going.

At this point, Ade happened upon a mixtape containing a house mix by Glaswegian DJ and Sub Club resident Harri and played it repeatedly. He saw an article in *Generator Magazine* titled 'Harri: Britain's Finest DJ?' and went down to the magazine's offices on a mission to try to get the DJ's contact details – which was how things worked before the internet. Finding culture was a hide-and-seek that could take months, endless bus rides and result in multiple dead ends. This mission was successful, and Ade secured Harri's services.

Harri's house-based Fridays R Firin' signalled an upturn and the start of a five-year residency for the Glaswegian, as did the arrival of Kenny Hawkes, who ran pirate station Girls FM, first in Brighton and then in London. *Muzik* magazine editor Ben Turner wrote an article calling Plastic People 'the second best club in the world' and started running his own nights, called Who's in Town. Turner had a deep, rich contacts book and would ask visiting DJs to come and play the tiny club, unannounced. House legends Masters at Work and Deep Dish obliged, as did Daft Punk and Chicago's DJ Sneak. Soon, there were hundreds of people outside every week, and Ade could buy back his jazz records. House music had saved the day. The packed dancefloor, full of music-loving regulars, created a sense of shared values and initiated relationships that would later bear fruit. This was a human-sized space, just large enough to offer new connections and small enough to correlate with the number of people we can know and care about.

In 1999 the lease expired on 37–39 Oxford Street. Ade briefly toyed with the idea of renaming the club Wasp, but eventually decided to stick with Plastic People, even though they'd be in a new venue. Graphic designer Ali Augur's final flyer for the Oxford Street sessions shows Ade behind the washing machines, with Jon Lucien's 'Would You Believe in Me' and Donald Byrd's '(Fallin' Like) Dominoes' in view. Before we walk down the stairs and onto the dancefloor at Plastic People Mk II, in the basement of 147–149 Curtain Road in Shoreditch, east London, let's zoom out to look at the bigger picture.

———

Many UK councils had adopted a positive attitude towards nightlife in the early 1990s, because they recognised that night-clubs and the dancers within them supported their strategic plans for urban regeneration. Grayson Perry once said that artists were the 'shock troops' of gentrification, but I think that the dancers were their unwitting predecessors. This pro-dance agenda changed in the early 2000s, as a number of structural alterations gradually shunted old ways of doing things into the past. The Licensing Act of 2003 required late-night dancing venues to obtain new 'Special Hours' licences, as well as a Public Entertainment Licence, giving clubs the opportunity to serve alcohol into the early hours if dancing was occurring – and giving councils and the police additional opportunities to object. The Act also offered greater scope for residents to complain.

Compulsory door supervisor licences arrived in 2004. The Alcohol Harm Reduction Strategy for England responded to a media and government focus on binge drinking – which was often conflated with nightclubs – and came into play in 2004, too. This encouraged police and local authorities to enforce existing laws to reduce alcohol-related crime and disorder, enabling them to shut down premises where there was a serious problem or things got out of hand as a result of alcohol use. The smoking ban arrived in Scotland in 2006, and in Wales, Northern Ireland and England the following year. It changed the flow of a night as dancers left the floor to spark up and chat in the smoking areas. DJs had to learn to play differently in response to this particular type of movement.

Old formations were dropping away because the conditions were no longer suitable, giving new forms a chance to emerge. Laws changed things, and so did shifting social and economic forces. A December 2004 Mintel trade report, *Nightclubs, Leisure Intelligence*, found that the commercial nightclub market was already in trouble. Its value had been falling since 1999 due to increased competition from late-night bars, an increasingly corporate club world, superstar DJs pricing themselves out of the market – and an ageing rave generation, with younger kids coming up behind them wanting something different. 'There is a general feeling shared by many in the industry that the high street has become oversaturated with licensed premises and that there isn't enough trade to go round,' said the report, referencing a 25 per cent increase in UK licensed premises since 1980 and an almost 10 per cent increase in UK pubs and clubs since 1991 alone. This 'oversupply of premises' led the authors to predict a 12 per cent decrease in visitors over the coming five years, noting that the introduction of university fees in 2006 would affect students' disposable income. There were still plenty of places to dance at this point: an estimated 1,950 permanent nightclubs across the UK in 2004, with 12,200 late-night Special Hours certificates in force in England and Wales, and another 10,000 in Scotland. Visitors to nightclubs nationwide numbered around 15 million, with total admissions in the region of 180 million: around 12 admissions per visitor across the year.

———

There were other clubs playing specialist or underground music within walking distance of the new Plastic People, including 333 and Herbal, as well as a number of bars. The new space was a success despite the competition: in autumn 2000 writer–photographer Dave Swindells wrote in *Time Out* that 'Plastic People could easily be a template for the perfect club', noting its intimacy and 'the kinds of facilities usually associated with superclubs: a state-of-the-art sound system and proper air con . . . It's a lovely space, with a cherry-lined bar decorated with the ace series of flyers and posters featuring the towers of London'.

A year later, writer Arwa Haider described the weekly Blueprint Sessions at the club as 'heavy, like being at Carnival but indoors'. New Year's Eve 2001 saw Plastic People expand for one night only into a larger club – Planit on Bishopsgate – and featured a live set from spiritual jazz legend Pharoah Sanders, who was then 61 years old. The idea was that all the other floors would go silent while he performed.

Over the coming months, specialist promoters booked the club – as long as they followed Ade's music-first philosophy – and heavyweight DJs from the worlds of hip hop, jazz and house music lined up to play. Flyers included in designer Ali

Augur's book *Floor to Wall: Plastic People Flyers, 1998–2003* feature Questlove from The Roots; underground hip-hop hero
Madlib; Kenny Dixon Jr, aka Moodymann; and Chicago's
Ron Trent, whom we met talking about Mendel High. There
were jazz-dance specials and, in April 2002, Gilles Peterson
broadcast his BBC Radio 1 show live from the club. Ade's for-
mula – a small, dark space where people could dance freely
to high-quality sounds without being observed – was thriving.
(It's worth saying at this point that incredible promoters ran
iconic nights there, many of which aren't mentioned explicitly here, but which live on in the memories of everyone who
attended – and in the imaginations of the new generation who
know Plastic People as folklore.)

You entered Plastic People through a metal grille between
two shopfronts. Above the small red door was a neon sign stating the club's name (later replaced with a lightbox that showed
a silhouette of a woman and a man, mid-jive). Inside, a short
corridor took you past the person who'd take your entrance
money, then down the stairs into a bar area flanked by a heavy
black curtain. The curtain was a flexible wall, a form of material soundproofing that turned the evening of the bar on one
side into the deep night of the dancefloor on the other.

It always felt good to pass through the curtain. The sound
in this 100-square-metre room was exquisite – loud enough so
you felt it in your body, but pitched so that you could hear when
one friend turned to another to communicate with words, not
just the gesture of dance or the faces people pull at each other
when the feeling hits. The DJ monitors hung over the dancefloor, just low enough to be slapped as a sign of approval when
the energy rose above a certain point. Acoustically treated

material in the alcove on the left effectively turned sections of the wall into a bassbin, something poet Rob Gallagher referenced in 'Plastic People's Tinitus Nights', in his collection *The Dance Floors of England*:

> Ade has made the wall a speaker
> or the speaker a wall

There were four steel girders that punctuated the space, signalling an industrial prehistory. The bespoke floor was made of oiled 18-millimetre tongue-and-groove American walnut, which Ade cleaned every night with a specialist liquid that soaked down and moisturised the sponge supports underneath. During his Saturday-night Balance sessions Ade would set up broadcast-quality EMT turntables especially for his set, then if his guests didn't want to use them, would switch to the standard Technics – a task that would require three people to carry the concrete-like EMTs off the table.

Accumulated culture expressed itself through architecture and design, helping form a perfect space in which to midwife new music into the world. It turns out that perfection was simplicity: a dark room that had been sonically treated; a wooden floor; a fantastic sound system; DJs who desired and induced dancefloor unison; and a sophisticated audience who knew that something special happens when you listen and move at the same time. Plastic People was a singularity, sweeping up the ingredients required for maximum vibe and compressing them into a dancefloor big bang.

The sound was wraparound – it surrounded you as surely as clothing. It fitted snugly not because Ade had installed a bespoke system – it was an 'off the shelf' Funktion-One – but because he had treated the space with the help of experts James Hurst and Mark Murphy. A room, he learned, has its own tone, and you need to take action if you want the music to sound exactly as the musicians intended. They discovered that anything below 49Hz was echoed by the room – which meant anyone on the dancefloor would hear it twice. So they built a box to trap the reverberating sound waves. 'Imagine a wine bottle,' Ade says, by way of explanation. 'Imagine if the sound waves went into the bottle, and they couldn't find their way out again because of the shape of the bottle. So we built a box which was like a wine rack, so that when the waves come into the bottle, it catches them and we don't hear that sound again.' Such attention to detail would be best practice for a superclub, but remember – this was a tiny 200-capacity venue run by a person, not a corporation.

I began attending regularly about halfway into Plastic People's existence, circa 2006. It was a very London club, in the sense of being demographically porous. It attracted assorted people who shared a love of sound and movement, and was cool without being exclusive in the usual sense: people who were physically beautiful and stylish, as well as average-looking individuals in unremarkable t-shirts. Plastic People was a Black-run space, in which I saw people of all ethnicities. It was co-run with Charlotte Kepel (who moved from the dance-floor to club management in 2006) and attracted music-lovers of all genders. If I do a 360-degree turn around the room in my mind, I can see people I knew who worked as scaffolders, students who grew up outside of London, and others with jobs in offices or shops. Ideas and partnerships percolated between like-minded people who might otherwise never have got to meet each other, and new collectives emerged.

Artists who could headline festivals chose to run their own regular nights at the club – Kieran 'Four Tet' Hebden or Andrew Weatherall – because they knew they'd be in communion with musically sophisticated and open-minded dancers who wanted to be pushed beyond the obvious: to hear the greatest record they'd never heard before and do so in a suitable environment. The sounds on a Monday or a Thursday would be differentiated by rhythm, instrumentation, style and cohort, and therefore dancing. Sometimes the room was occupied by highly skilled dancers moving to the music style known as broken beat, at a much-loved night like CoOp, run by Demus, Dego, IG Culture and the late Phil Asher. Other times there was deep, rich house and techno from Detroit's finest (including the esteemed Theo Parrish or Moodymann), where aficionados could two-step in the dark; and there was skanking with Aba Shanti-I or Dennis Bovell, who scored the soundtrack to *Babylon*. Each and every time the DJs and the audience were separated only by a low wooden booth. This is relevant because it brought the people playing the music into close proximity with the people responding to it, amplifying the relationship between the two entities: so-called performer and so-called audience.

'A club is a community in the process of educating itself,' wrote Josephine Macalister Brew way back in 1943, in her book *In the Service of Youth*. She was talking about youth clubs, but it's a phrase that translated accurately within the walls of Plastic People. A good example was the regular night CDR, which turned the club into a laboratory where upcoming producers could test out new tunes in this room which had been treated like a drum – tuned. Founder Tony Nwachukwu had been on the dancefloor and behind the booth at both iterations of Plastic People and considered the venue and the people within it as extended family. 'Plastic felt like home from the get-go,' he told me. 'There's only a few of us Black Africans in this music space in London, in the UK. So there was a kinship, fundamentally, with Ade. But there was also a kinship around the politics of the space; a really strong music policy that was amplified by the sound system. It was not just a commercial enterprise.'

CDR began when Tony was coming out of a bruising major-label experience as part of the band Attica Blues. He could see the digital revolution arriving in music, recognised that big business would try to extract maximum profit, and decided to build a community buffer where artists could experiment on their own terms. 'Plastic People was this analogue, real-life environment where a digital transformation could be embedded. I was committed to creating a safe space for artists and producers to experiment and take risks that the industry doesn't allow.' Monthly CDR sessions created a community in which artists were able to flourish individually and collectively. Some regulars went on to start labels (Alexander Nut's Eglo Records, for example); some already ran labels (Tic, A&R at XL and then Young Turks, now renamed Young); and CDR was an early incubator for acts that now have mainstream success, such as Sampha, Floating Points, Maya Jane Coles and SBTRKT. Adele came down. CDR travelled, taking music-production workshops and listening sessions across the UK and to France, Germany, Spain

and Croatia – and is still spreading artist-to-artist encouragement today.

A significant proportion of dancers in the space more generally were absorbing the environmental information, picking
up on the signal of contribution. Some became DJs or producers, and a number of regulars during this mid-point of Plastic
People's life went on to become festival headliners themselves (for example, James Blake, Floating Points, Skream
and Artwork). Others spun the sweetness into new shapes,
like the now-international NTS radio station, which *The New
Yorker* described as having 'reshaped how musicians and fans
around the world saw and heard each other'. NTS was started
by Femi Adeyemi, who met founding presenters like Marsha
'Marshmello' Smith at the club. 'Plastic People's eclecticism
and bold curation was a huge inspiration and a major ingredient for NTS,' says Sean McAuliffe, CEO of the station, who
also co-ran the Nonsense night. 'We essentially turned the
Plastic dancefloor into a radio community.' The record label
Hessle Audio exists because two of the founders – David
'Pearson Sound' Kennedy and Ben UFO – got chatting in the
queue, and writer John Eden told me that his sound-system
fanzine *Woofah* was 'made up in my head' during a night at
the club.

There are other examples: BBC Radio 1 DJ Benji B regularly collaborates with Kanye West and was hired by the late
Virgil Abloh at Louis Vuitton as their music director. Benji
was a regular from the earliest days of the club, sometimes
playing at Balance, CoOp and Nonsense; other times inhabiting a favourite spot by the speaker. 'There is no single club
space I have spent more time in, and no public space or sound

system that has had more influence on my life, than Plastic People,' he says when I message him. The man known as Elijah used his time on the dancefloor at Plastic People to turn his grime blog into a label and party (Butterz, 2010–22), and in 2021 began sharing ideas and conversations about music and community on social media in the form of handwritten statements and questions that became known as Yellow Squares. He received thousands of comments and DMs in response and has now transformed Yellow Squares into a live experience. 'That's the club I've been to most times,' he tells me. 'The way I DJ and release music takes that mentality of bringing different worlds together.' On a much more small-scale level Plastic People supported those in the community who were studying for formal qualifications: a regular at the dubstep and grime-based FWD>> night would often sit at the back with his laptop, finishing his economics coursework before rejoining the dance.

For a decade and a half this small dancefloor was responsible for a disproportionate amount of culture, generating and nurturing DJs, producers, designers, promoters and writers, as well as at least one entirely new genre of music – dubstep. The weekly night FWD>>, which ran here after moving from the Velvet Rooms in central London, is credited with inventing the genre. A regular, Lee Darkside, returned to Curtain Road in 2022 to stick his own blue plaque outside the building where Plastic People took place. It read: 'Dubstep Heritage Landmark. Foundation dubstep events took place here.'

One important ingredient in Plastic's successes was darkness. The room was sonically loud and visually quiet, relying on the emergency exit signs for illumination and, if necessary, a small light Ade installed in the ceiling above the turntables. The DJ could pull the cord, get a little light, find their next record, then turn it off again. Darkness in this environment was an amplifier. 'Plastic was absurdly dark,' says DJ, producer and writer Martin Clark when we chat. 'You couldn't show off even if you wanted to. Imagine you wanted to impress some-one with some sick move, get someone who had caught your eye to notice you – impossible! It was pitch black.' Which is in contrast, he points out, to vogue and ballroom or Chicago footwork circles, where fabulous, vivid dancing is centred and highly visible. It's also in contrast to the requirements of social media – the authors of a 2022 marketing report, 'What Do Gen Zers in the UK Want from Nightlife?', wrote that 'more aes-thetic spaces translate, rather than grimy underground venues that don't look good on video'.

The darkness was designed to deepen the dancer's experi-ence. 'By one or two o'clock, [with] a little alcohol, low lights so your senses are more concentrated in the sound, the sys-tem all around you,' says Ade, 'I think even the shyest person will get into the spirit of the dance.' The 'shyest person' in question might be Ade himself. 'I'm quite a terrible dancer,' he says, before pausing. 'I'm going to tell you something I haven't told anyone before.' This telling begins with a nec-essary preamble. He had transcended the usual methods of buying records from record shops and had graduated to per-sonal purchases from the mysterious breed of individuals who operate as record dealers. Ade would head over to north or west London, Kilburn maybe, and sit on the dealer's sofa while the dealer spun through the music he had on offer. 'After ten tunes, you're not feeling it, but he's made all the effort, so I'm going to have to buy something, just to make him feel better. I'd be thinking, "Why am I doing this? I'm losing money, how am I going to get out of this place?" Then he plays one track, and oh my god! What the fuck! It's an amazing track. I'll buy that record, and the first place I'll go is Plastic People by myself and I'll put the record on and I'll dance. Literally, I can play the same track for hours and dance, and I'm thinking, "I can't wait to play this on Saturday. It'll kill everyone!" It's the most joyful thing I did from secondary school until the age of 30, when I had my first child.'

Ade's experience of Plastic People as 'joyful' is shared widely by the music lovers who were lucky enough to have attended. It was perfect, I tell him. 'I'm glad you say that,' he replies. 'I can't, because otherwise they'd say Ade's gone big-headed. I did my bit. I got a room, I treated it the way I wanted to treat it. I put the guys I wanted in there. I turned off the lights. That was my job done.'

One of the guys he put in there was the doorman and community icon known mononymously to the Plastic People community as Winston, a notable individual among the 95,000 door supervisors operating in the UK in the mid-2000s. Acknowledging Winston while in the queue was part of attending Plastic People. 'Everyone'd say hello, no one ignored me,' he says. He was, after all, the protector of the realm, and this was a family situation in which not knowing Winston's name would have shown a lack of manners. He started out on the dancefloor in the 1980s, at clubs like Kisses in Peckham, Porky's in Streatham Hill or the Electric Ballroom in Camden, getting busy with 'a bit of breakdance, a bit of R&B, aerobics dance, a bit of house', and then working the door at places like the Podium in Vauxhall, before gradu-ating uptown to West End clubs.

The door person transmits the vibe without having to say a word because they communicate through gesture, stance and, in Winston's case, a laminated piece of A4. It explained that the club played underground music, and he'd show it to people who looked like they might need to know this impor-tant fact. 'I'd just look for people who looked a bit dodgy, just to check,' he says. 'Plastic People was just to have a good time, to listen to the music. Everyone who come here come to listen to the music.' What are we communicating when we dance? I ask him, defaulting to the profound and looking for meaning that isn't always there. 'I got a few things,' he says. 'What's your name? Can I have your number?' He chuckles. 'It's true, innit.' Once the club was full, and if the music was good enough, Winston would find a spot near the DJ booth for a tune or two. Ade might join him, if he wasn't having to cover the bar or deal with someone from the council who'd appeared at the entrance, or having to fix a 'disgusting' leak in the toilets.

Plastic People's ability to offer memorable individual and collective experiences became limited in February 2010, when the Metropolitan Police applied to review the licence of the club, citing reasons of prevention of crime, disorder and public nuisance. Derek Walmsley wrote about developments in *The Wire*. 'I find this disturbing and bizarre,' he said. 'Plastic People is one of the most welcoming and trouble-free places I've ever been to. Compared with the rest of the Shoreditch area – one of the most densely populated places for strip clubs and brothels in the whole of the UK due to the nearby presence of the City

– it's baffling how police could conclude that crime prevention would be well served by focusing their scrutiny on this intimate club, where you'll generally find 200-odd fairly well-behaved music fans.' The problem, he wrote, was that 'the police are essentially the sole arbiter of what constitutes safety in the context of club culture. From the outside, it appears they're more comfortable with busy, boozy pubs and superclubs than intimate and self-regulating underground events.'

A petition was launched by Ben Simons, who co-ran the Nonsense night at Plastic. It asked supporters to agree with a list of statements, the first of which related directly to the Met's stated issues with the club. Signees confirmed that they had never experienced issues with staff or other people within the space, and that they'd never been offered drugs at the club. Another part of the petition summed up the central relationship between the space and movement. It read: 'The darkness of the dancefloor enables you to dance freely without people watching, allowing you to express yourself with focus purely on the music.' Eight thousand people signed, and double that number joined the Save Plastic People Facebook group. The Met's application to review the licence was withdrawn before the relevant sub-committee meeting, but damage had been inflicted that played out over the coming months. In November 2010 writer Dan Hancox blogged about the conditions that had emerged: police 'hovering outside in a massive van every night, interrogating the crowd' and 'airport-style' security for what he described, in capitalised irritation, as 'the only fucking club in Shoreditch that NEVER HAS ANY TROUBLE'.

Strict searches are appropriate when you're entering an airport or government buildings. Moody security guards don't make you feel like you're entering a space where communities can form through individuals dancing freely in the dark and where new creative life can be born. I remember queuing up outside the club around this time and feeling affronted, as if a security guard was asking me to prove my acceptability before being allowed back home.

'Plastic People, of course, has been plagued by problems in recent years,' wrote *FACT* magazine three years later, 'and although for some the club has never managed to quite recapture the atmosphere of its pre-police interference prime, those who've attended in recent months will attest to the fact that it remains one of London's best spots.' The many upsides of Plastic People's life after 2010 included residencies run by top-flight DJs and producers from the US and UK, including James Blake, who was a Plastic People regular before winning the Mercury Prize in 2013, an Ivor Novello the following year and a Grammy in 2019. Communities emerged from this phase of the dancefloor, too. Wayne Francis recognised the value of an intimate, music-first dancefloor while attending the CoOp nights, and credits the experience as giving him the inspiration to create his weekly Steam Down jam, where live musicians improvised new music into existence for a room full of dancers. Alexis Blondel, who founded the influential Total Refreshment Centre, went a few times. He added the experience to the bag of encouragement and inspiration that he poured into his own space when he and his friends began transforming a derelict chocolate factory into a hub for London's new wave of jazz. Touching Bass founder Errol Anderson caught the final days of the club, describing it to me as 'confirmation that being intentional is important'. There were fundraisers, including one after Typhoon Yolanda hit the Philippines in 2013, featuring Jamie xx and Four Tet.

Ade finally closed Plastic People in January 2015. 'It just felt like time to stop,' he replies, when I send him a message asking the question why. 'It felt right to move on.' He painstakingly removed the floor and took it home. He didn't know what to do with this stack of walnut blocks, but he's retained them, ready for future use.

13: SPACE IN THE PLACE

Dancing to grime and dubstep in darkened rooms
flooded with sub-bass, 2006–2010

The dancefloor can generate new music. On rare occasions, it can create new genres, too, as with Chicago's home of house, the Warehouse. The style of music known as dubstep might have been concieved at a venue called the Velvet Rooms, but it was born at Plastic People, at a weekly night called FWD>> run by Sarah 'Soulja' Lockheart, who later co-owned radio station Rinse FM. The 140bpm music style had become sparse, with syncopated rhythms underpinned by expansive sub-bass, and was frequently instrumental. Their chosen name suggested a future-facing music, the fact that the music moved people – and an entire scene – in a future-facing direction, and the 'forward' of the reggae sound system, where dancers would request a tune be played again through gesture and sound. Many of the people involved in this dancefloor came from Croydon, with core crew arriving in a limo because it worked out cheaper than multiple cabs or a minibus – and because it was much funnier than a minibus. Resident FWD>> DJs Youngsta and Hatcha would play new dubstep and grime fresh out of the studio. Guest MCs like Wiley, Skepta or D Double E would 'bless mic' alongside regular host Crazy D, who'd slot signature phrases between the half-step beats – 'deeper and darker we go' or 'warm and easy' or the detuned poetry of 'woah woah woah', each 'woah' moving down and back up the scale – while young women in denim dungarees and Jordans picked up their knees and crunched down their waists. The crowd reminded me of the people I went to school with, which is unsurprising, given that St John Rigby sat on the borough boundary of Croydon, an important location for the emergence of the genre. (Prominent DJ Skream, in fact, went to the same school as me, starting seven years after I left.) A friend remembers a guy who'd turn up by himself and dance so intensely that he was allowed in for free, just because he brought such a vibe.

The acts of creation that took place weekly on the dancefloor at FWD>> existed within a network of physical locations, including Big Apple Records in Croydon and then-pirate radio station Rinse FM, which was based in any number of east London locations high enough to support a transmitter. There were nodes elsewhere, including the Kontakt club night in Leicester, and producers Oris Jay in Sheffield and Search and Destroy in east London. A compressed family tree of the music would show a direct connection to dub and reggae from the UK and Jamaica, and to the darker, stripped-down edge of UK garage – itself developed in response to the high-level energies of jungle and drum 'n' bass. Dubstep and the dancing that went alongside it evolved as the younger sibling of another genre – grime – which used similar lineage ingredients to create a different musical universe, into which we will take a short diversion.

Grime artists, DJs and dancers had been pushed out of city-centre venues by a range of issues, including, in London, the use of Form 696, which the Metropolitan Police first introduced in 2005 for events that featured DJs or MCs. The document purported to offer risk assessment but operated as a form of racial profiling. For the first four years of its existence it required details of audience ethnicity. By 2008 the head of industry body UK Music, former Undertones singer Feargal Sharkey, told the government that it was discriminatory. There was a long campaign against it, and it was eventually scrapped by London mayor Sadiq Khan in 2017.

Grime was hugely popular despite this and found fertile growth in the early 2000s in pre-Olympics east London venues like Stratford Rex. I interviewed Dizzee Rascal on a number of occasions around this time and recall him describing teenage dancers letting off energy, pulling each other's t-shirts, 'thuggin' out'. Mostly, though, grime grew on pirate radio, says producer and writer Martin Clark, when we chat about it, pointing out that pirates had the nominal set-up of a club (DJs, MCs, music, often an audience crowded into the studio) but no dancing, bar hyped-up, arms-out, upward-facing gun fingers. 'I'm convinced that this allowed grime to take sonic risks,' he says. 'It evolved, got weird, *because* there was no dancing. There was no real-time visual feedback from a crowd's motion.' There were some dancefloors, like the regular Sidewinder events in Milton Keynes, which combined popular garage outfits like Heartless Crew with up-and-coming young grime artists. Sixteen-year-old Dizzee Rascal was far from the youngest onstage – that accolade went to crowd destroyer Tinchy Stryder, who was first smuggled into the venue aged 13. Thousands attended these lively dancefloors, including Mercury Prize winner Ms Dynamite. 'Oh my goodness, Sidewinder, Milton Keynes,' she told me in a BBC Radio 1Xtra documentary I made in 2010. 'Vibe, energy, crazy.

About 50 MCs who weren't supposed to be onstage being onstage, at the same time – but the vibe being amazing, the crowd going crazy. Just not wanting the night to end.'

Grime was also popular with teenage dancers at Farringtons private girls' school in Chislehurst, in the furthest reaches of south-east London. More Fire Crew had a top-ten hit with 'Oi!' in 2002, and the crew were booked by students for an end-of-term social, which I covered for a magazine. The headteacher sat me in her office and explained that she originally thought the girls had booked a fire-safety event, but that she decided to go ahead because of her students' persuasive enthusiasm. More Fire Crew drove up the school's crescent-shaped gravel drive in a low white van, with smoke clouds puffing out of the windows like something from a cartoon. They sat in the staff room, huddled together uncomfortably on a bench, before being ushered onto the stage in Founders Hall, which had large oil paintings on each of the wood-panelled walls. The girls went berserk, throwing bits of paper with their phone numbers onstage, and one tried to pull Lethal B's grey trackie bottoms down mid-tune. When people talk about grime raves being risky, they are probably not imagining this scene.

———

A phrase I once heard from a drum 'n' bass MC rolls around my head whenever a lifestorm hits: 'Hold tight the ruff ride!' I was holding tight the ruff ride in early 2006, when I joined *Live Magazine*. It was a youth-run quarterly which sat within a forward-thinking marketing agency called Livity, and the main office was in Brixton, south London. I took over as editorial mentor from writer, promoter and all-round instigator Chantelle Fiddy, who was heavily involved with the early days of grime and dubstep. She ensured that *Live* was a high-quality, hilarious and locally famous publication, with the young writers interviewing the DJs, producers and singers they'd otherwise just be listening to.

Sometimes the *Live* office turned into a literal dancefloor, with contributors and staff bringing in and sharing the new and usually very accessible dances that were increasingly accompanying grime tunes. These preceded the wholesale reintegration of music with specific dance steps ushered in by the genre of afrobeats, and were disseminated through locally shot videos posted on new YouTube channels and out into raves, bus stops and school playgrounds. There would be deadline-inspired Migraine Skanks, for example, to the sound of Gracious K's tune of the same name. This happily simple choreography – see also Skepta's 'Rolex Sweep' and K.I.G.'s 'Head, Shoulders, Kneez and Toez' – was made even easier by instructional lyrics that spelled out the moves.

The office was a dancefloor in a more poetic sense, too. The so-called adults, none of us past our early thirties, and the so-called kids – many of whom had the life experience of people much older – were encouraged to try out steps and learn how to move in new ways. It was a rich, layered situation which, for a long time, contained no trained youth workers. Sometimes this allowed for incredible breakthroughs with the young people we worked with. Other times it skirted the edges of what anyone would consider wise. It was a formation dance which fell into tune and time more often than it fell apart.

The Dance

Live changed my life for the better, and it also offered me entry into another powerful and influential dancefloor. One of the two editors present when I joined was Jordan Jarrett-Bryan, who went on to work for Channel 4 as their lead sports reporter. He also happened to be the son of eminent DJ Bryan Gee, whom we met earlier playing brand-new jungle and drum 'n' bass tunes at the Haçienda's Phenomenon One. Jordan knew something strong and familial about the dance, not least because he sometimes helped out with his dad's award-winning weekly club night, Movement, which took place at Bar Rhumba on Shaftesbury Avenue in central London. We were in the office one afternoon, chatting about music. I mentioned that I wanted to go to DMZ, which played this emerging soundtrack called dubstep five minutes' walk away from the *Live* offices. Two previous attempts had failed, and I wasn't in the right frame of mind to go by myself. Clubs and the community that came with them could amplify fantastic times but could also ameliorate the worst of times, or at least the long recovery phases that follow. I couldn't change the size or shape of the waves that hit me or that I blew in, but I could equip myself to anticipate or even use them to carry me forward.

Jordan introduced me to one of our colleagues, who agreed that I could come along with him to the next bi-monthly session. The event was run by Mala and Coki (who operated under the name Digital Mystikz), along with their friends Loefah (pronounced 'loafer') and mic controller Sgt Pokes. DMZ had an alluring tagline: 'Come meditate on bass weight'. There was a lineage here, too: they had all attended Goldie's drum 'n' bass Metalheadz sessions, often arriving early to ensure they'd be first or second in the queue.

I was ready for another immersion, and it was going to be a big one. DMZ took its name from Digital Mystikz, not 'demilitarised zone', although it was a kind of demilitarised zone in the sense of carving out space for things to be different, in-between. The dance took place in a club called Mass, within St Matthew's Anglican Church, opposite Lambeth Town Hall – a church built in 1824 and big enough to be described in compass terms, with a West Wing. It was the first church in England to have electric lighting, powered off the same rig as Electric Avenue – itself carved into musical history by Eddy Grant's early-eighties pop reggae hit of the same name. Not unusually for an Anglican church, it has a patron saint. St Jude is associated with desperate cases and lost causes and is typically shown with a flame around his head, holding a stick-shaped weapon: a club. By 1975 congregational numbers were falling and work began to transform parts of this oversized, 2,000-capacity church into a community space. Various complicated evolutions meant that the church ended up with a basement club called Third Bass, and an upstairs nightclub, Mass, where I saw Daft Punk DJ in the late 1990s and where DMZ took place. There was a downstairs bar–restaurant in the crypt and, of course, a functioning worship space for the congregation.

Every other month between March 2005 and 2009 a line would snake around the edge of the church gardens as people waited to gain entrance to DMZ – unless they were friends and family, in which case they'd walk straight over to DJ and co-promoter Loefah, who ran the guest-list. Once in, a quick walk up two flights of the circular stairwell, through bass vibrations flowing down like wonky water, took you along a short corridor between the stairwell and the dancefloor, where producers would often stop to talk to mastering engineer Jason Goz, who only half-jokingly described it as his office. The dancing space itself was very dark, although you could still make out the big black-and-white banners, which had been designed by Mala and Loefah, the latter having studied fine art at Croydon College.

The only lights were from the bar, the exit signs or the occasional lighter sparking up, which meant that all of our attention was on the music – our eyes were turned off and our ears and bodies took over. In terms of dancefloor demographics it was mostly male, but there were women; it was mixed but mostly white; and the middle classes were in a minority, as they were on many of the dancefloors we've visited so far. A memory comes flooding back, of a conversation on the dancefloor at DMZ with a university-educated member of the community who loved the music as much as I did – probably more so, given how deep he went with it all. He told me that dubstep dancefloors 'didn't discriminate against middle-class people'.

There were hardly any phones on the dancefloor (in this period just before ubiquitous camera phones), and photography was not welcome unless you were Georgina Cook, who went on to publish *Drumz of the South: The Dubstep Years, 2004–2007*. The photographer had grown up going to family dances with her Irish relatives, picking up a camera in the spaces between steps. Her work exists in a lineage of photographer–dancers like Dave Swindells, whose pictures of strobe-lit acid-house dancers at Heaven had a strong influence on me as a teenager. These visual artists know what needs to go into the frame because they've danced it. Looking hard meant that Georgina noticed a lot, including changes to the ways people danced. For the first few years it was mostly nodding your head, slightly rocking, head down, eyes down: 'The music sped up and the dancing sped up.'

If you've been on enough dancefloors, you'll recognise the detail that she describes: that you'd have different types inhabiting different parts of the room, including a crew who'd hang out right next to the DJ booth, nodding their heads and attempting to read sharpie-written track titles on rotating dub-plates. 'You'd have people like [producers] Shackleton and Appleblim, who would be at the front, first in as soon as the doors opened. And they'd have pretty wacky moves as well, loads of freedom,' recalls Georgina. A second layer would be 'people that were really into it, really wanting to dance'. In the middle, more of a mosh pit, then 'towards the back the shyer people who didn't want to be seen, or who might be slightly too high for their own good, in the darkness'. Differing levels of energy in the room – higher in the middle than at the edges, for example – meant that it became very noticeable when a wave of support and agitation spread from the back to the front. There's a term for this in the reggae lexicon – a 'deep forward' that begins at the back of the room with the keepers of the cool, the ones who move only when they're really moved.

The ways people danced to this music had already gone through a few iterations. Martin Clark remembers the earliest days of FWD>> as being soundtracked by different beat patterns, from 'garage-influenced two-step to soca-beat, bruk, breakstep and 4/4 stompers'. The varying rhythmic patterns instigated specific body movements that related to speed, groove and intensity. 'How you dance,' he says, 'affects how

293

much space you need, who you touch – or don't – and the sense of norms and values in the community.' His observations remind me of feeling outraged when I later saw topless men moshing at DMZ, because this was in contravention of the unwritten rules I had absorbed. The rules, of course, were changing because the music and the culture around it were evolving. I had become old-school.

There are only a few clips in existence of dancing to dubstep in the mid-2000s, and they tend to reveal very dark club interiors and little else. A clip from the DMZ second birthday in 2007 contains the universal sound of deep human noise, a noise I have in my muscle memory because I was on the dancefloor, front left. It is a sound that can only be instigated by hours of dancing together, and it's a sound that indicates that the dance is at a high point. In the music of the dancefloor, it is a crescendo, the tip of a wave that is about to come crashing back down in sound. It is pure, compressed need and request.

At DMZ, little else existed bar the sound and the movement. Someone pulled up the tune, and you paused. A synth line or a snare signalled the opening of a big tune, and you prepared for the movement, winding up inside, becoming ready. The tune dropped and – pow! – there was a mass upsurge of arms and a collective dancing style that mixed a cockney knees-up with the militant skanking and stepping embodied by men and women at Brixton reggae dances three decades earlier. There wasn't enough room in the squeeze of bodies for fine footwork, but this wasn't fine-footwork music. This was the large muscles of the thigh moving together in time, like military drill. Gun fingers were common: either arms raised, fingers extended to mimic the barrel of a gun and articulated back and forth from the wrist; or sometimes emerging from chest level, in small half-circles towards the body and then up into the air. The language mirrored the physicality of the movement: '*Your chest!*' Sgt Pokes would shout into the mic. It was a contraction of a phrase common during jungle times – 'Big up your chest' – which itself came from 1980s Jamaican dancehalls in a lyrical translation of a positive physical posture: shoulders back, head up, chest out. In this context it was also about the bass weight pressing on your chest, in this room where tunes with acres of sub-bass were being played on systems that could accurately convey the deep and heavy low end embedded in the music.

In autumn 2006 dubstep DJ and producer Skream headlined the Croft Institute in Melbourne, Australia, a 200-ish-capacity venue known as a 'laneway bar', down an alleyway that runs off an alleyway. He was a scene veteran at the age of 21, having been in and out of clubs as a DJ and dancefloor regular since his mid-teens. The club in Melbourne was a squash, a mash, a madness – and an internet-collapsed, geographically dispersed celebration of brand-new music that wasn't that different from his home dancefloors. 'The crowd was a ten,' he told me during an interview for the Red Bull Music Academy. 'The crowd was amazing. It felt like being in London. People was freaking and it's good when you come this far away from home and people know what you're playing. I got asked to play tunes that I only cut last week. It's like, "How'd you know about that?" Obviously the internet, but it's just pretty freaky.' The web had begun dissolving geographical dancefloor boundaries.

The Dance

Six months earlier a south London teenager called Deapoh brought together hundreds of grime and dubstep radio shows and mixes that he'd recorded in shifts with another committed co-pilot, who went by the name of Boomnoise. He posted them on a site he'd coded himself and updated manually. Barefiles became a central conduit for the globalisation of these iterations of new UK music, meaning that people in Melbourne, Toronto or Johannesburg could now listen to Rinse FM shows like Skream's weekly *Stella Sessions* (tagline: 'Crack 'em') or Kode9's influential *Hyperdub* shows, almost at the same time as Londoners who could pick up the broadcast live. This proximity brought international dancefloors closer together.

Adegbenga Adejumo is better known as Benga, and for a long time was inseparable from his DJ partner Skream. They were regulars at DMZ and at Plastic People's FWD>>, where they would inevitably cause dancefloor mayhem, using half-speed dredge and high-tension production that had the capacity to be dread and hardcore, funny and stumble-sweet, avant-garde and compellingly simple. They were mates, they came as a unit, frequently DJing back to back and later hosting a BBC Radio 1 show together.

I hadn't spoken to Benga for years, so when I rang him to ask about dancing we spent many minutes cracking up at the comedy of the situation. The laughter was also a release: his ultra-marathon of DJing in clubs with people who were having the most intense night of the year, and doing so every night, led to a serious breakdown.

Benga is a multi-talented individual: good enough at football to play for the Arsenal youth team, he also won dance competitions at school. 'I was spinning on my head and all sorts,' he says, laughing. 'I started dancing to 2Unlimited, stuff like that. So I'd breakdance, but not to hip hop.' His first tune, released in 2002, when he was 15, was titled 'Skank'. It is a word with multiple meanings, one of which describes the dance with reggae roots, in which the knees are lifted in a stepping motion. 'When I used to skank I'd use my arms,' he continues. 'Some of the records made you feel like you wanted to put some aggression in it. Everyone attacked it slightly different, but we all did the same kind of statement in terms of timing. You'd look around the room and see people doing different things, catching different parts of the rhythm.' The dubstep skank had a huge influence on the growth of the music, he says, because it was a leveller – anyone could do it, dancing in the dark and moving together. As we're talking, I can feel the room reconstructing around me, like real-time CGI. I'm standing between the bar and the DJ booth with Benga, a decade and a half younger than we both are now, and the music is billowing out of the speaker stacks in dread blocks of bass, rivers of sound, heavy showers of bass and drum. I see myself standing next to him, both moving to the music. I remember how much I needed the release of dancing like this, surrounded by hundreds of people. It helped me repair – which also benefited the people around me. Dance can benefit the community in this way, too.

Sometimes the dancefloor moved location, as with the occasional DMZ coach trip to the West Indian Community Centre in Chapeltown, Leeds, to combine forces with Iration Steppas in a historic cultural building with bassbins that made you feel as if you might be blown across the room like a stray leaf. It was powerful, in every sense of the word, although that didn't stop antisocial and culturally deaf new arrivals later forcing the West Indian Centre's management to apply volume limitations. The question of who has the right to object to collective sound and movement isn't just a problem of the past. Today's priests are property developers and new residents who bring suburban expectations into gentrified cities, or entitled individuals who attend to their own unhappiness by squashing the pleasure of others. Complaining about noise from the West Indian Centre is like asking Mount Fuji to stop blocking the view. It is literally anti-social.

The morning after the coach trip to Leeds, Benga created a scene-famous tune called 'E Trips'. Other tunes were designed to socialise dancers differently. For 'Night', which has become a cross-genre, all-ages banger, 'me and [co-producer] Coki put the snare on the half. It was meant to try and get people not just to do the dubstep skank, but to full-on dance ... I wanted to get people to move, creating energy.' Each bar starts with what a dancefloor compadre calls 'the pigeon noise' – a staccato, bleepy *buh buh buh* – which suggests two moves per bar, before the sound speeds up, pigeon-max, and gives rise to more dance moves in each bar of the music.

Like 99 per cent of the DJs and producers who came through at this time, I'd often see Benga on the dancefloor before or after he'd DJed, or when he wasn't even booked to DJ, shocking out to the music. In many ways it's obvious why he and his fellow producers were on the dancefloor. This was a community of people working it out through the doing. 'Everybody working out the camp,' as James Young from the band Darkstar once described it to me. They were still just mates, all in it together, even though the mates were now being booked to travel all over the world, with the attendant schisms and personal damage success can bring.

I asked Benga anyway: why were you on those dancefloors when you weren't booked to DJ? 'Because the music was good, the vibe was good, the systems were great. I could hear everything, get inspired. I could get out of the rave feeling good, feeling excited, feeling happy.' I understood what he meant. Powerful dancefloors can be tied up with feelings of repair, of becoming whole again. They can offer acceptance and belonging and family, of being part of a formation, of contributing to building the space that is collectively required.

The listening entity on dancefloors like DMZ's indicated what it collectively wanted through gesture. And what a small but growing part of the dancefloor wanted was even more energy. This request, made with gun fingers and a grimey pogo, resulted in a record that perhaps contains more energy than any record ever made: a 2007 release by top producer Coki titled 'Spongebob' (no relation to the Baltimore dance style). It begins with a pitched-down sample of the cartoon character's laugh, which in Coki's expert hands sounds like a maniac wasp that has just realised it is trapped behind a window. Within 30 seconds it explodes into the kind of controlled chaos that only the most dextrous producer can pull off. The 'Spongebob' wasp has turned into Godzilla and is taking over the entire dancefloor, the whole building, the city. The 30 seconds of intro before Godzilla took over were repeated through the medium of the rewind at DMZ, better to charge up the dancers, better to power the inevitable explosion of torsos and limbs and hand gestures that pow-pow-powed into the air above the dancefloor. It was impossible to hear Coki's record at this time without endless rewinds – like five, six, even eight. The rewind is usually enacted by the DJ or sometimes the MC in response to crowd hype, or to create crowd hype. At DMZ it was a little more free-form, with certain members of the dancefloor feeling empowered to lean over into the DJ booth and stop the track themselves. Benga says he and Skream would always talk about Coki's records. 'Then,' he says, of the period after 'Spongebob', 'it became less about dancing and more about losing your mind.'

The b-side to 'Spongebob' was called 'The End', and in many ways this excess of sonic energy marked the end of one phase and the beginning of another. Coki's record was absorbed into the everstream and became a singularity from which producers in North America and Canada made spin-off tunes that riffed heavily on this particularly energised strand of the sound that Coki had magnified in his tune. Inevitably their translation picked up its own flavours and became its own thing. In 2012 the question 'What is dubstep?' was one of the top ten most googled phrases in Canada (along with 'What is Instagram?' and 'What is YOLO?'). In the hands of punk-schooled producers like LA-based Skrillex, the sound built at DMZ and FWD>> would be transmitted – supersized – to huge festival crowds, sonically and visually repackaging large rock concerts. Two years after Skrillex released his dubstep-based EP *My Name Is Skrillex* as a free download on his MySpace page he was nominated for five Grammy awards, winning three. A year later he won five Grammys and continued to win or be nominated for them for the rest of the decade. The response to 'Spongebob' in the US created evolution and mutation in the shape of a whole new dance style. The new movement style known as 'dubstep dancing' was entirely unrelated to the reggae-skank-meets-cockney-knees-up that accompanied the music as it was evolving in the UK; it was more an updated form of body popping, with a focus on fluid robotics and off-centre spins, pinned to the floor by the toe of a red and black Jordan. Top dubstep dancer Marquese Scott has millions of followers on social media, and the style has entered the pantheon of dance forms. There are now dubstep dancers across North America, in South Korea, Japan and Russia – all countries which excel at pro-level street dance. The genre began with small numbers of people on the dancefloor, eyes down, in the dark. The offspring culture reversed that: festival headliner DJs being watched onstage by large crowds, all facing the stage; and countless views of dubstep dancers online, with an individual centred on the screen. We couldn't possibly have imagined this as an outcome of the collective rhythmic movement we drummed up together while dancing to Mala, Loefah, Coki and the long list of incredible DJs and producers who responded to our dancefloor formation.

———

More than a decade after my dubstep excursions, I spoke to Dr Peter Michael Nielsen about epilepsy, ADHD, depression and low-frequency oscillation. He's a neurology specialist and senior consultant in the Stroke Unit in the Geriatric Department of Holbaek hospital in Denmark. He has a black leather recliner in his office, but it's no ordinary recliner. It is a bass chair which he helped invent because he believes applied bass can improve the symptoms of a number of ailments.

The Dance

The bass-chair work was published in neuroscience journal *Brain and Behaviour* in 2019. It investigated low-frequency musical stimulation as an add-on treatment for clinical depression. Doses of bass are delivered into the gut, where they are picked up by what the doctor calls a 'low-frequency microphone' in the abdominal cavity. The participants who received the applied bass found their symptoms improved, with no side-effects reported, bar one patient feeling tearful. Nielsen's hypothesis is twofold. Firstly, that we perceive low frequencies through Pacinian corpuscles, a set of sensory cells found on the skin and in all internal organs. It's a starting point with which the scientific community broadly concurs. But Nielsen goes a step further, into new territory, arguing that the Pacinian corpuscles in the abdomen can potentially trigger healing body processes that can rebalance out-of-sync stress and relaxation responses, with knock-on health benefits including a reduction in seizures and improvement in inflammatory diseases like IBS and rheumatoid arthritis. Low frequencies, he thinks, can also heal us through the vagus nerve – the longest nerve in the body, which in the necessarily interconnected way of things, links brain, face and gut. It is a main component of the parasympathetic nervous system – which itself controls mood, immune response, digestion and heart rate.

Nielsen's formulation delivers optimised vagus-nerve stimulation through the bass chair, using music he produces himself in his home studio. I'm used to dosing my central nervous system with a whole-body bass bath in the dance, and I told him about a thought I had on a dancefloor once: that the bass was dancing me on the inside. He nods, agrees. 'It's physical. The bass stimulus is in the air and is coming from the floor.

It is integrated in the process of the dance . . . the bass will come through the body.' The healing effect of his bass chair is, he says, 'quite physical, quite chemical and quite neuro-chemical'. To paraphrase, it is a calm-down button, a hug from the inside. Specifically, Nielsen believes that bass stimulation of the vagus nerve can balance out two chemical substances: stress hormone norepinephrine and gamma-aminobutyric acid (which we will refer to by its acronym GABA), which produces relaxation. Too much norepinephrine, especially in the lower layers of the brain, will produce chronic depression, chronic pain, anxiety, even epilepsy. Vagus-nerve stimulation, Nielsen says, will 'actually produce a healing effect in balancing this norepinephrine–GABA system in the bottom of the brain'.

I absorbed some of Nielsen's knowledge to make my own bass chair when I was being battered by Covid-19 in the pre-vaccination phase of the pandemic. In the worst of it, I had a feeling that things were going badly downhill. What to do? I didn't have the capacity to explain. My hands took my wireless speaker off my bedside table, which in my extremely weak state was an effort. I struggled through the epic mountain-climbing mental work of googling 'gong bath' – I'm not exaggerating, at this point I was deep in the minus lands – and placed the speaker on my belly. The oscillating tones vibrated through my body, and I slept. At a moment of extreme illness my body reached for the low end.

Part Three

AFTER THE DANCE

Photo on previous page: looking into Total Refreshment Centre, 2016
Photo credit: Lex Blondel

14: STEPPING INTO THE STUDIO

Contemporary dance and dyspraxia, mid-to-late 2010s

Dancefloors also exist outside of nightclubs. I had spent much of my teens, twenties and thirties making the most of late-night basements. And while there had been pauses – new parenthood, or in the other lull points that quietly refresh a cultural life – speaker stacks in dark rooms had been a constant. The dancefloor occupied a position that church might have if I'd not lapsed, or football if I'd followed my dad's side of the family into the hallowed realms of Plymouth Argyle FC. Collective, citizen-built dancefloors are constantly changing, shifting in response to what's required. People also change throughout their lives, and I needed a new place in which I could move my body. It was time to step off the dancefloor.

Oxleas Woods, on the border of Greenwich and Bexley, offered an alternative. I went there regularly, writing a monthly column about this half-moon of ancient woodland for the crew at nature and culture website Caught by the River. I couldn't help but see the woods through a nightlife lens. The trees looked like living expressions of the dancefloor, unpolished and uncut. Trunks presented themselves as the source material of the sound-system speaker box. I dreamed up impractical schemes to bring musicians and DJs into the woods as a way of reconnecting the elements. There is music in the woods, too, in the sound of ash tops whispering in the wind, a woodpecker tapping out a beat or a jeep driving past and leaving a dissolving bassline suspended in the air. There's dancing as well, as birds skim the hedge-rows and sweet-chestnut branches move moodily from side to side. Eighth-century Sufi poet and Islamic saint Rabia of Basra felt the connection divinely:

> He is
> sweet that way
> trying to coax the world to dance
> Look how the wind holds the trees in its hands
> Helping them to
> Sway

The woods were lovely, but it wasn't enough. I needed other people, and I needed more music. It took a few attempts to find the right location. First, I tried a class at Pineapple Studios in central London. I'd been there once before, in the late 1990s, when publicity-averse Detroit techno originators Underground Resistance used it as a location for a press conference. They walked in in a line wearing balaclavas and sat down behind a long desk, answering questions from us one by one.

Dance class in the mid-to-late 2010s was a very different situation. I wished I'd had a balaclava to hide behind as I struggled to match the teacher's pop-video moves. Later I took a much more enjoyable class at the studio, but at this point I was the wrong kind of learner at the wrong point in my dance-class journey. I was hyper-sensitive, imagining that people were looking at me and judging me. I was extremely uncomfortable. This was not a dark nightclub; this was a dance studio, with windows through which I could be seen and mirrors in which I couldn't help but see myself. I wanted to stamp my foot like a child.

Stamping is a very human response and one which sits at the centre of much movement. 'There is a dance which contains that stamping of the foot, like the European drum's primeval beat: the Polish folk dance, the Russian, the Irish, and of course the Spanish flamenco,' wrote Jola Malin in her book about recovering from terrible grief, *Carry a Whisper*. The stamp tells us to stop and listen, she writes, because something important is happening: 'The dancer goes on to tell you – through their dance – of their depth of anger, sorrow or pain. About being fully alive.'

My friend, poet Kate Ling, encouraged me not to give up. We were walking across Blackheath, and we stopped by a tufted mound that is an anomaly on this piece of flat common land in south-east London. The mound is fairly large – it takes a few minutes to walk around it – and it's covered in broom, gorse bushes and wild-seeded trees. It's a natural Speaker's Corner with a rich and rebellious history – Wat Tyler apparently delivered speeches here during the 1381 Peasants' Revolt, and by the early 1900s local suffragettes used it for meetings and rallies. Kate and I were sitting on a bench on the edge of the mound, when she told me about a contemporary dance class she'd taken at the Trinity Laban Conservatoire of Music and Dance in Deptford. 'There aren't many places for middle-aged women to take up space,' she said. 'And it's good for middle-aged women to take up space.'

Her words hit home. I went along and immediately loved it. The teacher was funny and accomplished, and Simone, the accompanist, improvised beats on his MPC Live, altering the music to suit our needs and abilities. I didn't need to exaggerate the emotional content of my moves, as you might imagine in a comic version of the class, in which we'd open like flowers or spill about like rain. My emotional state became very clear to me as I moved, just as emotion is visible in hunched shoulders or an open chest. The movement phrases we built on week by week might contain the suggestion of a feeling – tenderness or a certain heft – but I couldn't help but bring myself to it. The phrases became short choreographies that moved us across the diagonals of the studio, and they moved us, too, shifting sadness or frustration as we laughed and concentrated and approximated our teacher's fluidity and groove.

However, if sequences of movement are the 'carriers of the messages emerging from the world of silence', as Rudolf von Laban believed, then my silent world was expressing that I was terrible at learning dance steps. I spent most of the first year finishing dance phrases and facing in the opposite direction to everyone else. I turned right when we were supposed to turn left, and I'd have to improvise whole sections in the middle until I could find the steps again, my memory blanking out instructions like an out-of-control delete button. This was extremely annoying, especially given my years of fluency and confidence in the dark corners of a club. I'd stand still, about to practise a phrase we'd just learned, with absolutely no idea of how the phrase started, let alone how it continued. I attempted to learn by speaking the movements into my voice notes. I tried writing the phrase down in the shorthand we used in class: sweep right, raise arm, shampoo your hair.

I asked my teacher if I could video a phrase so I could try to practise at home. Nothing worked. My legs were dyslexic.

The way I danced was expressing something intimate about my neurology. I didn't have dyslexic legs, I had dyspraxia. The International Dance Teachers' Association describes dyspraxia as a condition in which poor balance affects co-ordination – a 'faulty passage of messages from brain to the muscles responsible for an action' – suggesting that one in ten of all children experience this to some degree. Dance class allowed me to recognise that a number of things that I thought were 'just me' were actually just standard for the non-neurotypical. I have a higher than average chance of bumping into things, for example, and I can't do even simple maths in my head. My poor sense of direction is a source of comedy to my friends, and I've always been better at improvising than following instructions. I discovered that dyspraxic symptoms commonly occur in people like me who have an underlying neurological disorder. A study showed that over 60 per cent of children with the same diagnosis had serious motor problems, often alongside Attention Deficit Hyperactivity Disorder (ADHD) and Autism Spectrum Disorder. The difficulty I experienced in learning steps could be explained by the chromosome on which a genetic mutation sits. It was a strange relief to understand myself on a cellular level.

Dyspraxia offered additional challenges to my weekly dance class, but I had added one of my own: I was trying to dance head first. One day in the changing rooms I was complaining about not being able to think myself into the steps, when a lady looked at me. 'You can't think yourself into it,' she said. 'You just have to feel it and trust that your body knows where to go.' This was quite a revelation. Trust my body! Radical. I did as the woman in the changing rooms suggested. I stopped thinking about the moves and began to feel them, seeing if my body knew where to go. It turned out that my body knew my left from my right better than my mind. I no longer finished phrases facing the wrong way, and my Laban sessions began to flow and ameliorate through the medium of trust. It was joyful.

Verbal instructions are difficult for neurodivergent dancers because of issues with processing and synchronisation. Dr Julian Ahmed spent years making techno, drum 'n' bass and jungle records and spent many hours 'getting lost in the music, windmilling around the dancefloor in front of a massive bassbin'. Now he's a consultant in Audiovestibular Medicine at Portsmouth's Queen Alexandra Hospital, with a specialism in the vestibular system. This is, he tells me, the body's 'internal compass', explaining that it integrates with the eyes and muscular-skeletal information to keep us upright. 'In simple terms,' he says of dyspraxia, 'information from our eyes and muscles doesn't match up or get integrated in the co-ordination centre of the brain. We know what we want to do, but the body doesn't obey.' I certainly experienced dance class in this way, knowing what I wanted to do, in a body which was less than compliant. Ahmed explains that 'complex integration activity' like dance or martial arts can have lasting effects, above and beyond becoming a better dancer. 'These activities start to get things back into sync,' he says. 'With dancing, you're paying attention to your body, to perception and to your position in space, but there's an emotional component, too. You're dancing to music. There's cross-sensory input, and it's this cross-sensory input that helps trigger and re-synchronise stuff.'

Ahmed's interest isn't entirely clinical, because he was diagnosed with ADHD at the age of 38. Knowing what he does about complex integration activity, he decided to self-medicate through skateboarding and by taking up jive, because he figured that the spins, manipulation and fast leg work required by the dance style would help re-sync his signals. 'I know with hindsight that the periods I did a lot better with my ADHD symptoms were when I was going raving, dancing all night,' he said. 'After that I did martial arts. These were coping strategies that worked. Where I've destabilised is when I changed jobs, had to start commuting, and couldn't keep stuff up.'

Recent research by paediatric clinical psychologist Gopika Govindan offers further ballast. She concluded that 12 weeks of dance movement therapy – the therapeutic style which uses dance-like movement and strategies – reduced the symptoms of ADHD in children, particularly in relation to emotional dysregulation. Mental-health conditions, more generally, often feature poor balance – and other research has suggested that the relationship might go both ways: that working to improve your balance might improve your mental health, too. Balance can be improved by 'combining sensory information from the eyes with internal sensations from the vestibular system of the inner ear' – or, in simpler terms, 'eyes open, head moving', according to *New Scientist*, an instruction which sounds a lot like dance class or a night out on the tiles. Improving symptoms through dance can improve the dance itself, and vice versa. It's a positive loop, as I discovered.

Contact improvisation also helped, despite the fact that I initially treated the idea with horror. It is a practice during which you move with someone through what contact improv originator Steve Paxton calls the 'sensorial palette of a dancing body'. This means applying or receiving pressure to a shoulder or a hip so that two people briefly share a centre of gravity, as the gymnast-turned-dancer describes in a slim volume, *Gravity*. In it, he explains what happens when he cartwheels: 'Inside, my body was radiating energies, not passively accepting them.'

The line put the idea of cartwheels into my head. My flat is a bit too small for a cartwheel, so I tried a handstand instead. It took a minute of belief to get up there, against the door, but I did it. Later that day I was walking with a friend through Greenwich Park when I saw a patch of grass that just invited some basic acrobatics. Hardly anyone around, why not? I can confirm I can still reach up, then a moment airborne, before my palms reach the floor and my feet pass over my head. I can't confirm if I felt my body radiating energies because I was concentrating too hard to know. A small child appeared from behind a tree and pointed at me: 'Nice cartwheel!'

———

Tara Brandel is the CEO of Ireland's leading integrated dance company, Croí Glan, over in Cork. She trained at Laban in the 1980s, and is dyspraxic. She struggled through her dance degree. 'It was brutal,' she says. 'I didn't have any support and I didn't have any language for it.' Her report at the end of the first year spelled it out: 'Tara is not a naturally gifted dancer. She is gawky and awkward.' Years later, she took the sting and turned it into a dance piece. The recording of *Gawky and Awkward* contained not only her choreography, but also her voice:

Do you see my shyness, my vulnerability, my courage?
Do you see the struggle or the technique? I'm hoping
     you see both.

Unlike many of her peers who received more complimentary reports from their professors, Tara is still dancing. 'I'm the only person in my year who is still performing and dancing professionally at age 52,' she says. 'I didn't burn out, because it's always been so hard for me.' She began her life as a dancer by chance. She moved to England from Ireland in the mid-1980s, aged 14, and ended up living near the experimental arts college in Dartington, Devon. Her mum approached one of the professors, asking if there were any classes her dance-mad daughter could join. It was a request that landed Tara in the epicentre of modern dance.

Dartington College of Arts has a long history of offering space and support to artists, notably Rudolf von Laban, whose work underpins much Western contemporary dance and whose name was bestowed upon the south London centre where Tara trained. Laban came to Dartington in 1938 on a temporary visa, after a circuitous route out of Nazi Germany. The Hungarian was head of ballet at the Berlin State Opera when the Nazis came to power, and was then appointed director of the Deutsche Tanzbühne, with a brief to organise and promote German dance. He fell seriously out of favour when his 1,000-dancer piece for the opening of the

1936 Berlin Olympics was cancelled at the dress rehearsal for being insufficiently pro-regime, an artistic decision which had ramifications. Laban remained involved with Dartington for the rest of his life, running the Modern Dance holiday course from 1949 to 1951. Other dancers followed, including choreographer Merce Cunningham, who performed there in 1964, accompanied by John Cage and artist Robert Rauschenberg.

The classes that the teenage Tara Brandel attended between 1983 and 1987 were run by North American pioneers of contact improvisation, such as Steve Paxton, who taught at the annual Dartington dance festival. 'I was just a kid. I thought they were nuts, and I loved it,' says Tara. 'I went back every year. I went to every workshop, went to every performance, stayed up all night, sucked it in like a little sponge. It was a complete shock to me that they all became successful.'

By the time Tara got to Laban in south London, the New Yorkers, who had her rolling about on the floor in workshops and watching dance performances in which someone changed a bicycle wheel, were evolving into the next wave of contemporary choreographers. Their movement was still far away from the establishment, and decades away from being codified and taught at dance schools. Nowadays it's standard fare.

Improvised dance engages with societal structures, wrote Paxton, allowing individuals to 'proceed to a mind and body sure of that inner strength to rebuild human systems in terms not of the bottom line, but the top line'. That's a dance joke, the top line being something they talk about on *Strictly Come Dancing*: a dance term that relates to the shape our arms and shoulders make. In-joke aside, Paxton's right. Improvised contact and movement can allow us to build nuanced human systems through gesture, shoulder connected to shoulder, even if these exist only in the small arena of a wooden dance-floor. Dancing our bodies can influence our minds, and it can influence our relationships. 'It was amazing to start contact improv so young,' says Tara. 'It really separated sensuality from sexuality. I think all teenagers should learn contact because it really helps you separate what it's like to be physically intimate with someone from what it's like to be sexual. You get those boundaries in your bodies really young.'

Tara learned similar lessons in nightclubs. 'I came out in 1987, and the whole queer culture of that time was all about being in clubs,' she says. She was a podium dancer at Venus Rising at the Fridge in Brixton and was a regular at Heaven. When she finished her studies at Laban she moved to Berlin. 'It was just a few years after the wall came down. These little old butchers' shops in East Berlin were becoming tiny techno clubs. I was a go-go dancer at a queer women's club. It was my life support for years, clubbing. It was my whole way of knowing who I was and celebrating my queerness.'

I experienced celebration through dance movement in 2013, when I visited Rwanda on an exchange programme with two editors from Brixton's *Live Magazine*. We were visiting the girl-run Ni Nyampinga in the capital, Kigali, and spent a week or so sharing story ideas and plotting cross-continental collaborations. On the last night we all went out dancing at a couple of spots, including the Hôtel des Mille Collines, which, like every building in the country, contains history in relation to the 1994 genocide. This building's particular story was told in the film *Hotel Rwanda*. We arrived at a diverse dancefloor, comprising middle-aged Congolese businessmen in blue shirts, blingy young Rwandan entrepreneurs and artists, plus we three Londoners. At the very back of one of the disco rooms there was a small handful of young men dancing Jamaican dancehall-style, dipping down and winding their waists in a manner I perceived as gendered, in the sense of being associated with the way women move. I assumed something about their sexuality. This says more about me than it does about their reality or the way they might identify. My response was cultural. Regardless, these were young men finding a small corner of the world in which they could move how they felt, which is a universal need.

———

I met up with Meg, my mum, in a café at Waterloo station, before I tried out a new kind of dance experience. I was heading to an Open Floor expressive dance session, making myself go even though I was sceptical to the point of outright prejudice about what I'd find there: wafty, middle-aged, middle-class women with little self-awareness and terrible moves; sanctimonious self-appointed leaders who'd found themselves through expensive wellness routes, despite having vast resources at their disposal; blinkered hippies; people who thought they'd invented spiritual dance, when in truth it was mostly invented by people without vast resources.

Meg laughed when I told her where I was going and what I was expecting, and then she gave me a look – a very specific, laser-guided look, which she'd inherited from her mother Máire, and which Máire had probably inherited from her mother. It is a look which can be evoked only through a certain kind of provocation, and it's the kind of look that changes the light in your eyes, in a very clear example of eyes as a visible extension of the brain. I've also inherited it, which means I know exactly what it means: a context-dependent variant on the phrase about pots calling kettles black – 'Will you look at yourself!' – in which no words are needed. She was right. I was just anticipating a mirror, one in which I wouldn't like the reflection.

I was using the phrase 'expressive dance' because I didn't want to say what I was really doing. The Open Floor session is an offshoot of the 5Rhythms™, a phrase with the capacity to make me recoil. I want to put it in inverted commas, better to distance myself. The 5Rhythms world of wafty, middle-aged, middle-class women is a reflection I really don't like.

The movement meditation was put together by the distinctly kick-ass Gabrielle Roth, who was born in San Francisco in 1941. She learned ballet from brutal stick-wielding nuns at her Roman Catholic school and paid her way through college by teaching at-risk kids, elderly folks and bipolar in-patients at Agnews State Hospital in Santa Clara, California. The sleevenotes to her meditation soundtrack *Endless Wave, Volume 1* describe a dream in which the newly graduated Roth meets legendary flamenco dancer La Chunga and says, 'I want to dance like you.' In the dream-exchange, La Chunga counters Roth's admiration, brutally: 'Then dance like you, fool!' This feels like an essential movement truth, and it's one that has appeared repeatedly in this extended sashay into movement and music, whether it's Toni Basil passing on the phrase 'dance your history' or Frankie Valentine saying 'dance your story'. I feel like La Chunga, stamping out an instruction through these pages: 'Dance like you, fool!'

Roth's whole life was a weaving tapestry of big cultural moments: years spent as the movement specialist at the Esalen Institute and retreat in Big Sur, at the same time as Alan Watts, LSD evangelist Timothy Leary and psychologist Abraham Maslow, whose Hierarchy of Needs theory, with its triangular diagram, was updated by an early meme, with the addition of the scribbled word 'internet' as the most basic of needs.

She taught movement to people attending the first Gestalt therapy classes with theory founder Fritz Perls and spent time with film-maker Alejandro Jodorowksy and Bolivian philosopher Óscar Ichazo. In 1977 she opened the Moving Center in New York, where she evolved her ideas about movement meditation into a codified form known as 5Rhythms and set up a theatre and music collective called The Mirrors, where she held classes and trained teachers until she died in 2012. There are now over 400 certified 5Rhythms teachers in more than 50 countries, running classes that move participants through five distinct phases: flowing, staccato, chaos, lyrical and stillness. Roth's interpretation of spiritual movement and ecstatic dance is an easily understood system that is beloved by the 100,000-plus people who take 5Rhythms classes worldwide. There's also a not-for-profit outreach element, founded in 2007 to bring her techniques to the prison population, cancer patients and demographics commonly described as underserved. I didn't know anything about Gabrielle Roth when I first went to an expressive dance class. I went to test myself, to test my prejudices – and because, deep down, I suspected I'd like it, although obviously I was going to maintain the opposite stance for as long as possible.

So there I went, down the ramp, round the back of Waterloo train station, and into the Waterloo Action Centre (WAC). Housed in the former public library where George Orwell wrote *Down and Out in Paris and London*, which subsequently fell into disrepair, WAC became a powerful community space, operational since 1973 thanks to the combined efforts of the local people who rebuilt it and Lambeth Council, which agreed a peppercorn rent. At the point I attended their dance class, WAC had 30,000 users and was open every day, offering multiple activities for older people. It was home to the longest-running free legal advice service in the UK (set up by Helena Kennedy QC), a welfare benefits service, six churches and the London School of Samba, which had been drumming and dancing in the space for over three decades. Hall hire was kept purposefully cheap so that as many people as possible could participate – something expressed in the regular dance sessions, from rock 'n' roll and jive to zumba and tea dances. A decade of austerity had undermined or destroyed many community-run facilities, and WAC immediately struck me as precious and increasingly rare. I walked in, aware that I was entering the building equivalent of an endangered species. How long until someone managed to finagle a sizeable private profit out of the place? Another thought followed, about the difficulty of measuring the endless social profits the building contained. Such notions were unfortunately prescient, because in 2021 Lambeth Council proposed withdrawing the peppercorn-rent arrangement, replacing it with a subsidised but vastly higher rent – which, of course, threatens to make the whole endeavour unsustainable.

The receptionist at the front desk was weary, even though it was only 10 o'clock on a Monday morning. I asked her about the dance class, and she pointed me past some bookshelves, towards some double doors. There was a lady in a red hat just behind me, and her interest had been piqued. As I moved off she asked the receptionist what kind of dance class was happening. I hung around behind the bookshelves, desperate to hear the answer, because my comedy radar was pinging quite hard and I imagined that the receptionist might share some of my preconceptions about what I was about to do. 'I think it's . . .' She stopped, aware that I was hanging around behind the bookshelves. She paused, using the silence and withheld speech as a suggestion that I should move out of earshot, and then quickly gave up. 'It's a modern dance,' she told the lady. 'They just float around.' I sniggered and moved on, into a square hall with a wooden floor, high-beam ceilings and windows that looked out onto tiny parcels of the Waterloo skyline. I was getting changed alongside a woman who took off her perfectly serviceable leggings to put on colourful silky trousers. I was already judging the degree of unnecessary expressiveness she'd bring to the dance.

There was no musician, just a man and a woman who ran the session. The man stood behind DJ equipment and played the music, occasionally getting on the mic to give us grounded-sounding instructions: 'feel the space', 'notice the architecture of your bones', 'move with someone'. There were two decent speakers on stands at either side of the hall, and people were warming up, freestyle, to quietly ambient classical music. We were a mix of around 20 people, mostly women, mostly around 30 to 45 years old, with a couple of younger ones and a solid number whom I'd assume were 45-plus. We were a fairly homogeneous demographic, mostly wearing shades of what a friend calls 'middle-class grey'.

After a while the man got on the mic and encouraged us to move in whatever way we felt like moving. For most people this involved a lot of arm movement, dramatically sweeping and swooping. The excess of arm was making my own limbs magnetically attach to my sides, as if I could differentiate myself from the rest of the people in the room – just in case someone happened to walk in, they'd be able to see, clearly, that I was different to this lot.

No one was telling us what to do, so I just decided to feel the music on the inside and see what my body did. I was pretty sure I wouldn't be back, so none of it mattered, even though it was nice just to find a pulse in music without drums, and to see how it felt to adapt my little two-step, to find how it fitted with violin and cello. The music amped up and began heading into more familiar territory: electronica, house, gentle techno. I just decided to dance like I'd dance if I were in a club, feeling expressive rather than trying to 'dance expressive'. I express myself with my little two-step; I convey my shyness and my reserve; I communicate my extreme need to not take up space, to stay small, to dance on a tea tray, a tiny square of space in which I can speak volumes with my hips and my feet. I communicate where I've been – specifically, thousands of late-night, musically expert, speaker-powered events. I indicate where I'm going.

'Dance with someone,' said the man on the mic. My partner was the youngest woman present. She was a beautiful dancer who was happily spinning and dipping around the room. We faced each other, smiled, and continued to mirror and reflect and adapt. Some of us in the room were very far from her freewheeling control and the relaxed humour she brought to her movement. Some of the older women moved cautiously, hyper-aware of their limits and of what would happen if they breached them. Some of us were doing the equivalent of high kicks at the school disco. They might have been enjoying themselves, but it was a bit jarring, at least to my hyper-critical and self-conscious eye. A woman who looked about my age began to skip around the room. Two women followed her and, for a moment, it looked like we were going to have a full-on conga, but it dissipated and she was off, quietly following her own moves without ever breaching the spatial awareness that I appeared to require from everyone around me.

After a while I found my spot, by the speaker. This dance session was helping me identify and recognise a feeling, to feel it. Emotion was moving around; energy in motion. I was transported back to a steamingly hot jam in Deptford where musicians were improvising new music out of old favourites in collaboration with the audience. I was standing at the back one week, when I became aware of my feelings relating to a very difficult situation I'd encountered in my voluntary role as a school governor. I felt like all the emotions related to it suddenly washed over me. A lid had opened in my chest and everything tumbled out in a way I hadn't anticipated. I knew I was upset, but I hadn't felt it. I was updating my reality when I danced, and it happened without thinking about it. It happened when I 'felt' about it, when it was just me and my body. The above scenario will be familiar to professional counsellors, therapists and parts of the wellness industry as the concept of somatics and embodiment – centring the body in therapeutic work – becomes increasingly mainstream.

Here, in a community centre in Waterloo, dislocated by time and space from my usual habitat, it was really obvious: dance provides a key to the body. The people around me were dancing their stories. A couple of women were rolling about on the floor and creating little moments of comedy or tragedy by themselves or with each other. Others were lying on the floor with their legs raised, shaking them.

A circle emerged, and I was marginally horrified because I knew this was an invitation to enter, solo, into the middle. I must have gestured this because the woman next to me responded, mid-dance, 'Don't do anything you don't want to do.' I watched as one of the men took the centre, and then another man joined him, and then the woman in the colourful trousers, and they swished about until there wasn't a circle any more, just people dancing in the middle of the room. Of course, I stayed on the edge. The middle of the room was centre stage and I wasn't going anywhere near centre stage, OK? The only time I've ever purposefully moved into the middle of a dance circle was with friends, working abroad, and I made myself do it as a statement of intent and an introduction.

We finished, and there was silence. I was sitting on the floor, and I thought of a writer friend, Nadia Gilani, who explained to me that yoga exists to exhaust the body so that the mind is prepared for meditation. For once, I wasn't thinking. I was pleasantly empty, hearing the silence and our breathing, and the sounds of Waterloo traffic and the trains seeping back in through the walls and the skylights. It felt good to sit removed from the hubbub outside, which was quieted by the walls of the building and our breath.

The organiser asked if there was a question or reflection that we wanted to put into the space. His question caused me to immediately stare at the floor, because this was another circle I did not want to enter. A woman spoke up. She was in her late forties, wearing greys, hesitating, close to tears. 'I don't want to put this in,' she said, 'but I feel like saying it. I've lived a long time in pain, for 20 years. I came four weeks ago and I keep coming back, and now I'm not dancing to stop the pain. I'm just dancing with what I have, and it feels so good.' If expression is the action of 'pressing out' or making interior feelings known to outsiders, then this expressive dance class had done its job, beautifully.

By now I was feeling ashamed of my judgement. I could see what it took for her to come here, and I could see how much it meant to accept the movement she had lost and learn to live within the movement she had. I thought of my school friend Dawn, living with ME – the energetic equivalent of a battery that's only ever 5 per cent full. I wondered what movement Dawn would have if she came here, and if we would dance like we were 14, transported by the dancefloor back to the Civic, where we could dance our way out of a tight spot and into the nightclubs uptown. And yes, I went back the following week.

———

The best kind of expressive dance is one that responds to a feeling, like the ten-second video I watched online, where photographer, dancer and choreographer Benji Reid got out of a car. He had parked in front of a painted mural of the rapper Ty, who was much loved and who died of Covid-19. The mural, in Valencia Place, under the railway lines by Brixton Market, was based on one of Benji's photographs, in which Ty has his eyes closed and is holding a crown made of pencils – a reserved and humble king. The photographer stepped out of his car, stepped back to better see the image, and danced. He danced just a few steps, but it was a dance that expressed friendship, grief, joy and release. It was a momentary dance of life. It was kinetic expression, more than words could say.

15: ONE MORE!

Dancefloors in South Side Chicago and under railway arches in Deptford, late 2010s

Dancing is about release, but it is also about solidarity, with others and within ourselves.

The word 'solidarity' stresses interconnectedness. It ultimately derives from the Indo-European word '*solh*', which means whole, and refers to an agreement of feeling or action. The everyday dancers we've met created temporary agreements around sharing space and moving together in it, and in doing so created the building blocks of togetherness. Sometimes this occurred within a single demographic; other times across different ones. The dancefloor is a technology of togetherness. It improves balance, the ability to problem-solve and symptoms of stress for individuals. And it supports wholeness collectively: in 2015 the journal *Biology Letters* published a study by University of Oxford dancer–researcher Bronwyn Tarr. She and her colleagues asked teenagers from a Brazilian high school to dance to fast electronic music in groups of three, and found that those who danced in sync with each other felt closer to their dance crew than to others in the class. A year later, in 2016, the Oxford Institute of Cognitive and Evolutionary Anthropology found that simple dance moves such as swinging arms or stepping from side to side drew children together emotionally, with participants reporting that afterwards they felt closer to the groups they'd danced with.

One More!

I found a new and unexpected opportunity to experience collective togetherness at Total Refreshment Centre in Hackney, east London. TRC was an under-the-radar music venue run by Alexis Blondel with a community of friends and artists, and which also comprised artists' studios, a rehearsal space and recording facilities. I ended up writing and publishing a book, *Make Some Space*, in order to tell the story of the music and dancing that was happening there – and had been happening, through various iterations, for decades. I'd arrived at TRC through a circuitous route. I'd stopped going to clubs and decided to start going to see live music instead. In my mind, live music was decoupled from dancing, as different as Brazilian jiu-jitsu and synchronised swimming.

Then a friend took me to see Sons of Kemet at Rich Mix in 2015, and I was transfixed. Shabaka Hutchings oscillated between power and tenderness on sax and clarinet. Two drummers weaved percussive patterns from either side of the stage, and the tuba player spun melodic bass around the room. It was everything I loved about producer culture, but in a band; live music you could dance to. I took note and began heading to gigs where I knew they'd be playing – which eventually led me to TRC. As soon as I walked in, I knew I'd be back. I'd found all my favourite spaces rolled into one: a mutable, music-first location where you didn't need to know the line-up to know that it was going to be great. Before long, I was on another dancefloor, in a whole new slipstream, moving with hundreds of similarly energised folk to bass guitars, drum kits and saxophones.

In the mid-to-late 2010s TRC became an important part of a network that supported then-upcoming musicians like

KOKOROKO, Ezra Collective, Sarathy Korwar and Emma-Jean Thackray. It attracted and developed sophisticated audiences who moved to the music and could recognise a good tune, even if they'd never heard it before. Sometimes TRC attendees would bop to Can covers at the Krautrock Karaoke sessions; other times they'd swing and sway, stepping to groove-oriented South Asian or South American vinyl. BBC Radio 1Xtra DJ Tash LC was a regular who observed that people were 'ready and open to dance. It attracted people who just genuinely liked to move and were in a space where they felt comfortable to move,' she told me for *Make Some Space*. 'There was no idea of "this is a dancer" and "this isn't". Anyone could dance.'

The dancefloor at TRC created a new connection between the cities of London and Chicago. Scottie McNiece had been looking for a European location to which he could bring artists from the International Anthem label he co-ran, to record, play live and hang out: 'A home base conducive to magic-making,' as he described it to me. He landed upon TRC thanks to DJ and curator Tina Edwards and booked two consecutive shows for October 2017, along with recording sessions and a Sunday-afternoon event where beatmakers could take the raw recorded material and create something new, live. The events were billed as CHICAGOxLONDON, and explicitly brought together artists from both cities, mixing up the configurations onstage. In the middle of trumpeter jaimie branch's slamming set, two other Chicago musicians – Ben LaMar Gay and Angel Bat Dawid – appeared in the crowd, adding to the improvisations from within the dancefloor. The vibe at the shows was high and lively, and people were tuned in, dancing, hard. At one point during Makaya McCraven's incendiary set with Londoners Joe Armon-Jones, Nubya Garcia and Theon Cross, I heard someone shout from the back of the room, '*Oi, oi!*' It's a demographically specific call that I hadn't heard since the dubstep days of FWD>> and DMZ; before that it was a regular cry at the funk and soul weekenders of the early eighties. I'd been dancing for long enough to enjoy the long view and become totally convinced that no music style or movement ever dies but instead evolves, nourishing whatever comes next.

The following summer I booked a flight to O'Hare International Airport to visit the Chicago crew I'd met at TRC. There was a tag team of visits going on between like-minded souls in the two communities, and we were solidifying the connections we'd made. The trip was also a kind of homecoming, because I was visiting the place where house music emerged, and which had been my springboard onto the dancefloor.

Chicago was having a heatwave – it was hot, even by Mid-Western standards. I ate Mexican ice cream to cool down before taking the L to another memorable night in another tiny venue, where John Simmons, whose father ran the sound system at Mendel High, was chopping up samples and making new music at an improvised producer-led event called Fresh Roasted.

I was soaking up the music and culture, shown around by friends I'd made on the dancefloor at TRC who were themselves deeply embedded in Chicago's musical communities. They invited me to the Back Alley jazz festival, which honoured the regular jams where musicians had carved out space in the 1960s by running sessions in and around people's homes

331

– because, of course, commercial venues weren't always available to communities of colour. We were standing in someone's back garden when I saw tap dancer Jumaane Taylor add percussion to a performance, and the penny dropped that dancers could be beatmakers, too. The musician Angel Bat Dawid told me about the South Side drummers who meet every Sunday by the beach at 63rd Street – so I took a cab down and watched a lone dancer enter the circle while they played. He was an ordinary dancer and he was feeling it, and he stayed within the body of the circle, moving to the music. Hip-hop dancer and music producer Damon Frost once explained the circle to me in a way that made me inhale sharply and make the '*ohhhhhhh*' sound that often follows a realisation. 'The circle is a zero,' he said. 'You add to it.'

I saw footwork at the Promontory in Hyde Park. The venue is dedicated to 'celebrating the eras when spacious ballrooms and jumping jazz clubs made Chicago's South Side the capital of American music'. On this night it was celebrating the super-fast and highly technical style which grew out of a tuff and stripped-back strand of the house music Mendel High kids danced to in the 1980s. The event was being co-hosted by Teklife, a leading Chicago record label, and by dance crew The Era, because the music and the dancing are inseparable, two strands of the same DNA. Each aspect is just a reflection of a bigger truth: that to move your hands up and down a musical instrument, or to move notes around a computer screen, is not that different from moving your feet around the floor. Both exist to reflect, express and update lived reality.

The room was full of Chicago's finest footworkers, which was like being at a ballet jam with the Bolshoi. There were circles, plural. Individuals took their place in the centre to respond to what went before and to invite the next response, and the people comprising the circle added notes and accents made of body language, gesture and stance. Tempo was easy to recognise because he had his name down the back of his t-shirt, fusing ultra-fast kicks and knee grinds with the smoothest movements, like double-speed jazz-dance on rollerskates. Two guys arrived together in matching Air Jordans and took their place in the circle next to a young man in a white shirt, a Panama hat and dinner shoes, and another who was dressed all in white like a South Side *sangoma*. The movement was relentless, dancers dealing in hyper-speed from doors open till doors close. They were marking out and amplifying new productions, as well as the occasional classic being thrown down by the DJs, who were playing back to back in their own reflection of this push for new levels of music, movement and concentrated collective joy.

We don't have to be doing the dancing to reap some of the benefits of moving to music, which was good news in an environment like this, where I wasn't going to do anything more than a simple bounce. A dance-movement therapist in the north of Chicago named Erica Hornthal once explained to me: 'Dancing releases endorphins. You can get the same mood enhancement watching someone dance as you can doing it yourself.' Which explains the automatic smiles that wash onto my face when I watch krump or flamenco or any of the gazillion dance videos available on the gorgeous side of the internet. In fact, I might just change all my settings so I see only dance videos online, so I can dancescroll, not doom-scroll. Watching dance might be good for you, but it doesn't do everything. 'I always joke: it's good for you but it doesn't use the same amount of calories,' Erica said. 'For that you have to do the dance yourself.'

It requires solidarity to generate a circle and it requires a solid base to enter it. The circle appears in many dance forms, including b-boying and breaking. It is a clearing, a space consensually generated in which dancers can communicate grace, fury, comedy and sensuality. In the circle, dancers respond to the moves that have just happened and instigate the dance still to come. Dhanveer Singh Brar described the footwork circle in his book, *Teklife/Ghettoville/Eski: The Sonic Ecologies of Black Music in the Early 21st Century*, as an 'ecological nerve centre', and the metaphor extends perfectly. Clear a space in nature, and new things can grow, as I discovered when I pulled a tonne of ivy off the stony bit of garden outside my flat. A year later there were poppies, elegant grasses, magnetised dots of low-lying white flowers. I didn't plant anything. I just made some space, and the environment did the rest. We're not so different: seeds of possibility floating in the hot air of a dance, ready to land and grow new shoots. Actor and choreographer Adesola Osakalumi was talking about New York house clubs during choreographer Camille Brown's 'Social Dance for Social Change' lecture series when he said, 'The circle is a communal showcase, a stage,' but his words rang true in this Chicago room, too. 'It's a testing ground: iron sharpens iron,' he continued. 'It encourages you to go and do the work. It's to sharpen you up.'

Of course, there was also house music at the Promontory. I went back a few days later with two friends of friends, who, like me, were visiting Chicago, and – also like me – had a long-standing relationship with dance music. The three of us headed to a club night that followed the annual Silver Room block party and which featured DJs we've appreciated for decades. Chicago house-music innovator Ron Trent, whom we met earlier starting out at Mendel High, was playing back to back with New York's Joe Claussell, who has similarly esteemed status within house culture. The queue was a good indicator of what was to come: Robert Williams, who brought Frankie Knuckles to Chicago to start the Warehouse back in the early 1980s, was standing right behind me, wearing a flat cap. This configuration lasted only until Mr Williams was noticed by the guy on the door. 'Hey, Godfather!' said the door guy, waving him up the stairs in mock outrage at his humble queuing style. 'Come on through!'

Inside, there was deep and soulful house music all night long, and all-ages dancers. A man in red velvet slip-ons with gold embroidery dropped his shoulders in the circle, and two women in their fifties danced up close and personal. A liquid-drunk twenty-something slid down the back of a chair on the edges of the room, attracting a dour side-eye from the young woman he was with. She remained on the dancefloor, half dancing, half disdaining. I didn't sense nostalgia in this room or any idea of it being a 'Back to the Nineties' event, as this line-up might suggest in the UK. It felt like a living lineage of house music expressed through everyday dancing. Hardly anyone had their phones out, and to me, as an outsider – white in a Black space; a Londoner in Chicago – it appeared that this dancefloor existed in the everstream, and that it offered a warm embrace, like home-style cooking; a house-music family, dancing together in unity of feeling and action.

The ladies' toilets at the Promontory offered a different perspective on family. What I hadn't clocked from my cultural remove was that house-music crowds could include hard girls. The bathrooms were organised in a long rectangle, with a mirror by the door. A group of women in their late twenties were in time-honoured fashion turning the bathroom into a break-out space, and the energy levels were high and hilarious. When I left the stall, they'd all gone, and I was briefly alone. It was a momentary pause, because the doorway between the club and the bathroom then flew open. It had been pushed, hard, by a woman with glassy eyes who stormed up to me and engaged in the kind of body language that looked very much like she was deciding whether or not to headbutt me.

'Where's the fucking bitch?'

Obviously I didn't know anything about the bitch, let alone where she was, but because I was sensing that she was still weighing up whether or not to headbutt me I decided there was only one thing for it: to inhabit a side of myself which is confident in any south London situation. I shrugged to communicate my lack of knowledge and pulled my face into the non-committal scowl I'd learned from the hardest of dancefloor hard girls and which leapt across time and space to this moment now, in the early hours of the Chicago morning. Next thing, she's kicking in the door of a stall. This could have been where the bitch was, but I didn't stick around to find out. There are limits to dancefloor solidarity, after all.

———

One More!

In spring 2018 I'd begun attending a weekly jazz jam called Steam Down that took place in the back of a beautiful Jamaican restaurant called Buster Mantis in Deptford, south-east London. I'd go down after contemporary dance class, and if the queue outside Steam Down got too long, I'd go instead of contemporary dance class, because I didn't want to risk not getting in.

It's not coincidental that this dancing occurred in a restaurant tucked away in arches that support the railway tracks, and not a nightclub. It relates partly to where I was age-wise – less comfortable in youth-focused club spots – but also to the broader picture. There were hardly any nightclubs left. Between 2014 and 2019 £200 million had been wiped off the UK club market amid a 15 per cent drop in the number of adults attending a club at least once a month. By 2015 half of UK clubs had closed due to a pincer movement of shareholder-serving property development and masses of home entertainment.

Steam Down combined West African musical inspirations with North American hip hop and London jazz, and quickly made its way into fictional representations of the dance: British–Ghanaian writer Caleb Azumah Nelson included a scene from the jam in his best-selling debut novel *Open Water*. The dancefloor also reflected changing British demographics. In 2016 the *Economist* reported that 'Britain's black population is now about two million, or just over 3% of the total', adding that until 2000 most had Caribbean forebears. Between 2000 and 2011 the population with direct African ancestry doubled. Data analyst Tholani Alli wrote in 'Mapping London's African Community' that over a million adults born in Africa (excluding

South Africa) were living in the UK in 2016, and noted that the most common country of origin was Nigeria, followed by Ghana. A year earlier the mayor of Brent, Michael Adeyeye, had stated that a million people with Nigerian heritage were living in Britain. These demographic realities made their way onto the broader dancefloor, as detailed in Christian Adofo's brilliant book *A Quick Ting on Afrobeats*. In it, he explains how West African-originated music and dances, like the Azonto, were nurtured in the UK at family-based hall parties, at university African–Caribbean society raves, and by building on the dance crazes popularised by late-2000s grime artists, as strands of the music evolved into a new sub-genre, UK funky.

All of this fed into the music and dancing at Steam Down. I'd find a tiny space at the back, happy to be in the presence of generative greatness, and let my body find the beat and the groove, allowing myself to be dragged like a pebble by the waves of sound that were improvised into being each week. Sometimes the musicians would riff on a well-known melody from, say, a hip-hop classic like Slum Village's 'Fall in Love'; other times they'd rework songs that had been built from scratch in the room and gradually became bubbling Steam Down anthems like 'Free My Skin'.

It was tropical hot, like Flann O'Brien's Irish rural dance, and it was blissful, transportative. A photographer friend, Yusaku Aoki, snapped me at the end of one session. The image shows my hair slicked back with sweat and my skin reflecting the light, peachy with heat and happiness. I am smiling widely, head turned towards Yusaku, who is also drenched in the feeling-full moment, but my body remains facing the source of the sound, deep in the catching of all remaining vibrations, like the last moment of a spectacular sunset. Standing just out of the frame is a friend I hadn't seen since the dubstep era at DMZ and Plastic People, who came along that night because he'd heard that something was happening. His radar, like mine, was well tuned, and he soaked up the music and the vibrations as enthusiastically as we had standing in front of low-end bassbins a decade earlier.

Dancing can unlock memories and aspects of your personality that you had forgotten, and once a feeling has been danced into your body it's there for life, ready to be reawakened. It is lifelong socialisation in its most universal form: learning how to understand yourself and the people around you; learning how to share space with other people; and discovering the space and movement you need at whatever point of life you're at. It allows you to communicate what you want and need, and to sense the wants and needs of those around you.

The dancers were as important as the musicians who played at Steam Down, and the musicians represented an A-to-Z of London's new wave of instrumentalists, as well as international guests who'd pass by when they were in town, like Kamasi Washington or Nigerian trumpeter Etuk Ubong. The music drew a line back to the jazz dancers we met earlier in Leeds, or to Trevor Shakes at Spats, but the entry requirements were minimal, dance-wise: a two-step, a skank, a sway. Many good dancers spent time on this dancefloor, some of whom had had professional training that amplified the everyday dancing they'd gained at home and from being young Londoners out and about. There were sometimes small circles in which the dextrous ones could shine. Dancers from across the skill divide conducted, mediated, encouraged and expressed the music, using their arms or an energetic bounce to call for a heavier synth line or a new chord from the keyboards, and to respond when the drummer cut up the drums to their most sparse and effective. This was whole-body listening and whole-body responding.

In *As Serious as Your Life*, a history of free jazz in 1970s North America, Val Wilmer quotes drummer Andrew Cyrille telling her that the drummer shapes the music 'like the skeleton in a body'. It's a line which makes me think of the dancing body itself as a drum: both encased in skin, both resonant. The dancers at Steam Down – and all the places like it – laid down a new seam in the geology of the city's cultural life, and they laid it down in their bodies. They added to the song, if the song is the ongoing way in which humans express their specific sorrows and their specific joys, and in doing so linked back to all our collective sorrows and joys. The dancers at Steam Down also pointed forward to how things could be.

Sometimes I'd see Amarnah Osajivbe-Amuludun at Steam Down. She's a professional dancer who started her training at Laban, in Deptford, as part of their programme for talented youngsters, took a degree at the London Contemporary Dance School and followed that up with a Master's degree at the Northern School of Contemporary Dance in Leeds. She also knows a lot about the kind of dancefloors we've been visiting over these pages. She made underage forays to Madame Jojo's in Soho, took teenage trips to Shoreditch clubs like 333 and Catch, went to squat raves playing drum 'n' bass, jungle, garage and dubstep, and had a three-year stint where she went every month to a long-standing and hippyish clubland staple called Whirl-y-Gig, which in nicely circular style I had attended decades previously. Since the mid-2010s she's been adding gestural notes to music made by the UK's new generation of musicians, and she's also part of south London-based collective Scrapbook Mixtape, making music informed by a decade in the dance. Her most recent release was titled 'Stumbling', which is funny, given the grace with which she moves. She's well placed to articulate the experience of moving to music with other people. 'It's a space for me to experience my body with others,' she tells me, 'and to connect to something that's more than just form and shape, which is what I normally think of when I'm performing as a professional dancer.' Communal dancing spaces offer her the opportunity to 'drop down out of my brain, into my heart, into my stomach. To let the vibrations affect me and let me affect the vibrations.' What do you think dancing does for us collectively? I ask. 'It's a chance for people to be together, communicating without necessarily talking. A chance for people to open themselves up to contact and communication, to bypass the social norms of appearance, dress sense, style, even culture sometimes, and to connect as peoples, as one. It helps people communicate in a way they don't get to daily. Usually we use words, and that's only a tiny percentage of communication. Most of it is in the body.' I understand what she's saying. I feel it, quite literally, in the muscle memory built up on the dancefloors I've inhabited over the years. We finish up our chat. 'It's funny, that thing people say – "I'm not a dancer,"' she says, evoking a typical dancefloor conversation. 'But I just saw you dancing. You're a dancer.'

———

I'm not very comfortable being photographed at the best of times – apart from when someone catches me unawares. It was, therefore, quite a leap for me to agree to be photographed dancing by a professional photographer for an article I had written about dancing with dyspraxia. I am not a dancer in any technical sense – I'm just a grown version of that child who loved dancing to *Top of the Pops* in a swimsuit, connecting enjoyment of music to enjoyment of movement. I'm also a shy dancer, happiest on the edges, doing my own thing in a small glass rectangle. I decided to accept the editor's suggestion precisely because it was uncomfortable. 'I'm writing a book about collectively moving to music,' I thought. 'I'd better do the same.'

I agreed with the photographer, Camilla Greenwell, that we'd shoot the artwork on a bridge over Deptford Creek, in sight of the Laban centre, where I took contemporary dance classes, and a ten-minute walk from Steam Down. It's a place that connects to the sound-system past, too, as many iconic locations are within walking distance, including the paint-peeled doorway of 51 Storm, where young sound-system operators chatted lyrics on the mic. A plaque commemorating the Battle of Lewisham is ten minutes away, as are the locations used in the reggae film *Babylon*.

Camilla was calm and reassuring, and we ended up talking about movement. She's been photographing professional dancers for a decade, including a recent session with an organisation called Move Dance Feel, which runs classes for women affected by cancer. She's younger than me, in her early thirties, and she described what she calls 'a con' – the constant deferral that comes with bodily connection, especially if you're a woman. The time when you're able to enjoy your body, or appreciate it, is always out of reach. It's either ahead, in the suggestion that you'll be more relaxed about your body when you're five or ten years older, or it's in the past, in the experience of seeing a photograph and realising how good you looked. It is rarely synchronised to the now, which is, of course, the only moment we actually have. Moving our bodies to music, whether we're 15 or 50, gives everyone a chance to inhabit and enjoy the way we're configured right now. I think that improvised, ordinary dancing also allows you to arrive back at a version of yourself that's less tainted by the illusions that society places upon individuals based on ability, gender, sexuality, class or ethnicity – which perhaps explains why certain people are less likely to dance freely, given that those illusions benefit them.

We stood on the bridge that crosses Deptford Creek, and I pulled out my wireless speaker. Camilla positioned herself further up the bridge so she could place me in the frame. I started moving. Just a little two-step. Just a little sway left to right. The DLR trundled past. I ignored the people who might possibly be looking at me, their eyes a source of shame, and welcomed the sound waves that emanated from the railway tracks as an additional rumbling bassline. I was moving, my borrowed jacket dropping slightly off my shoulders as I dipped and stepped a little to the side, a little to the back and a little to the right. I was wearing a heavy black skirt that I bought to interview an influential musician because it gave me feelings of strength and groundedness, solidity. I dug into those feelings and felt the skirt move heavily around me, adding to the lines and curves that my body was marking out in the air. I had come some distance from being stilled into shame at a school disco. I was dancing a new story.

A South African friend, Siviwe, popped into my mind – memory unlocked by movement. He runs gumboot-dancing classes for kids in his neighbourhood, just outside Cape Town. 'Emma!' he'd say. 'Flow like water!' He'd mimic my dancing, making flowing shapes up and down his tall frame as we stood outside a community centre. This shared moment of move-ment reflection was communication and a gentle teasing joke. It was conversation, a bridge, and a gift.

I wanted to show Camilla a place that I visit regularly because I am endlessly fascinated by the invisible stories it contains. We walked down to the River Thames, arriving at the ten-foot wall that surrounds the site of Deptford Royal Dockyard, which (between 1513 and 1869) built and refitted warships and vessels designed for exploration – 'the cradle of the British Navy', according to author Jess Steele. Matthew Sheldon of the National Museum of the Royal Navy wrote that state-built vessels were 'a key guarantor of the colonial system', making Deptford Docks a foremost location from which the British Empire sprang, with all the dark histories that entails. It was also the centre around which companies profiting from enslavement grew, including the East India Company, with Royal Navy expertise being used directly and indirectly to build, refit and stock company ships. There are multiple stories here: about workers, about state power (a letter in the nearby Maritime Museum was written by 17th-century naval officers who 'desire and direct' that men be press-ganged onto the King's ship) and about the historical realities that underpin so many aspects of British life.

This momentous geography is invisible, at least from where we were standing, by the stone steps that lead to the river. I could see colourful graffiti that has visual roots in North America, and some buddleia, a plant which arrived in the UK from China in the 1890s, but no blue plaque. Last time I came there was a fading information board about kings and queens that a previous developer had left behind, but even that had disappeared. The site of Deptford Docks itself is empty, although not for long, because luxury flats are being built here, despite the World Monuments Fund adding it to their watchlist of threatened heritage sites in 2014, alongside the city of Venice and the ancient stone structures and stairways at Gran Pajatén in the cloud forests of Peru. A swan swam past, down the Thames.

For now this place is a pause, an interregnum. There is silence regarding the deep international histories and the national narrative that rests so closely within this specific place on the planet, where the Thames rises and drops before rolling back out to sea. Behind the high wall there's an absence in which Britain's national story is stashed away, out of sight. The old story of 'Rule Britannia' and glorious empire is ageing, and we haven't developed a new one that enough of us can believe in. The old narrative begins here, because Britain as we know it started here.

Maybe a new story begins here, too. I think that the seeds of new ideas about who we collectively are can be sown when people with a rich range of identities move to music underneath arches beneath railway tracks or in the back rooms of restaurants. This version of Britishness acknowledges that we're all from everywhere, and that 'everywhere' begins with the realities expressed through Deptford Docks. Recognising this might be a starting point from which we can improvise ourselves into a more realistic and recognisable place. We need a more accurate story about Britishness and Englishness that better matches our reality.

Perhaps ordinary dancing, collectively, is one way of developing new stories that more people can believe in. 'I am not naive enough to think that dancers can single-handedly get us out of our present troubles,' wrote choreographer and educator Gill Clarke, in her 2007 essay 'Mind as in Motion'. 'But I do believe their concerns, expertise and knowledge are ever more vital in connecting us back into our living, moving organisms, to a sense of relationship within ourselves and with the world.'

You might think it's not that deep, it's just dancing. You can think what you like, but I believe that moving to music is an effective way to see ourselves and each other, and to resynchronise and rebuild, regardless of what has been demolished – hopes and dreams, an economy, the future. To dance you must let go of self-consciousness, embarrassment, pride and prejudice, and embrace what you actually have. The more we improvise movement, together, the better chance we have of thickening our relationships, building the necessary connections we need for a future that looks increasingly low-resource and local. Motion is tidal, flowing around obstacles like water round wood, wearing them down with repetition. It reshapes the environment and it reshapes us. We're all dancers, I think, regardless of where we come from or where we're going. We're dancers because we're human, and we're more human – or perhaps more humane – if we dance together, especially when we make it up on the spot.

One More!

Hallelujah, then, for everyday dancing. Respect to the generation who have created and absorbed a vast library of moves thanks to online dance crazes. Pre-teens all over the world are extremely dance-literate, thanks to the internet, with an ability to know and name multiple steps. They know how to dance, and this amplifies and builds on all the work, hardship, joy and release of previous times. Countless millions are sharing their own dancing online, which transmits encouragement. All of this builds on the foundations of dancing, which contain our deep, interconnected roots. It shows solidarity.

If these roots flourish, it'll be thanks to all the people creating space for dancing together, in a moment in history where dancefloors everywhere are being rolled up and transformed into low-quality student blocks or overpriced rabbit-hutch housing. Salutations to the people running dances in citizen-salvaged venues; to school leaders who keep dance on the curriculum when the existing systems strongly encourage the opposite; and to volunteers creating impromptu neighbourhood street parties. They are acting in a deep lineage of basement raves, of seasonal dances on the village green, of step dancing on the crossroads.

Out to the dancers, all of you.

Epilogue
CLOSING STEPS

There was less communal dancing during the writing of this book than at any other time in my life. The pandemic separated us into our own box-sized dancefloors, and those who wanted to move found new ways of doing so: families learning dances together; people bopping to DJ streams alone or with housemates; the collective discovery that online classes can work, and that any kind of dancing can improve a miserable day. People approximated communality: an acquaintance's Zoom dance class culminated with everyone turning off their lights and dancing, as if together, in the dark.

I found my own way into movement by writing about it. Sometimes, I'd try to remember a specific dance – the Running Man, the acid-house jack or the dubstep knees-up – and rummage through my records for the right piece of music to see if I could reconstitute how I'd moved when those moves were new to me. Of course, this was an impossible piece of time travel because my body is stratified with gestural information, and this can't be reversed. Sometimes, though, for a moment or two, the movement would unlock a sense of how things really felt at the time, in the same way that a scent or a piece of music can transport you. On other occasions I'd just put on some music and dance in response to the feeling of love, or sorrow, or a specific kind of giddy hyperactivity that I'm prone to.

Epilogue

Once the pandemic eased off – and once I'd recovered from long Covid – I ran a dance project with the children of a Deptford primary school that is situated as close to the Thames as it's possible to be. I invited writer Kieran Yates and artist Zezi Ifore to join me for the sessions. I'd first met them during my time on *Live Magazine* and, over the years, we'd moved from a mentoring relationship to one of extended family and creative collaboration. We shared a belief that dance is important and undervalued: Kieran once half-jokingly suggested that we should nationalise dance, putting TikTok dance profits back into communities, and Zezi dreamed up events that brought together dancers across the generations. Neither of them were trained dancers, which was important because the idea of the programme was to strip away the underlying connotations of skill from the act of dancing. We wanted the children to dance their story, regardless of technique. It was an opportunity for a very specific kind of dance-up.

Each week, the three of us asked classes of children aged between 8 and 11 to make up simple choreography in response to pandemic-related prompts like 'hand sanitiser', 'bubble' or the admittedly tricky 'one-way system', and they did so to our chosen soundtrack. The playlist mostly contained house music, because it's so easy to dance to, with the odd grime instrumental thrown in. I'd expected the children to be shy about dancing in front of each other, but this wasn't the case. Each class, without exception, threw themselves into the task. As the sessions evolved, I began using a handy phrase: 'It's not about being GOOD, it's about being YOU.' Some of the children were, of course, good at dancing. All of them, without exception, were good at being themselves.

Imagine them now, a group of four boys who have placed themselves at each point of the compass, close to each other. One is on his knees. He is the virus, and he attacks the others one by one, turning them into viruses, too. Close your eyes and see other groups making up dances about not being able to see their friends – by running at an imaginary wall, then falling back, or by using flat palms to indicate being stuck in a glass box. The children created complex shapes that described the boredom and inertia of home schooling (a dramatic slide down a wall; staring at the ceiling; remaining stuck to a chair), or went straight to gaming, which, of course, involved pinging around the room, imaginary console in hand. The children were able to access layers of their experience that would have been inaccessible if they'd been asked to write an essay about the pandemic. Words aren't always enough.

We planned the sessions but improvised around what was happening, as with the 'emotion conga' that Kieran invented in response to supply-teacher energies that briefly began percolating at one point. 'OK!' Kieran said. 'Conga round the room! Show us an emotion!' The impromptu idea evolved and became part of the sessions, and we'd try to catch their intention so that we could reflect it back at them.

Conga aside, there were cartwheels and many dances that ended with children hugging dramatically and throwing themselves around in circles. Even the shyest scowler got involved, approximating some breaking and flinging his jumper around to illustrate release from lockdown. There were hopeful dances where vaccine-related prompts allowed for enjoyable jabbing manoeuvres. Others ended with everyone dying, often in a fit of giggles. The children used fewer of the popular dance steps than we'd imagined – there was just an occasional dab or hints of whatever new dance their older siblings were learning from the internet. The children just used the moves they had, to express whatever they felt like expressing. They needed it. We needed it, too.

Acknowledgements

I'm grateful to all the people who helped me with this book. Individuals took the time to read large sections, including Lexy Morvaridi, Julian Brimmers, Kevin Braddock, Kate Ling, Joanna Kirk, Anna Wood, Simone Sistarelli, Nadia Gilani and Georgina Cook. Other people took the time to comb through specific chapters, and I'm very grateful to Kieran Yates, Les Back, Lez Henry, Tamika Abaka-Woods, Ali Augur, Colm Carty, DJ Mantra and the EQ50 crew, John Burgess, Paul Benney, Nuala Ginty, Mark Gurney, Naomi Brown, Chris Waywell, Annette Richardson, Deanna Heer, Georgina Hirsch, Charlotte Kepel, Martin Clark and Tony Nwachukwu. Special thanks to Seema Khera, Kingsley Deckon and Ekowa. Thank you to Dan Papps, Mo Hafeez and Rachael Williamson at Faber. Alexa von Hirschberg did a brilliant job as editor. I'm grateful to Hannah Knowles, who edited it into the final stretch, and to Ian Preece for his copy-editing skills and proofreader Ian Bahrami. Thank you to Cathryn Summerhayes at Curtis Brown. All mistakes are, of course, mine.

Generous people offered time to discuss the dancefloor: Piotr Orlov, Jo and Chad Vill, Louis 'Loose' Kee, Jazzy M, Cassie Kinoshi, Jason Goz, Claudia Wilson, Tyrone Isaac-Stuart, Azizi Powell, Robbie Wojchiechowski, Dave Tindall,

Acknowledgements

Jolyon Green, Irfan Rainy, Michael Barnes-Wynter, Sophie McCready, Scott McCready, Dave Waller, Ffion Wyn Evans, Angela Samata, Dr Iris Bräuninger, Prof. Theresa Buckland, Dr Anthony McCann, Geoff Amos, Lubomir Jovanovic, Glyn Andrews, Ed Williamson, Avi Del Mono, Nicole Mckenzie, Alasdair Hood, Mark Nightingale, Ed Stutt, Kester Rymaruk, Jeff Barrett, Cally Callomon, Tony Crean, Ross Allen, Fergus Murphy, DJ Debra, Coco Maria, Gilles Peterson, Clark Tracy, David Dunne, Beverley Bogle, Katie Cambridge, Katherine Griffiths, Mark Davyd, Dr Adam Behr, Mialy Rama, Janine Neye, Martyn Ware, Tina Edwards, Cecil B, Dave Swindells, Charlie Dark, Grand, Deapoh, Subeena, Lisa Der Weduwe, Tedra Wilson, Dr Stephaun Elite Wallace, John Simmons, Alejandro Ayala, Scottie McNiece, Raluca Simiuic, Ian Calvert, Amy Kaherl, Sisanda Ntshinga, Siviwe Mbinda and Sifiso Ngobese.

Gratitude to the people who lent me things or helped me track down things: archivists at Sheffield City Archives, the Manchester City Archives, the National Youth Archive at De Montfort University, and the British Library. Paul Byrne, Nadine Andrews, Ruby Savage, Leo Zero, Rosa Methol from All Hands on Deck, Borge, Tigs Ikkos-Serrano, Beverly Bennett, Tanya Tempa Benz, Bill Brewster, Frank Broughton, Damian Lazarus, Karen P, Rahul Verma, DJ Sappo, Johnny Jay, Pete Shepherd, Ben Wilmott, Johannes Kompa, Belinda Zhawi, Joshua Idehen and Jesse Bernard, Katherine Green at Rendezvous Projects, Craig McLean at *The Face*, Claire Thynne at the Killaloe Diocesan Office, Sue and Judith at the Museum of Slavery and Freedom, Colin Steven at Velocity Press, Sharlene Small from Manchester's Got Talent Youth,

Acknowledgements

and Vicki Cuff, Alison Webber and Angela Cudmore at Invicta School. Hawkwood College and the Francis W. Reckitt Arts Trust supported development with a week-long artist residency.

Other folk offered support, helped with ideas or are otherwise part of the story. Out to Richard King, Emma-Jean Thackray, André Anderson, Carolyn Roberts, Ben LaMar Gay, Tej Adeleye, Gus Fairbairn, Dawn Pearcey, Darren White, Graham Styles, Emma and Alex Pheby, Maria Taylor and Sophie Nicol, Annie Nicholson, Cyndi Handson-Ellesse, Mark James, Jason Page, Kalise and Khari Cross, Frances Eccleston, Harriet Green, Will and Florence Nicholls, Hayley Joyes, Marina Blake, Haseeb Iqbal, Rebecca Salvadori, Hanna Bächer, Davina Pobee, Mari Kimura, Parul and Matt from the London Writers' Salon, Larissa McGoldrick's Covid Recovery Class, and to Anne Davey, Claire and Nic Davey and Pete Warren. If I've not named you, apologies. If you answered a DM, responded to a request or otherwise helped me out, you know who you are. I'm very grateful.

And, of course, Meg, Detta, Paul, Danny, Nats, Karl, Jim, Katy and all the nieces and nephews.

Acknowledgements

Keeping Together in Time: Dance and Drill in Human History by William H. McNeill, Cambridge, Mass.: Harvard University Press. Copyright © 1995 by William H. McNeill. Used by permission. All rights reserved.

'Lines Written a Few Miles Outside Blackburn, On Revisiting the Site of the Sett End Pub, April 10 2021' originally appeared in *Flashback: Parties for the People by the People* (Rough Trade Books).

Alice Walker, *Hard Times Require Furious Dancing: New Poems* (New World Library, 2010). Introduction, p. xvi, used with kind permission from the author and publishers.

BBC Radio1Xtra documentary *Classic UK Clubs*, produced by Folded Wing, broadcast 4 December 2011, used with permission.

'A Lover Who Wants His Lovers Near' from *Love Poems from God: Twelve Sacred Voices from the East and West* by Daniel Ladinsky, 2002, used with permission.

The section around dancing with dyspraxia first appeared in another form in The Wellcome Collection's 'Stories' strand. Parts of the Deptford Docks section first appeared in *The Developer* magazine.

Notes and References

Epigraph

The opening quote is taken from a 2016 Facebook post by Detroit DJ and producer Theo Parrish, in response to the killing of Alton Sterling and Philando Castile by police. It stated that he was 'embarrassed' at the lack of overt commentary from the art form of dance music, which is 'rooted in reaction to racism, birthed in struggle'. Posted 16 July 2016 and reprinted with kind permission from the artist. https://bit.ly/3OsUp3d.

Introduction: Opening Steps

I was taking part in a programme for grass-roots social innovators . . . Between 2013 and 2019 the soft-drinks brand Red Bull ran a social enterprise programme called Amaphiko. The programme worked with community entrepreneurs in South Africa, Brazil, the US and the UK. I worked on it, which is why I was in South Africa.

'*England through the looking glass*' . . . from the poem 'Dirty Little Smithfield'. Robert Gallagher, *The Dance Floors of England* (Diabolical Liberties, 2019), p. 29. Gallagher was the vocalist and original member of the band Galliano.

PART ONE
1: Dance Your History

Barbara Ehrenreich, *Dancing in the Streets: A History of Collective Joy* (Granta, 2007), pp. 23–8.

The house dance workshop where Toni Basil went viral in 2016 was run by choreographer and dancer Ousmane 'Baba' Sy.

Edwin Denby claimed it began . . . Edwin Denby, *Dance Writings* (Alfred A. Knopf, 1986). The text comes from two sections: '*ballet began* . . .' on p. 566 and '*a simple bounce*' on p. 509.

Notes and References

Egil Bakka, *Contemporary Dance, Universal Claims, Colonialism* (Academia Letters, 2021), pp. 2–3.

Rudolph Laban described the 'kinesphere' in *Choreutics* (Macdonald & Evans, 1966), p. 10.

Experimental spinal surgery . . . Thank you, NHS, and Mr T. T. King at the Royal London Hospital.

Dancing increases opioid production in the brain . . . Bronwyn Tarr, *Dance and Social Bonding: Synchrony and the Endogenous Opioid System, a Thesis* (unpublished, Hertford College, University of Oxford, 2014), p. 247.

More calories than cycling, swimming or running . . . 'Dancing Burns More Calories Than Running – And Makes You Happier', *Argus*, 23 December 2015.

Dance stimulates the brain . . . Scott Edwards, 'Dancing and the Brain', an *On the Brain* lecture, Harvard Mahoney Neuroscience Institute, winter 2015. Other studies unearthed remarkable results, as was the case with PhD student Carine Lewis at the University of Hertfordshire, who showed that 20 minutes of improvised dancing improved divergent thinking. Dr Peter Lovatt, *The Dance Cure* (Short Books, 2020), p. 86.

The Association of Inter-Church Families was established in 1968 after a couple tried to involve their Catholic and Protestant churches in the baptism of their child, without success.

Edwin Denby, *Dance Writings*, ibid, on birds murmurating, p. 573; observations on the way people walked in different cities, p. 544.

2: National Dance

Martha Bayless, 'The Fuller Brooch and Anglo-Saxon Depictions of Dance', *Anglo-Saxon England*, December 2016, Volume 45, pp. 183–212 (Cambridge University Press).

Reminds me of a song from a different context: St Vincent's soca maestro Skinny Fabulous . . . There are multiple dancefloor connections and similarities that span time and space, but it is important to remember Skinny Fabulous's specific context of being Caribbean, with all the histories that involves. Skinny Fabulous (real name Gamal Doyle) is a hugely popular soca musician from St Vincent and the Grenadines.

In the crypt of St Paul's, just off Deptford High Street . . . The Crypt was run by Canon David Diamond. His obituaries in the *Independent* (8 September 1992) and the *Guardian* (21 September 2012) give a strong sense of the man.

Martha Bayless kindly sent me her notes from Bernadette Filotas's *Pagan Survivals, Superstitions and Popular Cultures in Early Medieval Pastoral Literature* (Pontifical Institute of Mediaeval Studies, 2005).

Notes and References

Church during feasts threatened with excommunication . . . Jerome Bertram, *The Chrodegang Rules: The Rules for the Common Life of the Secular Clergy from the Eighth and Ninth Centuries. Critical Texts with Translations and Commentary* (Routledge, 2005).

The section on language, and Italian in particular, comes from a conversation with dancer Simone Sistarelli, who runs Popping for Parkinson's, a social enterprise.

The English word 'shout' relates to movement . . . Albert Raboteau, *Slave Religion: The 'Invisible Institution' in the Antebellum South* (Oxford University Press, 2004; first edition, 1978), p. 71.

Folk song would 'stimulate the growth of the feeling of patriotism' . . . Cecil Sharp, *English Folk Song: Some Conclusions* (Simpkin & Co., 1907), p. 135.

Sharp 'dominated the organisation . . .' Sharif Gemie, 'The Oak and the Acorn: Music and Political Values in the Work of Cecil Sharp', *Musical Traditions*, 17 April 2019.

The 'Stepping On' conference took place at Cecil Sharp House on 16 and 17 November 2019. It was organised by the Historical Dance Society, English Folk Dance and Song Society, Instep Research Team and Dance Department, University of Roehampton. All speakers are listed on the event's Facebook page, and there is an article about it in *English Song and Dance*, spring 2020. https://www.efdss.org/about-us/what-we-do/news/10104-stepping-on-a-meeting-of-minds-and-feet.

King Charles and Pause Eddie's footwork video was titled *How to Do Chicago Footwork* and has over a million views at the time of writing. It was posted on 19 April 2014 on Pause Eddie's YouTube channel. https://www.youtube.com/watch?v=tlVbzuARvh0.

The introduction to his 1909 publication . . . Derek Schofield, 'Cecil Sharp and English Folk Song and Dance before 1915', *Country Dance and Song Online*, vol. 1, April 2016.

Cecil Sharp was not alone in the early 20th century in thinking that national identity needed rebuilding, that dancing contained key information about this, and that dancing could be corralled in service of identity. Folk dance was part of the process of nation-building in the newly independent states of Norway and Finland, and not in the established states of Denmark and Sweden. Egil Bakka, *Emergences and Struggles, Dance and the Formation of Norden* (Tapir Academic Press, 2011).

Folk dances aren't just something that existed just in the past . . . Dr Anthony McCann describes 'a commodifying logic' to the way the past can be reused by the present. Particular aspects of what people think of as tradition become privileged, he says, things that are 'very thin, low-somatic, non-body context'. Zoom interview, July 2020.

Dance as ritual . . . Theresa Buckland, 'Th'owd Pagan Dance: Ritual, Enchantment and an Enduring Intellectual Paradigm', *Journal for the Anthropological Study of Human Movement*, 2002, p. 415.

Dave's brother's wedding Greebo. https://www.youtube.com/watch?v=ljAQ7WUdLNU.

Barbara Ehrenreich . . . quoted the historian Cornelius Nepos . . . Dancing in the Streets, ibid, p. 48.

Vladimir Putin . . . waltzed with Austrian Foreign Minister Karin Kneissl . . . Kate Connolly, 'Ex-Austrian Minister Who Danced with Putin at Wedding Lands Russian Oil Job', *Guardian*, 2 June 2021.

Maxine Leeds Craig, *Sorry, I Don't Dance: Why Men Refuse to Move* (Oxford University Press, 2013), pp. 17–18, 185, 190.

African–Roman legions stationed . . . David Olusoga, *Black and British: A Forgotten History* (Pan Macmillan, 2016), p. 29.

DNA sequencing of people buried in the east of England . . . Clare Wilson, *New Scientist*, 1 October 2022, p. 22.

We have been seen by visitors from afar . . . Mirza Sheikh I'tesamuddin, *The Wonders of Vilayet: Being the Memoir, Originally in Persian, of a Visit to France and Britain in 1765* (Peepal Tree Press, 2002). Detail taken from Amrita Satapathy, *The Politics of Travel: The Travel Memoirs of Mirza Sheikh I'tesamuddin and Sake Dean Mahomed* (Institute of Technology Bhubaneswar, 2020).

Mayim Mayim, which is also danced by schoolchildren in Japan . . . The Israeli Mayim Mayim dance, where people hold hands and move around in a circle, became popular in Japan in the post-war period through American GIs. The tune that usually accompanies the dance also ended up in a Studio Ghibli film, *Only Yesterday*. Mackie Lorkis, 'How an Israeli Folk Dance Became a Hit in Japan', 25 November 2020, Heyalma.com.

Paul Gilroy, *The Black Atlantic: Modernity and Double-Consciousness* (Verso, 1993).

I pulled together the detail on the genesis of the Electric Slide through a number of sources, including 'Marcia Griffiths on the Electric Slide', *Dancehall Magazine*, 26 February 2021. Writer and archivist Azizi Powell has two excellent blogs – Zumalayah.blogspot.com and Pancocojams. blogspot.com – and she was kind enough to point me towards two entries, the latter of which features Ric Silver in the comments, Ric Silver's website and an interview on SECTV in October 2015 (from 21 mins). I emailed Silver but didn't get a reply. http://the-electricslide. com/ https://www.youtube.com/watch?v=e7uByEP8XEY.

A group of protesters are doing the Electric Slide . . . Sanjoy Roy, 'How the Electric Slide Became the Black Lives Matter Protest Dance', *Guardian*, 11 June 2020.

3: Down with Jazz

Malcolm Rifkind wrote to the home secretary . . . National Archive, Prem 19/2724.

Electronic: From Kraftwerk to the Chemical Brothers at the Design Museum, London. July–December 2020.

Dutch film-maker Jan Beddegenoodts made a film about the Bassiani promoter titled *Naja: A Portrait* (2021). https://www.youtube.com/ watch?v=Je69_iOmc_I Bassiani.

'No Dancing' poster from Tokyo . . . I was in Tokyo the year before the no-dancing law was removed and can attest to the nervousness with which the law was still approached, which was all the sadder given the gorgeous sound quality and attention to sonic detail in so many of the city's bars.

Changes to welfare benefits in 1984 . . . Alan Booth and Roger Smith, 'The Irony of the Iron Fist: Social Security and the Coal Dispute, 1984–85', *Journal of Law and Society*, vol. 12, no. 3, winter 1985.

At the time of writing, it is illegal to dance in public in Kuwait . . . Ramadan Al-Sherbini, 'Kuwaiti Dance at Concert Sparking Outrage from Conservatives', *Gulf News*, 21 October 2019.

The authorities in Iran . . . Ban Barkawi, 'Iranian Musician Faces Jail Over Women Dancers and Singers', Reuters, 28 August 2020.

Dance was being explicitly quashed in Saudi Arabia . . . Bill Bostock, 'Saudi Arabia is Admitting General Tourists for the First Time', Insider.com, 9 October 2019.

Breandán Breathnach, *Folk Music and Dances of Ireland* (Mercier Press, 1971). The descriptions of dance styles come from pp. 41–3. The book came with a unique addition for the time: a cassette that illustrated the dancing Breathnach wrote about.

South African gumboot dancing . . . Nicola F. Mason, 'Gumboot Dancing and Steppin': Origins, Parallels, and Uses in the Classroom' (Eastern Kentucky University, 2019), published in *Slavery to Liberation: The African American Experience*, pp. 27–8. Dr Mason also writes that the African American form of dance known as steppin' drew from traditional African dance, tap, military drills – and gumboot dancing.

Culminated in 1695's Penal Laws . . . 'Before 1695 there were many penal enactments against Irish Catholics, but they were intermittent and not persistently carried out. But after that date they were, for nearly a century, systematic and continuous and as far as possible enforced.' Patrick Weston Joyce, *A Concise History of Ireland* (Longmans, Green and Co., 1903).

A child would sometimes wait outside Mass, ready to indicate imminent danger by tapping out certain rhythms with their feet . . . Mark Knowles, *Tap Roots: The Early History of Tap Dancing* (McFarland & Co., 2002), p. 13.

Large enough to contain a ballroom . . . James Nott, *Going to the Palais: A*

Social and Cultural History of Dancing and Dance Halls in Britain, 1918–1960 (Oxford University Press, 2015), p. 13.

Dance venues sprang up in cities and large towns . . . Méabh Ní Fhuartháin, 'Parish Halls, Dance Halls and Marquees: Developing and Regulating Social Dance Spaces, 1900–60 (Éire-Ireland, Irish–American Cultural Institute, vol. 54, nos 1 and 2, spring/summer 2019), pp. 233–4, p. 242.

The list of places where people would dance comes from a range of sources, including Méabh Ní Fhuartháin, ibid, p. 222.

She was one of just under 10,000 women who emigrated at this time . . . 'Between 1926 and 1936 an average of 9,420 women left the Free State every year compared with 7,255 men.' Louise Ryan, 'Leaving Home: Irish Press Debates on Female Employment, Domesticity and Emigration to Britain in the 1930s', *Women's History Review*, vol. 12, issue 3, 2003, pp. 386–406.

Half a million Irish women emigrated to England in the mid-20th century. Twenty-five thousand went to Birmingham, working in transport or nursing. Sarah O'Brien, 'Britain Was No Paradise for Irish Emigrant Women', *Irish Times*, 1 March 2019. By 1951, 11 per cent of nurses and midwives in Britain were Irish. https://greencurtaintheatre. co.uk/irish-nurses-in-ww2.

I'm one of an estimated six million people in the UK with an Irish-born grandparent . . . Simon Maybin, 'How Many Britons Are Entitled to an Irish passport?', bbc.co.uk., 2 September 2016.

There is a significant repository of information about the Public Dance Halls Act on Setdance.com.

In the context of tuberculosis . . . Dr Méabh Ní Fhuartháin, ibid, p. 239.

John Porter, 'The Public Dance Halls Act, 1935: A Re-examination', *Irish Historical Studies*, vol. 42, issue 162 (Cambridge University Press, 2018), and from a lecture he gave as part of the Trinity Research Centre for Contemporary Irish History Seminar Series. https://soundcloud.com/ tlrhub/the-public-dance-halls-act-1935-a-re-examination.

Dublin's Stardust Club . . . Rachel O'Connor, 'Stardust Tragedy', *Irish Post*, 14 February 2020.

Empowered clergy, who reportedly set them on fire . . . Martin Dowling, *Traditional Music and Irish Society: Historical Perspectives* (Routledge, 2015), p. 135.

Simon Price in The Rabble . . . Quoted on the blog History Is Made at Night (which runs with the tagline 'The politics of dancing and musicking and other dark matters'). 'Public Dance Halls Act 1935 in Ireland', 18 February 2013.

Described jazz-dance disparagingly as 'a cross between a waltz and all-in wrestling' . . . Eileen Hogan's quote from the Dáil comes from Teachta Dála Mr Kehoe, and the original quote is located in Dáil Debates, 26

Notes and References

March 1936, vol. 61, section 377–8. Eileen Hogan, *Earthy, Sensual and Devilish: Sex, 'Race' and Jazz in Post-Independence Ireland* (JRJ, 2010), p. 73.

Phil Murtagh's band . . . 'tip top' . . . 'Well Known in Tramore', *Waterford News and Star*, 4 April 1941, pp. 8–9.

In November 1929 the tradition-focused Gaelic League issued a jazz ban . . . Philip Martin, 'Gaelic League Bans "Jazz"', Irish News Archive, 6 November 2019.

It's worth remembering that making sense . . . Garry Bushell and Rick Sky, *Sun*, 12 October 1988, p. 15.

The bishops of Ireland released a statement titled 'Evils of Dancing' . . . https://lxoa.wordpress.com/2012/02/16/irish-hierarchys-statement-on-dancing-1925/.

The Down with Jazz march in Mohill in 1934 has been reported broadly by people interested in this area. I used these blogs, among others: https://www.theirishstory.com/2011/07/01/the-anti-jazz-campaign/#.YdSwVRPP0Wo; https://leitrimannals.com/2014/07/28/jazzing-every-night-of-the-week/.

There is now a monument to this dancehall hero . . . 'Large Numbers Expected for Gralton Unveiling': the *Leitrim Observer*, 1 September 2016, reported that 'large numbers are expected to assemble at the site of Gralton's "Pearse Connolly Hall" at Effrinagh, County Leitrim, on Saturday morning next when President Michael D. Higgins formally unveils a monument to the memory of the famous Leitrim Socialist Jimmy Gralton'.

The phrases 'orgies of dissipation' and 'pernicious consequences' appear in the Carrigan Committee report, paragraph C28.

wrote a civil servant . . . from Jim Smyth, 'Dancing Depravity and All That Jazz: The Public Dance Halls Act of 1935', *History Ireland*, 1993, p. 53. Having served on committees as a school governor for some years I would suggest that any civil servant who wrote down the phrase 'wanders quite far from the terms of reference' was doing so with masses of understatement.

The full name of the Carrigan report was *Report of the Committee on the Criminal Law Amendment Acts (1180–85) and Juvenile Prostitution (1931).*

[The Public Dance Halls] Act was passed without being debated in the Dáil . . . Taken from the final paragraph of Jim Smyth's paper 'Dancing, Depravity and All That Jazz', ibid.

'The Country Where Clubs Are Illegal' . . . Mark White, *Muzik*, June 1999, pp. 52–4.

Former premier Albert Reynolds, who himself ran a network of dancehalls . . . Conall Ó Fátharta, 'Business Brain Made Albert Reynolds the Dancehall King', *Irish Examiner*, 22 August 2014.

Notes and References

Another campaigning group – Give Us The Night . . . This is an independent
volunteer group of night-time economy professionals founded by
DJ Sunil Sharpe. They continue to campaign for 'positive changes
to nightlife in Ireland', with a focus on licensing laws, 'with a view
to influencing legislative changes that lead to a more vibrant and
profitable night-time industry'.

Father Gildea's statements appear in the full Carrigan report, which is
available here: http://the-knitter.blogspot.com/2005/06/full-carrigan-
report_24.html.

The reports from the *Irish Times* on closing times come from Dean
Ruxton, 'Scoundrels of the Lowest Type: When the Priests Took on
Dancing', *Irish Times*, 1 April 2018.

Jim Smyth, 'Dancing, Depravity and All That Jazz': ibid, p. 53. The file
also contains letters from surveyors describing overcrowding and duty
evasion at dances, and others, from gardaí, blaming outdoor dances for
cases of unmarried pregnancies.

A mammoth hall-building exercise . . . John Porter, 'The Public Dance Halls
Act, 1935: A Re-examination', ibid.

*Ironically, dances then became necessary in order to meet the construction and
maintenance costs* . . . Dr Méabh Ni Fhuartháin, ibid, p. 223.

He holds up a note and kisses it . . . *Down with Jazz* was broadcast on 29
September 2020 on RTÉ One. Director Colm Kirwan told me that the
footage came from the series *Changing Face of Ireland*, first transmitted
on 27 July 1965, from an episode titled 'Of the People, for the People'.

The Dromakeenan Fianna Fáil Club . . . *Nenagh Guardian*, 5 October 1935, p. 3.

It's hard to know what to make of some of the reports from the licensing
sessions. In autumn 1936 William Ryan applied for a licence at Nenagh
District Court. The *Nenagh Guardian* reported a cross-examination
by an Inspector Lavan. Ryan stated that the proceeds from previous
dances had gone to the IRA, that he was aware that this was an
unlawful association, and that he was a member. The inspector then
asked if there had been any fights at his dance, to which he answered
that there might have been, but that he'd been in Dublin undergoing
an operation. 'Did you strike anybody yourself?' asked the inspector.
'No,' said Ryan. There followed some discussion about the hall being
three miles from the Garda station and therefore hard to supervise,
and about sanitary accommodation. The Justice said he would allow
the application to stand over for some time, when it could be renewed.
Nenagh Guardian, 10 October 1936, p. 10.

John left in the summer . . . D. M. Leeson, *The Black and Tans* (Oxford
University Press, 2011), p. 10.

Flann O'Brien wrote about dancehalls in the literary magazine The Bell . . .
The Bell, vol. 1, no. 5 (February 1941), pp. 44–52. Conservative opinion

continued to hold sway. In 1954 the *Redemptorist Record* published 'The Devil at Dances' by Bill Gerrard, and later published his article as a popular pamphlet. 'Dancers should not be allowed to dance cheek-to-cheek, even if they are man and wife – the dancefloor is no place for intimate demonstrations of affection,' wrote Gerrard. 'They should not be allowed to dance with the woman's arm around the man's neck, not with body tightly clasped around body. Those who offend should be warned on the first offence, on the second expelled from the premises.' Bill Gerrard, *The Devil at Dances* (Juverna Press, 1955), p. 12.

The first céilí in London's . . . Dr John Cullinane, *Aspects of the History of Irish Céilí Dancing, 1897–1997* (Antonio Pacelli, 1998), p. 24.

The word 'jig' links to the Hindu deity Lord Jagannath . . . Mark Knowles, ibid, pp. 7–8.

15 sounds per second with their feet . . . Mark Knowles, ibid, pp. 12–13.

Dewitt Fleming Jr described the connections between tap dance and Irish dance . . . *Steps of Freedom: The Story of Irish Dance*, broadcast by RTÉ, 16 December 2021, and BBC4, 13 March 2022.

Mark Knowles offers another, brutal, connection between Irish dance and tap when he describes stolen people being forced to dance, including to jigs and reels, during the middle passage. *Tap Roots*, ibid, pp. 25–6.

Heel Up: Damhsa ar an sean-nós, 9 December 2006, RTÉ Radio 1.

Horse skulls that people would bury . . . 'Why Were Horse Skulls Buried Under Floors in Great Houses of Ireland?' IrishCentral, 8 August 2018.

There are various spellings of the word 'hoolie', but Pat O'Dea suggested I use this one.

Popping for Parkinson's run free classes (their website states 'we do not want to profit off disability') and was founded by Simone Sistarelli, whom I met when he was the accompanist at the dance class I took at Laban.

Argentinian tango also held up well . . . Lötzke, D., Ostermann, T., and Büssing, A., 'Argentine Tango in Parkinson Disease: A Systematic Review and Meta-Analysis', *BMC Neurology*, 2015.

Terrence O' Dwyer, 'Italian Doctor Finds Cure for Parkinson's Disease in Irish Dancing', IrishCentral, 11 January 2020.

Dr Daniele Volpe, 'A Comparison of Irish Set Dancing and Exercises for People with Parkinson's Disease: A Phase II Feasibility Study', *BMC Geriatrics*, 4 June 2013.

4: Deep Roots

Lloyd Bradley used the phrase 'the soundman revolution' when I interviewed him for a BBC Radio 1Xtra documentary *Classic UK Clubs*,

Part 1, produced by Folded Wing and broadcast on 4 December 2011. He talked about sound systems in more depth on my Worldwide FM radio show, 4 April 2018.

Linton Kwesi Johnson used the phrase 'electric hour of the red bulb' in his 1975 poem 'Dread Beat an' Blood'. Linton Kwesi Johnson, *Selected Poems* (Penguin, 2006), p. 5. It originally appeared in his collection of the same name, which was published by Black-owned independent publisher Bogle-L'Ouverture. The poem also titled his 1978 album, released on the Front Line label, which was produced by LKJ and his school friend Vivian Weathers, and featured artists including Dennis Bovell.

The quotes from Jazzie B come from interviews I did for the BBC Radio 1Xtra/Folded Wing documentary *Classic UK Clubs, Part 1*, broadcast on 4 December 2011.

The detail on Norman Jay and the Good Times sound system comes from my interview with him for the Red Bull Music Academy in 2010.

Fabio repping Jah Shaka: Tony Nwachukwu, 'The Art of DJing', *Resident Advisor*, 7 December 2019.

Shy FX . . . https://tileyard.co.uk/community/shy-fx/.

So Solid Crew began life in a sound system called Killawatt . . . Peter Lyle, 'Street Kids', *The Face*, August 2001.

DJ Magazine profiled a number of influential DJs and producers from the 1980s onwards who had roots in their parents' or older siblings' sound-system histories. Carl Loben, 'Children of the *Windrush* Generation: Pioneering DJs Who Paved the Way for UK Dance Music', *DJ Magazine*, 22 June 2018.

With grime artists including Wiley (whose dad ran a sound) . . . I wrote a long read for Red Bull Music Academy, 'Wiley: The Eski Boy', *Daily Note*, 26 May 2015.

Lloyd Bradley's phrase 'logic and ambition' comes from the BBC Radio 1Xtra/Folded Wing documentary *Classic UK Clubs, Part 1*, ibid.

Let's not pollute this book with the name of the specific Conservative health secretary, but you can find the 'big up' tweet here if you wish: https://twitter.com/matthancock/status/1084878231960989696.

The *Windrush* scandal affected thousands of people. '*Windrush* Generation: Who Are They and Why Are They Facing Problems?' 24 November 2021, bbc.co.uk.

A staggeringly high percentage of the jungle and drum 'n' bass tunes . . . apart from the ones that people cut elsewhere to avoid everyone hearing your secret tunes, as discussed in this Red Bull Music Academy article: Todd L. Burns, 'Nightclubbing: Metalheadz at the Blue Note', *Daily Note*, 2 April 2013.

Notes and References

I asked Ed Rush and Optical if they remembered what tune they were cutting that day, and they said that a good guess would be 'Sick Note' or 'Bacteria'.

Producer Teebone's half-hour conversation with Leon Chue is on YouTube: https://www.youtube.com/watch?v=qRBfszxN-3Y.

This blog post explains more about the Reggae Walk, which was organised as part of Goldsmiths' '70/50 Bass Culture' events. It also contains a video of one of their walks, along with the reggae map which Lez and Les built as part of the research: https://cucrblog.wordpress.com/2018/10/12/the-reggae-map-of-new-cross-by-les-back-and-william-lez-henry/.

Lezlee Lyrix's lyrics, reprinted with kind permission from the artist:
Me say me nah go ah church and go bow to no priest,
the priest ah make them money out ah lies and deceit,
them worse than the muggers who ah roam Britain street,
an ah rob poor people on the cold concrete,
because them take people money in the name of the lord,
go buy fast car and ah posh up them yard,
and pon poor people them love draw card,
ah take Jah Jah name and ah use it for fraud.

South London blog Transpontine have a selection of Saxon flyers here: http://transpont.blogspot.com/2011/06/saxon-archive.html.

Professor Henry spells his sound 'Ghettotone' in his book *What the Deejay Said*, but it's spelled various other ways on flyers and online.

This national story . . . as evidenced in this 2015 exhibition of Birmingham sound systems: Stuart Brumfitt, 'Delve into Birmingham's Sound System History', *i-D*, 3 August 2015.

The 2010 *Champion Sound* documentary tells the story of Coventry sounds: https://www.youtube.com/watch?v=kRydM-pOGPg.

This history of Huddersfield sounds tells the story through photography: Mandeep Samra and Paul Huxtable, *Sound System Culture* (One Love Books, 2014).

Shottsman and Holy Roller present *Two Big Sound, Part One: Seven Nights a Week* (2011). It was filmed by IG Culture, who is better known to music fans as one of the leading producers within the music scene known as broken beat. An article by Paul Bradshaw tells the story: 'Shottsman Comes with Two Big Sound', Ancienttofuture.com, 31 October 2011.

Vinyl Factory ran a history of the sound by David Katz, 'The Story of Saxon Sound System', Vinyl Factory, 21 August 2019. Saxon themselves posted an edited clip of a BBC programme about reggae which heavily features their crew: https://www.facebook.com/watch/?v=1640077002908961. There are various films online taken

from Saxon Studio International dances in the 1980s, including this one
from 1985: https://www.youtube.com/watch?v=IGGp1a3bvj4.

Janice prefers not to include her surname. She also has a strong
preference around the spelling 'shubeen', hence my decision to spell it
this way here (although I have used 'shebeen' elsewhere).

Steve McQueen's *Small Axe* anthology was screened by the BBC on 22
November 2020.

I talked to Dennis Bovell about his experiences in person and on my
radio show for Worldwide FM, 5 January 2017.

Melissa Bradshaw, 'Anti-Sus Sound Systems: An Interview with Dennis
Bovell', *The Quietus*, 2 February 2011. In it he talks about the raid on
the Carib Club and the subsequent legal case.

The 15th-century courtyard where I met Dennis in Rome was in a
building being used by the Red Bull Music Academy in 2004. Dennis
was interviewed by Fergus Murphy for a long-form couch session:
https://www.redbullmusicacademy.com/about/projects/rome2004.

We attended the pub after one of Dennis's regular Soho Radio shows in
autumn 2019: https://sohoradiolondon.com/profile/dennis-bovell/.

Orphy Robinson demonstrated shuffling in the back garden of the
Brownswood Basement after appearing as a guest on my Worldwide
FM radio show, 3 September 2021.

*The Story of Lover's Rock: The Secret World of a Generation and the Birth of a
Reggae Genre*, directed by Menelik Shabazz (2011). It includes dancer
and academic Dr Kwame 'H' Patten deconstructing the dance style.

Oxytocin helps create feelings of warmth and attachment . . . 'Oxytocin
Enhances the Experience of Attachment Security', *Psychoneuro-
endocrinology*, vol, 34, issue 9 (October 2009), pp. 1417–22.

Lovers rock drew on a lineage of Jamaican versions of big soul records and
gained its name after husband-and-wife team Dennis and Eve Harris
invited Dennis Bovell to join them as sound engineer, producer and
in-house musician, along with musician and producer John Kpiaye. The
label was named after Augustus Pablo's 1973 record 'Lover's Rock'.
They recorded in the Eve Recording Studio on Upper Brockley Road, a
short walk from 51 Storm and other locations that comprised the musical
geography of that area of south-east London. Lloyd Bradley went into
more detail in my interview with him on Worldwide FM, 4 April 2018.

She described the dancefloor at a Shaka dance for a 1981 cover story . . .
'Big, Big Sound System Special', *NME*, 21 February 1981, pp. 26–9.
Paul Bradshaw told me that this was the *NME*'s first substantial
reggae coverage. He also told me that Leroy 'Lepke' Anderson, who
founded the heavily influential DBC pirate radio station, was a top
shuffler. Bradshaw knew this detail because he worked at the youth
club Lepke attended.

Notes and References

The Club Noreik footage was posted online by The Roots Shed, 23 May 2019: *Jah Shaka at Club Noreik Tottenham, London, UK 1978–79*. The text at the beginning by Cleve Macca states that it was shot at Shaka's last dance at the club, a month before Haringey Council's compulsory purchase of the building. Available at: https://www.facebook.com/rootsshed/videos/580649945791450.

Yaojun Li, 'Ethnic Unemployment in Britain, 1972–2012', the Runnymede Trust, 15 January 2014.

The phrase 'thinking on the move' appears on p. 34 of Les Back and Lez Henry's chapter 'Reggae Culture as Local Knowledge: Mapping the Beats on South-East London Streets', which itself appeared in *Narratives from Beyond the UK Reggae Bassline: The System Is Sound*, edited by William 'Lez' Henry and Matthew Worley (Palgrave Macmillan, 2021).

Paul Byrne, 'Warriors Dance: Interview with Kid Batchelor', *Test Pressing*, 26 February 2019.

Derek Bishton, 'Remembering *Shades of Grey*', derekbishton.com.

Shades of Grey was taken apart by Paul Gilroy in *The Empire Strikes Back: Race and Racism in '70s Britain* by the Centre for Contemporary Cultural Studies (Routledge, 1982).

I saw *Leave Taking* at the Bush Theatre in Shepherd's Bush in summer 2018 with my friend and theatre reviewer Ben Benjamin. The play was originally produced at the Liverpool Playhouse Theatre in 1987. In the introduction to Nick Hern Books' reprinting of the play, Winsome Pinnock explains how she became a playwright: 'I developed a passion for theatre and performance as a child of around 12 years old when, with generous grants from the GLC (Greater London Council), our school took us on visits to the theatre. I wouldn't have gone otherwise.' Winsome Pinnock, *Leave Taking* (Nick Hern Books, 2019), p. 33.

This interview gives an account of Franco Rosso's first encounter with a sound system – at the bottom of his garden, where the local church hall held weekend dances. PJ Grisar, 'Q&A Martin Stellman, Screenwriter of *Babylon*,' Forward.com, 6 March 2019.

Babylon writer Martin Stellman told me that the film's production HQ was a church-owned building – Methodist, he thinks – on Creek Road, Deptford, which was also used for the first sound-system scene.

From the Ashes of New Cross was a three-part series about the New Cross Fire on BBC Radio 4, broadcast on 26 October 2020. https://www.bbc.co.uk/programmes/m000nv68.

Other racist attacks had happened before, repeatedly, without anyone ever being charged . . . This is discussed in Elizabeth M. Williams's book *The Politics of Race in Britain and South Africa: Black British Solidarity and the*

Anti-Apartheid Struggle (Bloomsbury, 2015), p. 132. It is also discussed in the Lewisham 77 blog, in a post titled 'Racism and Resistance in South-East London: A Chronology', 26 July 2007.

The detail about the Waterloo Action Centre comes from a conversation with WAC trustee Jenny Stiles.

The local Moonshot youth club, which regularly housed dances, had been gutted in a firebomb attack . . . Reported on the Transpontine blog: http://transpont.blogspot.com/2011/01/new-cross-fire-bleakest-moment.html.

Column 88 had claimed responsibility . . . *Time Out*, 22–28 September 1978, pp. 16–18.

The National Front argued in their manifesto . . . Quoted in Worley, M. and Copsey, N., 'White Youth: The Far Right, Punk and British Youth Culture', *JOMEC Journal*, 9 (2016), pp. 27–47.

Margaret Thatcher spoke about the country being 'swamped' in a 1978 TV interview for *World in Action*.

I was able to piece together information about the Battle of Lewisham largely because Les Back generously gave me access to his collection of archive material. Goldsmiths University created a standalone archive of material relating to the events, including podcasts: https://www.gold.ac.uk/history/research/battle-of-lewisham/.

Aug 13: What Happened? directed by John White (Albany Video Productions, 1977). The film was made by editor/producer John White, with Mary Sheridan and Nick Fry on camera, and Pete Anderson producing: http://www.the-lcva.co.uk/videos/599c1e80201c4e2196cb18a5. Originally distributed on VHS to anti-racist groups in Deptford in the 1970s and early 1980s, the film was considered lost, until it was discovered in the archive of production company Spectacle. Detail on the route comes from the Albany video, at 18 mins, in which the speaker at a pre-march press conference shows the original route on a map. At 08:45 mins the narrator states that at the National Front's press conference before the march Front leader Martin Webster said, 'We intend to destroy race relations here': https://www.youtube.com/watch?v=3t0ujrSM2pE.

Lewisham Council asked the home secretary to intervene . . . This and the following details come from the Goldsmiths University history of events: https://www.gold.ac.uk/history/research/battle-of-lewisham/what-was-the-battle-of-lewisham/.

In his affidavit to the court, Ronald Pepper, deputy leader of Lewisham Council, wrote: 'The applicants are most concerned that the marches planned for August 13th are a danger to the people of the borough and that they will cause incitement to racial hatred and discrimination.' Chief of police David McNee responded, in his affidavit: 'Having considered all the circumstances I have no reasonable grounds for

Notes and References

apprehending that either of the processions will occasion serious public disorder . . . and I am satisfied that the police are able to maintain control of the situation and prevent any serious disorder occurring.' After hearing evidence for four hours, Judge Slynn dismissed the council's case.

Nicholas Roe, Christopher House and Richard Holliday, 'Police Besieged in Clash Over "Front": 111 Hurt, 214 Held', *Sunday Telegraph*, 14 August 1977, p. 1.

The demonstration at Ladywell Fields is covered in the Albany video from 10:05 mins and in this retrospective interview: James Rippingale, 'Lewisham, London 1977, Notes on Fighting Fascism: Balwinder Singh Rana, a 71-year-old anti-fascist, recalls the day he and thousands of others took on the National Front', Al Jazeera.com, 24 November 2018. The extraordinary mid-protest meeting between Lewisham's mayor and the chief of police appears at 21:22 in the Albany video.

The detail about music and dancing in the early stages of the protest comes from a Goldsmiths University podcast which features interviews with people who were there. Producer Kenya Scarlett talked to photographers Paul Trevor and Syd Shelton, and to Dr William 'Lez' Henry. Kenya Scarlett, 'The Battle of Lewisham: The Clashes', New X Change podcast, 2017.

Cameraworks, issue 8, p. 15, picture caption reads: 'New Cross Road. Anti-racists meeting before NF march.' John Tyndall's speech after the march was printed in full, including crowd responses, in *Cameraworks*, ibid, p. 6.

There is footage of the National Front gathering on Achilles Street in the Albany video, from which I took the detail about placards and banners.

There is only a fortnight to go to the West Indian carnival in Notting Hill . . .' John Smalldon and David Rosenberg, 'Why the Extremists Are on the March', *Sunday Telegraph*, 14 August 1977, p. 15.

Roger Godsiff's age is included in Robin Lustig's coverage of events in the *Observer*, 'Lewisham Counts the Cost', 21 August 1977, p. 3. The *Observer* reported at the time that the Met brought in 4,000 police to Lewisham. Ian Mather, Charles Glass and Kevin O'Lone, *Observer*, 14 August 1977, p. 1.

The National Front were escorted by the police to special trains . . . Euan O'Byrne Mulligan, 'Battle of Lewisham: 43 Years Since National Front Marched', *News Shopper*, 12 August 2020.

'A *short tribal dance . . . a secret arrangement' between police and the Front . . .* Will Ellsworth-Jones, John Ball and Michael Bilton, '214 Seized, 110 Hurt in Clashes at Front March', *Sunday Times*, 14 August 1977, p. 1.

Deep Roots, Channel 4, broadcast 2 November 1982, narrated by Mikey Dread. Episode one was titled 'Rebellion'.

Notes and References

Smiley Culture, 'Cockney Translation' and 'Police Officer', both released in 1984 on Fashion Records. There is a brilliant Fashion Records compilation on Soul Jazz titled *Style & Fashion: A-Class Top Notch Hi Fi Sounds in Fine Style* (2019).

David Allen Green wrote a blog post on Smiley Culture's death, ten years after the events, in 2021. 'The life and death of Smiley Culture, who died ten years ago this month during a police raid', Davidallengreen.com, 31 March 2021.

'Reggae Star Stabbed Himself in the Heart', *Daily Mail*, 17 March 2011.

'Smiley Culture Died from Single Stab Wound to Heart . . .' Amelia Hill, *Guardian*, 17 March 2011.

'Police Witness Tells Court He Left Musician Alone with Another Officer', Jermaine Haughton, *The Voice*, 17 June 2013.

'Impossible to Tell if Smiley Culture Stabbed Himself', Jermaine Haughton, *The Voice*, 25 June 2013.

The jury could not reach a unanimous decision . . . Leslie Thomas, QC, the barrister representing the Emmanuel family, on the Smiley Culture verdict: 'Smiley Culture Inquest Jury Return Suicide Verdict', Garden Court Chambers blog, 3 July 2013. The inquest jury decision is available on the Garden Court Chambers website: https://bit.ly/3U1zDbV.

The coroner requested that the full report not be made public or shared with Emmanuel's family . . . 'The Independent Police Complaints Commission (IPCC) conducted an investigation into Emmanuel's death. The summary of their final report – the coroner has asked that the full report is not made public or shared with Emmanuel's family – condemns the raid as significantly flawed and compels the Metropolitan Police Service to overhaul the way they plan and execute future drug seizures.' Amelia Hill, 'Smiley Culture Death – No Charges', *Guardian*, 29 November 2011.

'About a thousand' people attended the Justice for Smiley march . . . bbc.co.uk, 16 April 2011. https://www.bbc.co.uk/news/uk-england-surrey-13104094.

Additional detail on the Justice for Smiley march regarding the sound-system operation was obtained from Justin Boreland.

Street Beat was Marky B's management/record company. He used to manage the More Fire Crew of 'Oi' fame, who also appear in this book, performing at a private girls' school in Chislehurst.

William H. McNeill, *Keeping Together in Time: Dance and Drill in Human History* (Harvard University Press, 1995), pp. 4–5; p. 13; p. 42; p. 152.

PART TWO
5: Up the Youth Club

Unemployment for men averaged at 15.7 per cent in 1984 . . . John Salt, 'The Geography of Unemployment in the United Kingdom in the 1980s', *Espace, Populations, Sociétés*, 1985, issue 2, pp. 350–2.

20,000 schools were affected . . . Mike Baker, bbc.co.uk, 25 April 2008.

Resistance through the medium of working to rule . . . Kate Loveys, 'It's Back to the 1980s as Nativity Plays Are Threatened by Teachers' Work to Rule', *Daily Mail* Online, 17 November 2011.

Racism and discrimination impacted everyday life . . . The Swann Report, *Education for All: The Report of the Committee of Inquiry into the Education of Children from Ethnic Minority Groups*, March 1985 (Her Majesty's Stationery Office), p. xxi.

Statistical chances of being considered intelligent . . . Bernard Coard, 'Why I Wrote the *ESN Book*', *Guardian*, 5 February 2005.

Of being considered for jobs . . . Yaojun Li, 'Ethnic Unemployment in Britain, 1972–2012', ibid.

experienced a police force, not a police service . . . This remains unchanged: 'Based on self-defined ethnicity, individuals from a Black or Black British background were searched at a rate 7.0 times higher than that of those from a White ethnic group.' Home Office national statistics, 'Police Powers and Procedures: Stop and Search and Arrests, England and Wales, Year Ending 31 March 2021', www.gov.uk.

'Obituary: Diana, Countess of Albemarle: Chair of the Influential *Albemarle Report* Which Led to the Expansion and Professionalisation of Youth Work in Britain in the Sixties', *The Times*, 15 July 2013.

Becoming the chair of the Women's Institute, and later joining various royal commissions . . . Michael Pollitt, 'The Dowager Countess of Albemarle DBE: Devoted to Serving Norfolk and the Country', *Eastern Daily Press*, 14 May 2013.

Chairing committees as an art form . . . She told *The Times* in 1959, 'You know, I can come home one day and feel: "I've done a good committee," rather as a conductor might feel at the end of a concert. A chairman needs to develop some sort of antennae, which can sense what members have to contribute to the meeting. This is really more important than knowledge.' *The Times*, 15 July 2013.

The report directly referenced dancing . . . The Albermarle Report, *The Youth Service in England and Wales: Report of the Committee Appointed by the Minister of Education in November, 1958* (Her Majesty's Stationery Office, 1960), paragraph 196.

Specially designed youth centres . . . The Albermarle Report, ibid, paragraph 229.

Notes and References

Within hours of publication, the Conservative government accepted almost all the main recommendations . . . Michael Pollitt, *Eastern Daily Press*, ibid.

The government allocated £23 million . . . Bernard Davies, *From Voluntaryism to Welfare State: A History of the Youth Service in England, Volume 1, 1939–1979* (Youth Work Press, 1999), p. 61.

Bernard Davies was kind enough to send me *The Fairbairn–Milson Report* (*Youth and Community Work in the 1970s*, HMSO, 1969, paragraph 24), which states that for the period April 1960 to March 1968 starts were made on building work totalling £28 million, covering over 3,000 projects, and in the same period 160 youth sports projects totalling £2.4 million of building works.

10cc's Graham Gouldman, Kevin Godley and Lol Creme were friends who used to rehearse at Jewish Lads Brigade in north Manchester. 'Heirs to the Beatles: 10cc', *Jewish Chronicle*, 27 December 2012.

'Youth work, like any form of people-work . . . Bernard Davies, 'Part-Time Youth Work in an Industrial Community' (National Youth Agency, 1976).

Maltby Youth Centre . . . F. Ralph Bozeat, 'Buildings for Social Education', from *Youth Service Buildings*, 1 December 1967, pp. 883–5, via Bernard Davies.

Withywood Centre in Bristol . . . 'A Blueprint Comes to Life: Model Youth Club at Bristol', *Times Educational Supplement*, 23 August 1963.

'Original youth work' . . . 'Obituary. Diana, Countess of Albemarle', *The Times*, ibid.

Detail on Sheffield youth clubs in 1974: City of Sheffield archive, LD2230 (2-42), pp. 41–2.

The Greater Manchester Youth Association (GMYA) annual report from 1980 showed 250 affiliate clubs . . . City of Sheffield archive, Greater Manchester Youth Association Annual Report 1979-80. 522/G9/3.

Cheshire and Wirral had 130 boys' clubs and youth clubs . . . City of Sheffield archive, SASY/YASY County Co-ordinating Committee 522/G9/3

The Lincolnshire Association of Youth Clubs reported in July 1981 the official opening of a new disco . . . City of Sheffield archive, Lincolnshire Association LINKS newsletter 522/G9/3.

The National Association of Youth Clubs ran a disco-dancing competition . . . City of Sheffield archive, 522/G10/16.

Greater Manchester entered 65 teams in 1978 and 1979 . . . City of Sheffield archive, Greater Manchester Youth Association Annual Report 1979–80. 522/G9/3.

Detail about Barnsley, Rotherham and Doncaster youth clubs in 1983: City of Sheffield archive, 522/G9/4 Introduction, 1.3. The report noting detail about interest in discos, p. 9.

Rowlinson Youth Club contract, courtesy of Sheffield City Archives EDN

·1038/CA514 (101). The section describing what was inside comes from Winston Hazel.

Hurlfield architect drawings and detail. Courtesy of Sheffield City Archive. CA514 (122). It was designed by city planning officer and architect, Bernard Warren (no relation).

A SMAC-19 t-shirt was exhibited at the Manchester Hip Hop Archive exhibition, Central Library, Manchester, 1 July–28 September 2021.

I interviewed Winston Hazel alongside Radio 1's Toddla T and bassline don DJQ for a panel about the Steel City sound for Red Bull Music Academy, 9 November 2017.

The story of DJ Kool Herc is well documented, including on his website, djkoolherc.com.

They nurtured the early forward motion of grime . . . James Keith, 'The Last of a Dying Breed: London's Youth Clubs', *Trench* magazine, 22 November 2017.

29 per cent of the UK's 10-to-15-year-olds were still using a youth club . . . *National Council for Voluntary Youth Services Youth Report, 2013*. There's a good outline of youth-service devastation under the early years of the Conservative (coalition, initially) government: 'Mid-2014: The Wider Youth Work Context' by Storytelling in Youth Work (story-tellinginyouthwork.com.) See also: *Out of Service: A Report Examining Local Authority Expenditure on Youth Services in England & Wales* (YMCA, January 2020); for more on youth provision and serious youth violence: *Securing a Brighter Future: The Role of Youth Services in Tackling Knife Crime*, a report by the All-Party Parliamentary Group on Knife Crime and Violence Reduction, March 2020.

In 2010 there were an estimated 2,150 nightclubs in the UK . . . *Nightclubs, Leisure Intelligence*, December 2010 (Mintel report), p. 38.

JFM also offered community news . . . John Hind and Stephen Mosco, *Rebel Radio: The Full Story of British Pirate Radio* (Pluto Press, 1985), pp. 29–32.

Located next to Orpington train station, the Civic . . . Confusingly, this wasn't the only under-18s event taking place in the building. Olympic champion and TV star Brian Jacks ran discos in a hall he rented when he wasn't running his highly successful judo club, and DJs Scott Ralph and Andy Smith ran Sunday sessions and Thursday nights at the Norman Hall. Ralph told me that club owner George Cooper (who ran Happy Jacks in London Bridge) was involved. There were sister nights to the Civic happening in Chislehurst Caves and Crook Log in Bexleyheath. There had been regular mod nights at the Civic run by Radio Caroline, and David Bowie played his first gig with The Konrads there in September 1963.

The founders of St Anne's moved to Orpington from Bermondsey when the church found cheap land on which to build an orphanage, convent and the primary school I later attended. The 'family-style' group homes that Peter Thomas/Solar Angel lived in were built in the 1950s and 1960s and replaced the main orphanage. There's a short history of St Anne's written by nuns still in residence at the convent in 1994, including some who were teaching when I was at school. https://docplayer.net/21144822-An-outline-of-the-history-of-st-anne-s-convent-orpington.html.

Joseph Henrich quoted in Alun Anderson, 'Time to Rethink What Makes Humans Special', *New Scientist*, 9 December 2015.

The Sun *newspaper was writing* . . . Garry Bushell and Rick Sky, *Sun*, 12 October 1988, p. 15.

6: Slow Dance at the School Disco

'Headmistress Jailed for Theft' *Evening Standard*, 31 August 2003.

'The Grange Hill *generation'* . . . Phrase courtesy of Steven Hall, who ran Junior Boy's Own in the 1990s, from a social media post I made trying to find out when school discos started.

Two sixth-formers at John Rigby ran a mobile disco called R&B Groovin' . . . Out to Rodney and Bruce.

Many popular pre-19th-century European dances . . . John Playford's *English Dancing Master* was published in 1651. It contained 104 partner-dances, each presented with its own music. See Barbara Sparti (editor and translator), *On the Practice or Art of Dancing* (Oxford University Press, 1993), p. 58.

Caribbean quadrilles . . . In 2013 Beverley Bogle ran a project with Goldsmiths University titled *Quadrille: Exploring Cultural Dance*. Her Januka company dance and teach camp and ballroom-style quadrilles. See also Dr Tola Dabiri, 'Follow the Signs – The Quadrille, Intangible Heritage and the Caribbean Carnival', on Leeds Beckett University's Caribbean Carnival Cultures website, 2019.

New variants of the polka and the waltz arrived . . . Theresa Buckland, 'Dancing Out of Time: The Forgotten Boston of Edwardian England', in *Bodies of Sound: Studies Across Popular Music and Dance*, edited by Susan C. Cook and Sherril Dodds (Routledge, 2013), p. 57. *Transmitted by travelling orchestras playing new compositions in theatres* . . . Theresa Buckland, ibid, p. 61; *'A lounging closeness'* . . . Theresa Buckland, ibid, p. 67; *In which it was 'treason to talk'* . . . Theresa Buckland, ibid, p. 78; Elizabeth Hyatt-Woolf emphasised the self-expression that was possible when dancing the Boston: 'the modern fashion of dreaming the music' in 'Passing of the Waltz', *The Dance Journal*, March 1910, p. 5, quoted in Theresa Buckland, ibid, p. 72; *Sprung dancefloors began emerging* . . .

Theresa Buckland, ibid, p. 69; *Light classical composers often doubled up as conductors of dance orchestras* . . . Theresa Buckland, ibid, p. 62.

Travis Elborough, *A Walk in the Park: The Life and Times of a People's Institution* (Jonathan Cape, 2016), p. 225.

Mecca Ballrooms created novelty dances . . . James Nott, *Going to the Palais*, ibid, p. 112. And, on the Lindyhop becoming the Jitterbug and later, the Jive, see James Nott, ibid, p. 119.

A wave of pop productions arrived with simple, collective dance crazes baked in . . . Richard Powers, 'Teen Dances of the 1950s', Stanford.edu.

For more on the 'decline' of dance, see *Everything We Loved About Dance Was Taken*, report by One Dance UK, 2021.

A few wonderful schools have embedded dance into the curriculum . . . including Thomas Tallis, in south-east London.

Bonnie's appeared on Lewisham Council's 2017 list of pubs in the borough, at 28–30 Bromley Hill. In the late 1980s it was a south London acid-house stop-off, linked to the Downham Tavern and DJ Tony Wilson (no connection to the Factory Records founder) and his Fascinations events. It is not to be confused with another local high-street disco called Bon-Bonnies, or Bonnie's in Lower Sydenham, which was at 241 Southend Lane, SE6 4DD, which is the same postcode as the Saxon Tavern, previously the King Alfred pub, which held mod nights, jazz-funk nights and is now a Lidl, and which Janice identified as a place where she'd go to reggae dances.

The Harbour Lights survived until 2016, when it was turned into flats. Torpoint City Council considered the planning application and noted their support in the minutes: 'Members support the application as it is in sympathy with the Vision for Torpoint . . . it opens up the waterfront and improves the aesthetics of the area.' https://www.torpointtowncouncil.gov.uk/data/uploads/902.pdf.

Butlin's in Filey, Yorkshire, had been built with two large dance spaces . . . James Nott, ibid, p. 78.

An episode of the London Weekend Television programme Twentieth Century Box . . . 'Jazz Funk', broadcast 1980, and online via soul-source.co.uk.

'We Are the Ovaltineys' . . . The British Film Institute has the original *Meet the Ovaltineys* advert on the BFI Player.

7: Jackin' in the Gymnasium

House-music artists on the weekly BBC chart run-down Top of the Pops . . . Farley 'Jackmaster' Funk and Jesse Saunders's 1986 playground-famous *Top of the Pops* performance of 'Love Can't Turn Around' featuring Daryl Pandy is readily available on YouTube.

Notes and References

Jazzy M's LWR show *The Jackin' Zone* linked to Rob Olson's *Jack Beat* show in Chicago each week. Leo Zero, *Faith Magazine, Got the Bug*, vol. 3, no. 1, autumn 2020.

It's now global, and big enough to be celebrated . . . House music is also a deep and rich international music genre: Dan Schawbel, 'House Music Has Become a Global Phenomenon', *Forbes*, 9 March 2012.

There were high-school dances at other schools in Chicago – for example, De La Salle student senate presented 'De Is the Key, Part II' on 18 January 1985 in the main gym, featuring Steve 'J. M. Silk' Hurley of WBMX, with the party running from 7.30 p.m. till 11 p.m. *Beyond Heaven: Chicago House Party Flyers from 1983–1989* (Almighty & Insane Books, 2018).

Most famously in an intensely rough-and-ready club called the Warehouse . . . House innovator Jesse Saunders described the Warehouse as having a capacity of 150 to 200 people in the unreleased documentary *All We Wanna Do Is Dance* (directed by Gordon Mason). https://greenlit.com/project/all-we-wanna-do-dance.

There is an official history of Mendel High online: https://mendelchs.org/history/.

Hot Mix 5 DJs, who reached a million listeners a week . . . This fact appears in the introduction to *Beyond Heaven: Chicago House Party Flyers* . . . ibid.

Diana T. Slaughter-Defoe and Deborah J. Johnson (eds), *Visible Now: Blacks in Private Schools* (Greenwood Press, 1988), p. 46.

The detail about average tuition and fees comes from John J. Augenstein, *National Catholic Schools and their Finances, 1986*, National Catholic Educational Association, p. 27, Appendix A, under the 'finances' section. Mendel appears by name in Appendix H.

Mendel had a falling roll, according to a *Chicago Tribune* story about another school, a decade later. Flynn McRoberts, 'St Martin High Closing Its Doors', *Chicago Tribune*, 11 April 1997.

The Chicago Black Social Culture Map is put together by Honey Pot Productions and covers Chicago's Black social culture across the 20th century, from the First Great Migration through the birth of house music. Their growing archive includes information on social venues (featuring basic geo-spatial information), first-person stories and other media, all collected through collaborative community research. 'Drawing from blues, gospel, disco, and funk as well as dances such as bopping, stepping, and line dances, the archive explores an evolving embodied lineage of African American forms of making community and of cultural resistance.' https://www.honeypotperformance.org/about-the-cbscm.

She came up with 'Joining Academics with Music', or J.A.M., motivating listeners to get better grades . . . Phyllis Magida, 'Good-Grades Club to Hold a Dance Party', *Chicago Tribune*, 18 April 1986.

Notes and References

Describing the networks of spaces that schooled young dancers as 'stair steps' . . . Micah E. Salkind, *Do You Remember House?: Chicago's Queer of Color Undergrounds* (Oxford University Press, 2019), p. 93.

Channel 7's *Eyewitness News* footage is on YouTube: https://www.youtube.com/watch?v=O17kvAwh554.

In 1985 the House-O-Matics dance group, home to many pioneering dancers and DJs-to-be, was formed by Ronnie Sloan. They'd battle the likes of U Phi U and House Arrest 2 at local venues like the Warehouse and the Boys and Girls Club. Dave Quam, 'Battle Cats: From the Rise of House in the '80s to Today's Juke and Footwork Scenes, Chicago's Circle Keeps Expanding', XLR8R, 8 September 2010. Chicago's Twilite Tone discussed his dance crew Dem Dare on my Worldwide FM radio show, 9 October 2020.

Jose 'Gringo' Echevarria, *The Real Dance Fever, Book One: The Beginning* (Jose Echevarria, 2014), p. 173.

Barry Walters, 'Burning Down the House', *Spin* magazine, November 1986.

The Jackmaster Dick YouTube video which @DavidB's commented on: https://www.youtube.com/watch?v=os9kFpqw1uc.

In 1986 a graph showing HIV diagnoses in the city was only a small way up a steep line. By 1988 3,748 Chicago men and women . . . Overview of HIV Disease in Illinois, Department of Public Health, 2014.

The jack appears to be unpartnered, a 'stripped-down social dance' . . . Most of the quotes come from my interview with Dr McNeal, but I came across her work – and this phrase – in a 2014 interview, conducted by Micah E. Salkind for his book *Do You Remember House?* and hosted on the Columbia College Chicago's Digital Commons library. McNeal's work 'Navigating the Cultural Marketplace: Negotiating the Folk in Trinidadian Performance' appeared in *Latin American and Caribbean Ethnic Studies, Volume 8* (Routledge, 2013).

8: Smoke and Strobes

Started life as a large wine cellar for the hotel above . . . Heaven's website also describes its pre-history as a 'rundown rollerdisco called Global Village' and the opening of Heaven in December 1979 by Jeremy Norman. It also describes the purchase in 2013 of Heaven by G-A-Y founder Jeremy Joseph. There's more info here: http://cinematreasures.org/theaters/19908.

In April 1988 five Leeds United supporters appeared at Southwark Crown Court . . . 'Mob Chanted "Kill Queers"', *Hayes and Harlington Gazette*, 14 December 1988, p. 1.

Notes and References

The judge directed the jury to find them not guilty . . . 'Not Guilty of Attack', *Hayes and Harlington Gazette*, 28 December 1988, p. 9.

Resident DJ Colin Faver knew how to . . . There's a Colin Faver mix from 1988 titled *Psycho Acid Mix* on YouTube: https://www.youtube.com/watch?v=RnyCEaJYZE4.

'I try to kill people on the dancefloor' . . . Todd Terry on dancefloor destruction in *Jockey Slut*, January/February 1994, pp. 48–9.

William Gibson famously once said that the future's already here, it's just unevenly distributed . . . *The Economist*, 4 December 2003.

'Fiver for a Drug Trip to Heaven in Branson Club', *Sun*, 17 August 1988.

An edition of Time Out *from October 1988 included 70 nightclubs in the listings* . . . *Time Out*, 12–19 October 1988, p. 104. The previous week's issue included 306 spaces in the music-venues listings, 5–12 October 1988, pp. 93–8.

The Astoria, just up Charing Cross Road, was turning away 'up to 1,000 ravers every Friday and Saturday night' . . . *Thames Reports* documentary, directed by Ken Craig, Thames Television, 1989. https://www.youtube.com/watch?v=CZlKciFlpi4.

Trip had spilled out onto the street . . . Dave Swindells, 'Dancefloor Revolution: The Photos That Captured the Birth of UK Rave', *The Red Bulletin*, 12 August 2019.

The Bromley Contingent . . . Danny Rampling mentions Bromley's acid-house contingent five minutes into his Kiss FM show in summer 1988: https://www.youtube.com/watch?v=L_3ZI5UoxJA.

One journalist reported seeing 'thousands of ecstasy wrappers' . . . Robert Kellaway and Simon Hughes, 'Spaced Out!', *Sun*, 26 June 1989.

A policeman was asked for his perspective . . . I remember reading this report at some point between autumn 1988 and when I left home in autumn 1990, but I have not been able to source it. The detail about the policeman's confusion about people dancing alone stayed with me.

Holding or tensing up body parts . . . I first came across this idea of body defences in an MA thesis in the library at the Trinity Laban Conservatoire of Music and Dance: Iris Bräuninger, *Consideration of Children's Held Upper Body Posture as a Reaction to Stressful Events*, MA Dance Movement Therapy, 1993. Dr Bräuninger is now a senior researcher and co-director of the BA Studies in Psychomotor Therapy at Zurich's Interkantonale Hochschule für Heilpädagogik.

Apologies again to Pat Barry and Adam Maddison for the Shoom situation.

The club's flyers stated 'No ruffians!' . . . Matteo Sedazzari, 'When Positive Energy of Madness Met Danny Rampling, November 1989': https://www.linkedin.com/pulse/when-positive-energy-madness-met-danny-rampling-1989-matteo-sedazzari.

Notes and References

It was a 1,100-capacity venue that opened in 1979, with a heavyweight sound system . . . The Warehouse sound system and Greg James are covered in this excellent post by DJ and cultural archivist Greg Wilson: https://www.facebook.com/DJGregWilson/photos/big-thanks-to-dino-wiand-son-of-the-late-mike-wiand-who-opened-the-legendary-lee/10154585078205756/.

Author Bill Brewster also wrote about the Warehouse's history. Bill Brewster, 'Leeds Warehouse', billbrewster.co.uk, 21 December 2017.

One interviewee, Miller the Driller, benefited from a state school that included dance on the curriculum . . . He attended Harehills Middle School, where teacher Nadine Senior showed him that dance was a possibility. Ms Senior went on from her position of deputy headteacher to form the Northern School of Contemporary Dance.

Ian Hylton, quoted in Mark 'Snowboy' Cotgrove, *From Jazz Funk & Fusion to Acid Jazz: The History of the UK Jazz Dance Scene* (AuthorHouse, 2009), p. 115.

Club owner Saad Shaffi runs 24 Kitchen Street in Liverpool and offered a more contemporary perspective on racist door policies, on a panel I did with him. 'The thing about racist door policies,' he said, 'was that you sometimes knew the bouncer and you knew they knew you, but you couldn't put their job at risk by kicking off.' *Save Some Space*, Open Eye Gallery, 13 August 2020: https://www.youtube.com/watch?v=Xl4FGLBi6MI&t=1s.

Including approximately 120,000 young people living in Britain without full citizenship or secured status, 65,000 of whom were born in Britain . . . Aamna Mohdin and Dan Kopf, 'Thousands of Qualified People Can't Get UK Citizenship Because They Can't Afford It', quartz.com, 23 March 2018.

I got chatting to a guy in Liverpool about Voodoo after taking part in an event, La Violetta Società, 28 January 2020, where I was talking about *Make Some Space*. The event is run by the poet known as Roy.

Anna Wood, 'Lines Written a Few Miles Outside Blackburn, on Revisiting the Site of the Sett End Pub, April 10, 2021', from *Parties for the People* (Rough Trade Books, 2022).

There is a clip on the internet . . . *Quadrant Park*: https://www.youtube.com/watch?v=Ui-TaOq2gEU.

Picking notes out of the hot air . . . Youth worker Kev Henman used the phrase 'picking notes out of the air' when I interviewed him about youth clubs, and I have adapted his brilliant phrase in this section.

In December 1990 it was voted the number-one club by the UK's best-selling DJ magazine, Jocks . . . Email correspondence from resident DJ Mike Knowler, who still DJs.

The story of Quadrant Park provides an excellent example of the layered links . . .

Notes and References

The connections were illuminated beautifully by the artist Mark Leckey in his short film *Fiorucci Made Me Hardcore*, 1999.

Musician Reggie Andrews is quoted in Steven L. Isoardi's book about South Central LA, *The Music Finds a Way*, describing the long histories of high-quality music teachers and mentoring in the Black community. He believed he had a responsibility to carry the torch. 'I told myself, "Do I want to be another Herbie Hancock or do I want to create more Herbie Hancocks?" In his own way, Quadrant Park's DJ did the same for the kids in Merseyside who flocked to the club.

9: Northern Dancefloors

Sometimes the collective dance is atomised, in retreat . . . Ollie Plumb, 'An Incomplete List of Clubs in the UK That Shut Down in the 2010s', *Dazed & Confused*, 23 July 2019.

'The Cinderella' of academic dance studies . . . Theresa Buckland, 'Society Dancing: Fashionable Bodies in England, 1870–1920', *Victorian Studies*, vol. 55, no. 3, spring 2013 (Indiana University Press), pp. 531–3.

'Last Orders for Nightclubs' – the Mintel nightclubs UK 2016 report stated that annual admissions for the UK nightclubs industry fell by 23 per cent in the five years between 2010 and 2015, from 149 million to 115 million: https://www.mintel.com/press-centre/leisure/last-orders-for-nightclubs-uk-nightclub-attendance-drops-by-34-million-in-5-years.

Over 200 million admissions to nightclubs in the UK in 1994 . . . Sarah Thornton, *Club Cultures, Music, Media and Subcultural Capital* (Polity, 1995), p. 32. Another piece of research by economists at the Henley Centre for Forecasting claimed over 50 million attendances a year in 1993 at 'rave events' in the UK. Sarah Thornton, ibid, p. 31.

There were only 35.7 million people aged between 16 and 64, according to the 1991 census . . . StatsWales, national level population estimates by year, age and UK country.

Gina Yashere, *Cack-Handed* (HarperCollins, 2021), p. 180.

Sheffield University, which had provided dancing spaces . . . Funding resources per student per degree entered decline in 1990, according to the Institute for Fiscal Studies. Chris Belfield, Jack Britton, Lorraine Dearden and Laura van der Erve, *Higher Education Funding in England: Past, Present and Options for the Future* (IFS, 2017), p. 27.

'Britain's first rave dance agency' . . . Helen Mead, 'Work It!', *i-D*, February 1992, p. 56.

Matthew Collin on Greater Manchester Police taking clubs to court, from 'Club Column', *i-D*, June 1990, p. 79.

Notes and References

Yakub Qureshi, 'Revealed: Secret Documents Show Margaret Thatcher Helped Save Manchester Police Chief Sir James Anderton After Row Over AIDS Comments', *Manchester Evening News*, 4 January 2012.

Gil Scott-Heron, '"B" Movie' (Arista, 1981).

Speed or whizz, as it was often described . . . Elsa Sharp, 'Are You Ready for the Rush Hour?' *Independent*, 17 October 1994.

The demolition of Hulme began in 1991. 'Hulme/Manchester', the Academy of Urbanism, 18 November 2015.

The PSV had a pre-history in the shape of the Russell Club . . . Murph, *Red News* (Manchester United fanzine), issue 233. The detail about the cricket club and Sore Foot Sam's Caribbean restaurant comes from the comments on the online version of the article: https://www.manutdfansblog.com/raving-rolling-russell-club/.

There's an interview with the PSV founder's daughter and niece Jackie McNeish in the MDMA Archive: https://www.mdmarchive.co.uk/artefact/8729/PSV_CLUB_VIDEO_2011.

More detail on PSV: Seamus Quinn, 'Saturday Night Sunday Morning: Manchester's Techno Blues Club', *Mixmag*, April 1992; listings detail on the DJs and club nights at PSV: Nayaba Aghedo, *City Life*, 16 August–13 September 1990, pp. 25–8.

John Cage once said that utopia was a multiplicity of individuals who have the habit of respecting one another . . . Alex Ross, 'Beyond Delta: The Many Streams of Björk', *Bjork: Archives* (Thames and Hudson, 2015), p. 32. Ross is quoting Joan Retallack, *Musicage: Cage Muses on Words, Art, Music* (Wesleyan University Press, 1996), p. 293.

Daft Punk, *Muzik*, February 1997, p. 54. I also interviewed Daft Punk for *The Face* as DJs of the month, February 1997, p. 127.

Drum 'n' bass DJ Marcus Intalex . . . Marcus was a lovely guy who supported many other artists. He died in 2017, and the Marcus Intalex Music Foundation was set up in his name 'to nurture and guide music talent'.

The Ford Piquette Avenue plant was modelled . . . Jim Volgarino, 'The Building of Legend', Journal.ClassicCars.com, 22 September 2018.

Vron Ware and Les Back, *Out of Whiteness: Color, Politics and Culture* (University of Chicago Press, 2002), p. 306.

The Morris Federation explain their decision about blackface on their website FAQs: www.morrisfed.org.uk.

10: Phenomenal Basslines

East Londoners Shut Up and Dance, a couple of professional contemporary dancers . . . Brian Belle-Fortune, *All Crews: Journeys Through Jungle/Drum & Bass Culture* (Vision Publishing, 2004), p. 13.

Notes and References

High-ranking DJ Fabio was a dancer . . . Bill Brewster and Frank
Broughton, 'Musical Outlaw Fabio on the Birth of Rage and the Jungle
Sound', Red Bull Music Academy, 28 June 2016.

Phenomenon One was co-promoted by Nadine Andrews, who was
involved with many nights at the Haçienda and also worked for
Rob Gretton's Rob's Records. Devon is convinced that there were
two separate Phenomenon One nights at the club, but other people
thought there was only one. The YouTube recordings online are
labelled variously 1995, 1996 and 1997. My friend Ed is convinced we
went in 1996. It's proved impossible to be 100 per cent sure. Devon
asked me to note that DJ Dexterous and MC Rudeboy Keith, aka King
of the Jungle, did live PAs at Phenomenon One on 3 May 1995. The
flyer reads: 'It's time to experience the largest jungle flava Manchester
has ever seen . . . calling all conscious junglists.' Tickets were £10, and
the line-up in the main room included Grooverider, Jumpin Jack Frost,
Devious Devon and Bryan Gee, with MCs Navigator, 5–0, Crystallise,
Goodfella and special guest Baron Turbo Charge. Devon says that
Dillinja was booked for a PA but couldn't make it.

Edith Van Dyck, *The Impact of the Bass Drum on Human Movement*, Music
Perception (2013), pp. 349–59.

Underground Inna Moss Side, 1996. I contacted approximately 40
individuals, organisations and archives, including Salford University,
Channel M and Granada TV, to try to find out who made this. The
furthest I got was that it was made by someone called Derek. If you
know more, please let me know.

Alice Walker, *Hard Times Require Furious Dancing: New Poems* (New World
Library, 2010). Introduction, p. xvi, with kind permission from the
author and publishers.

*[A Guy Called Gerald] as writer, had a major role in 808 State's top-ten hit
'Pacific State'* . . . There were legal proceedings on this matter almost
immediately. *NME*, 2 December 1989, p. 3.

Rage: The Club that Inspired a Generation, directed by Karma London and
Paul Mortimore, 2019.

*Producer Lennie De Ice left a comment on a YouTube video of his 1991 tune 'We
Are I.E.'* . . . Luke Kessler, 'Classic Track: "We Are I.E.", DnB Dojo, 11
June 2020.

ST Holdings remember releasing about 'ten drum 'n' bass tracks a week . . .'
Detail via Indi 'Mantra' Khera, who contacted Chris from ST Holdings
on my behalf.

Robert Kazandjian, 'Edmonton, Jungle, Roller Skates and Me', *Trench*
magazine, 28 April 2020.

The LTJ Bukem feature appeared in *Jockey Slut*, October/November
1996.

Notes and References

Vision Publishing was started by *Knowledge Magazine* editor Colin Steven. It is now called Velocity Publishing and releases brilliant books, including the reissue of Brian Belle-Fortune's *All Crews*.

Mid-nineties pressure created deep seams of music . . . And deep culture, currently being protected and amplified by equality group EQ50 and archivists the Black Junglist Alliance.

The longest-running event worldwide, though, is DnB Tuesdays in Seattle . . . Dave Jenkins, 'The Story of the World's Longest Running Drum 'n' Bass Weekly', 5 November 2019, UKF.com.

825 million views of 'drum and bass dance' on TikTok as of August 2022: https://www.tiktok.com/discover/drum-and-bass-dance?lang=en.

The quotes about dancing styles, MC Det and Sting from Telepathy: Brian Belle-Fortune, *All Crews*, ibid, p. 97.

11: Household Bopping

Beatrix Bánkyné Perjés, 'Does Dancing Have a Beneficial Effect on the Fetus?', 25 February 2020, University of Peés. There is a video of her describing her work online: https://www.youtube.com/watch?v=eG-nndxPiCc.

Elizabeth Manejias, 'Pregnancy in Dance', Dance USA's Task Force on Dancer Health, 2020.

Exercise while pregnant, including dance, is considered broadly safe and beneficial . . . Jennifer Stahl, 'So You're Pregnant. Here's How to Keep Dancing Safely', *Dance Magazine*, 6 February 2020.

It is advisable to avoid very loud environments . . . 'Noise – Reproductive Health', The National Institute for Occupational Safety and Health (28 October 2019; updated 2 June 2022). https://www.cdc.gov/niosh/topics/repro/noise.html.

Moving to music during the first stage of labour . . . Caroline P. Toberna, Drew Horter, Kayla Heslin, Marie M. Forgie, Emily Malloy and Jessica J. F. Kram, 'Dancing During Labor: Social Media Trend or Future Practice?', *Journal of Patient Centred Research and Reviews*, 7, vol. 2 (spring 2020), pp. 213–17.

Morocco (C. Varga Dinicu), *You Asked Aunt Rocky: Answers & Advice About Raqs Sharqi and Raqs Shaabi* (Hypatia-Rose Press, 2013), p. 128.

Maxine Leeds Craig, *Sorry I Don't Dance*, ibid, p. 153.

Björk spoke about dancing with friends and family when I interviewed her for the Red Bull Music Academy, 25 September 2017. There is a transcript available: https://daily.redbullmusicacademy.com/2017/09/bjork-couch-wisdom.

I took part in two events at Berlin's CTM music festival in January 2020.

I moderated a panel on creating solidarity between musicians and
journalists and ran a 'Document Your Culture' workshop.

Lucy: My Transgender Life, directed by Melinte Reitzema (Cour Films, 2016).

Baltimore, August 2017 . . . I was in the city for the Red Bull Amaphiko
academy programme, working with grass-roots social innovators.

The Baltimore Ceasefire Weekend . . . This is an incredible idea, turned into a
powerful reality by committed individuals and communities, and which
deserves to be celebrated worldwide: www.baltimoreceasefire.com.

Dark City Beneath the Beat, directed by TT the Artist (Netflix, 2020).

Rob Nixon, *Slow Violence and the Environmentalism of the Poor* (Harvard
University Press, 2011).

The LA-born style of krump . . . I can recommend the documentary *Rize*
(dir. David LaChapelle, 2005) about Tommy the Clown and how he
invented krump as a dance style designed for kids' birthday parties in
South Central LA.

'The most influential party in history' . . . Piotr Orlov, 'Still Saving the
Day: The Most Influential Party in History Turns 50', NPR.com, 19
February 2020. Lucky Cloud was founded by Colleen Murphy, Tim
Lawrence, Jeremy Gilbert and David Mancuso.

Rachael Smart's viral tweet was reported in the *indy100*. Sinead Butler
wrote that former tap-dancer Smart responded with 'triple time steps':
'Woman's Beautiful Story About Grandfather Dying Goes Viral', 13
April 2021.

12: Searching for the Perfect Nightclub

Loyola College Class of 1980: www.lciclassof1980.com.

The building had been constructed in 1912 . . . Andrew Saint, *Survey of
London, Volume 53: Oxford Street* (Paul Mellon Centre for Studies in
British Art, 2020).

whose wife Lily was a campaigning suffragette . . . Lucy Handscomb,
Riverview Gardens History, 6 September 2014: https://riverviewgardens.
wordpress.com/2014/09/06/the-architect-delissa-joseph/. '. . . *well-
known for her musical voice* . . .': https://www.benuricollection.org.uk/
intermediate.php?artistid=36.

Fitzroy Facey, *The Soul Survivors* magazine, issue 90, February–March
2021, pp. 3–28. The detail about Sylma Laviniere and Lee Wickins
comes from issue 97, April–May 2022, p. 6.

I recommend this interview with Paul 'Trouble' Anderson, Terry Farley
and Roual Galloway on early-1980s dancers in London: 'The Dancers
in Their Own Words', the Daily Note, Red Bull Music Academy, 17
September 2015.

Notes and References

Travis Edwards made music in the rave era under the name Satin Storm, according to the comments on Simon Reynolds's blog. I bought myself a copy of his 12-inch 'Kick Up a Sound Boy' after hearing it here: http://energyflashbysimonreynolds.blogspot.com/2019/12/knickerless-parsons.html.

The always-reliable Red Bull Music Academy Daily (respect to Todd and Aaron) published a long read on Crackers. Stephen Titmus, 'Nightclubbing: Crackers', 11 March 2013.

Trevor Shakes's support slot consisted of a 45-minute solo dance performance, according to Fitzroy Facey. There is a small photograph of Trevor with one arm raised, dancing down a staircase, in *Smash Hits*. The caption reads: 'Support act Trevor does his stuff as the "no dancing" announcement is made.' Peter Martin, 'Wham! in China: The Full Story', *Smash Hits*, 8–21 May 1985.

Dez Parkes was interviewed by Carlos Guzman, 'Mr Black Music: Undiluted Soul', 6 November 2020, Soulradiouk.net.

'If Spats was the hip-hop Hadron Collider . . .' The post comes from the anonymous Bboyslippers.wordpress.com. and includes video from the club taken by Derek Jewell: www.bboyslippers.wordpress.com/they-reminisce/they-reminisce-1.

A positive attitude towards nightlife in the early 1990s . . . 'The concept of the "night-time" economy, understood here as a policy initiative articulated with urban regeneration, arose in the early 1990s in the United Kingdom. It was initially conveyed as a strategy for socio-economic revitalisation of central areas of cities affected by deindustrialisation in the 1970s and 1980s, continued suburbanisation that had occurred over the post-war period and the dramatic shift of retail to peripheral sites.' Jordi Nofre and Adam Eldridge (eds), *Exploring Nightlife: Space, Society and Governance* (Rowman & Littlefield, 2018), p. 165.

Artists were the 'shock troops' of gentrification . . . Grayson Perry, Reith Lecture 2013.

The Licensing Act of 2003 . . . Dr Lesley Mackay, *VivaCity 2020: Sheffield and Its Late Night Economy*, October 2005 (VivaCity report, 2020).

Compulsory door supervisor licences arrived in 2004 . . . https://www.services.sia.homeoffice.gov.uk/Pages/licensing-cri.aspx.

The Alcohol Harm Reduction Strategy, England, March 2004 (Cabinet Office Strategy Unit).

A December 2004 Mintel trade report . . . The report in question is *Nightclubs, Leisure Intelligence*, Mintel, December 2004 (see also pp. 5–13).

The first Plastic People club managers were Selom Amoa, known as Slim, and Bernard H. Koudjo. Final-era manager Charlotte Kepel told me via email that Bernard's son started a label, ec2a – Plastic's postcode – despite being too young to ever attend himself.

387

Dave Swindells, *Time Out*, 27 September–4 October 2000, p. 64.

Arwa Haider, *Time Out*, 'Blues Heaven', 21–27 March 2001.

Ali Augur, *Floor to Wall: Plastic People Flyers, 1998–2003* (Blurb Books, 2009).

Robert Gallagher, *The Dance Floors of England* (Diabolical Liberties, 2019), p. 49.

'*A club is a community in the process of educating itself . . .*' Josephine Macalister Brew, *In the Service of Youth* (Faber and Faber, 1943), p. 67.

Hua Hsu, 'Sublime Frequencies' Vision of What World Music Means Today', *New Yorker*, 29 April 2019.

Dubstep Heritage blue plaque: https://www.youtube.com/watch?v=uaXDOMasSgM.

Amelia Abraham, 'What Do Gen Zers in the UK Want from Nightlife?', *Canvas*, 8, 5 September 2022.

Derek Walmsley, 'Plastic People Under Threat', *The Wire* blog, 3 May 2010.

The Met's application to review the licence was withdrawn before the relevant sub-committee meeting . . . https://hackney.moderngov.co.uk/ieDecisionDetails.aspx?ID=550.

'Seminal Club Night FWD>> Moves to Dance Tunnel for Skream's Birthday', *FACT* magazine, 3 May 2013.

'Save Plastic People Petition Now Online', *FACT* magazine, 26 February 2010.

Dan Hancox, 'There Is a Light That Never Goes . . . Out?', dan-hancox. blogspot.com, 17 Sept 2010. Hancox attributed at least some of the pressure to gentrification in his blog post: 'This is just hearsay and rumour but I've heard a lot said about pressure to close the venue coming from people who've recently chosen (god knows why) to live on Curtain Road.'

Anyone interested in Ade's floor might also want to take a look at an article in *New Scientist* which suggests that treated wooden floors could generate energy if people walk up and down them – or perhaps dance on them. Matthew Sparkes, 'Wooden Floors Laced with Silicon Generate Electricity from Footsteps', *New Scientist*, 1 September 2021.

13: Space in the Place

The use of Form 696 . . . In 2021 the Horniman Museum in south-east London ran a series of events that responded to the form. They have a good explainer here: https://www.horniman.ac.uk/story/what-was-form-696/.

The Ms Dynamite quote comes from a documentary I made for BBC Radio 1Xtra. *Classic Clubs, Part 2* was broadcast on 11 December

2011 and was produced by Folded Wing: https://www.mixcloud.com/
FoldedWing/bbc-radio-1xtras-stories-classic-uk-clubs-part-2/.

More Fire Crew had a top-ten hit . . . I have not been able to discover which
magazine I wrote this for.

Jordan introduced me to one of our colleagues . . . Mark Gurney, who
contributed to the culture by starting a dubstep label called 2nd Drop.

*There was a lineage here, too: they had all attended Goldie's drum 'n' bass
Metalheadz sessions* . . . I interviewed them for a small piece that
appeared in a national newspaper, 'Rising Star: The DMZ Collective',
Observer, 4 March 2007.

St Matthew's Anglican church, opposite Lambeth Town Hall . . . Taken from
the history section of the St Matthew's website, stmatthewsbrixton.org,
and written by Neil Gilchrist.

Loefah . . . studying fine art at Croydon College . . . The DMZ artwork was
punky, ransom note-style, as if each individual letter had been cut out
and pasted onto the flyer.

I wrote the foreword for Georgina's book *Drumz of the South: The Dubstep
Years, 2004–2007*, which she put together and self-published in 2021.

Skream headlined the Croft Institute in Melbourne . . . The Red Bull
Music Academy interview with Skream is available at https://www.
redbullmusicacademy.com/lectures/skream-zen-skreamism.

Barefiles became a central conduit . . . 'I dedicated a lot of time and
effort to building and maintaining the site,' said Deapoh, when I
contacted him. He continued posting mixes on Barefiles until 2008.
'I taught myself and learned many things,' he said, with extreme
understatement. 'And it was good fun, albeit a bit stressful at times.'
There is a whole other sub-story about Barefiles, some of which
was documented on the scene-popular Dubstep Forum at the time.
When *Resident Advisor* wrote a retrospective feature on the forum,
they described it as a 'music and social time machine' and noted that
founder Dubway still pays for the servers so that it remains available
to the diggers of the future. I was an active user, although I'm not
disclosing my forum name. Richard Akingbehin, 'Ancient Memories:
Revisiting Dubstep Forum', *Resident Advisor*, 28 October 2020:
https://ra.co/features/3771.

They were regulars at DMZ and at Plastic People's FWD>> . . . There were
plenty of clubs in the UK at this point. In 2010 there were an estimated
2,150 nightclubs, although the dancing estate had tipped into a steep
decline and would lose over half its number over the following seven
years. A *Statistic Bulletin* from the Department for Culture, Media and
Sport in 2010 identified 46,406 premises for dancing in the UK. They
also reported that two-thirds of adults said they visited nightclubs,
although half of these went less than once a year.

Culturally deaf new arrivals . . . 'Leeds West Indian Centre to Implement Volume Limit on Sound System Events', *DJ Magazine*, 11 February 2020.

In 2012 the question 'What is dubstep?' was one of the top ten most googled phrases in Canada . . . Matt Hartley, 'Pinterest Named Top Trending Search in Google Canada's Annual Zeitgeist Rankings', *Financial Post*, 12 December 2012.

Top dubstep dancer Marquese Scott has millions of followers . . . His 2011 'Pumped Up Kicks' video was seen by more than 146 million people as of January 2022: https://www.youtube.com/watch?v=LXO-jKksQkM.

I first came across doctor–inventor Dr Peter Michael Nielsen at Danish electronic music festival Strøm, in Copenhagen.

The bass-chair work was published . . . Gudrun Agusta Sigurdardóttir, 'A Pilot Study on High Amplitude Low Frequency–Music Impulse Stimulation as an Add-on Treatment for Clinical Depression', *Brain and Behaviour*, 11 September 2019.

PART THREE
14: Stepping into the Studio

I wrote a monthly column titled 'A Year in Oxleas Woods' for Caught by the River throughout 2014. The following year I wrote intermittently about celebrating pagan dates in the calendar.

Rabia of Basra, felt the connection divinely . . . Rabia of Basra, 'A Lover Who Wants His Lovers Near', in Daniel Ladinsky, *Love Poems from God: Twelve Sacred Voices from the East and West* (Penguin Compass, 2002), p. 26.

There is no record of the Underground Resistance press conference on the internet, but I can assure you that it happened.

Stamping is a very human response . . . The quote comes from Jola Malin, *Carry a Whisper: Mourning a Suicide, Finding a Language for Loss, and a Search for Healing* (Yew Tree Press, 2018), p. 56.

Kate Ling is also part of the collective that runs the Agnes Kirk poetry imprint. She was interviewed on Mark McGuinness's podcast *A Mouthful of Air*, 4 January 2022.

It's a natural Speaker's Corner . . . The local historian behind the excellent *Running Past* blog covered Whitefield's Mount (or Wat Tyler's Mound, as it was previously known) in a 2014 post titled 'Whitefield's Mount – a Rallying Point for Protest and Preaching'.

Simone, the [Italian] accompanist . . . This is the same Simone who founded Popping for Parkinson's. He handed out cards relating to the project after class one day, which led to him joining the social enterprise project I was working on – the one that took me to South Africa.

Notes and References

'*Carriers of the messages . . .*' Rudolf Laban, *The Mastery of Movement* (Dance Books Limited, 1980), p. 87.

The International Dance Teachers' Association describes dyspraxia . . . From https://www.idta.co.uk/members-hub/general-interest/scoliosis-osgood-schlatter-disease-osd-dyslexia-dyspraxia-developmental-co-ordination-disorder-dcd.

60 per cent of children with the same diagnosis had serious motor problems . . . André B. Rietman, Rianne Oostenbrink, Sanne Bongers, Eddy Gaukema, Sandra van Abeelen, Jos G. Hendriksen, Caspar W. N. Looman, Pieter F. A. de Nijs and Marie-Claire de Wit, 'Motor Problems in Children with Neurofibromatosis Type 1', *Journal of Neurodevelopmental Disorders*, May 2017.

Dr Julian Ahmed told me by email that he also had a reputation for falling asleep or appearing to have passed out with his head in or near a bassbin: 'It turns out [this] was fairly stereotypical stimming behaviour.'

12 weeks of dance movement therapy . . . Gopika Govindan, 'Efficacy of Dance Movement Therapy in the Treatment of Children with ADHD', *Journal of Child and Adolescent Behaviour*, 2018.

'*Eyes open, head moving*' . . . Caroline Williams, 'Bad Balance: Why Dangerous Falls Are on the Rise Around the World', *New Scientist*, 7 October 2020.

'*Sensorial palette of a dancing body*' . . . '*Inside, my body was radiating energies*' . . . Steve Paxton, *Gravity* (Contredanse Éditions, 2018), p. 23, p. 6.

Tara Brandel's *Gawky and Awkward* was premiered at the Balina Arts Centre in 2013 and performed at the San Francisco International Arts Festival in 2015.

Marie C. Boyette describes the circumstances surrounding Laban's exit from Nazi Germany in her thesis *The Universality of Laban Movement Analysis* (Virgina Commonwealth University, 2012), pp. 10–37.

Running the Modern Dance holiday course from 1949 to 1951 . . . https://www.dartington.org/rudolf-von-laban.

Choreographer Merce Cunningham, who performed there in 1964 . . . https://www.dartington.org/merce-cunningham-at-dartington-from-the-archive/.

Strictly Come Dancing is a BBC TV series known internationally as *Dancing with the Stars*. It is the world's most successful reality-TV format, according to Guinness World Records.

The phrase *Ni Nyampinga* translates as 'a girl who is beautiful inside and out'. The magazine and radio shows are well known in Rwanda, reaching over 12 million people each year. There are now similar youth programmes nearby: *Yegna* in Ethiopia, *Zathu* in Malawi and *Tujibebe* in Tanzania.

The sleevenotes to her meditation soundtrack . . . Gabrielle Roth & The Mirrors, *Endless Wave, Volume 1* (Raven Recording, 1996).

There are now over 400 certified 5Rhythms teachers . . . Detail from 5rhythms.com.

Chris Waywell, 'One of London's Oldest Community Centres Is Under Threat', *Time Out* online, 20 April 2021.

Yoga exists to exhaust the body . . . Personal conversation with Nadia Gilani, author of *The Yoga Manifesto* (Bluebird, 2022).

The mural of Ty was created by artists Bunny Bread and Jason Caballero of Create Not Destroy, and replicates an iconic photographic image by Benji Reid.

15: One More!

It improves balance . . . Marie Fabre, Jean Blouin and Laurence Mouchnino, 'Enhancing the internal Representation of the Body Through Sensorimotor Training in Sports and Dance Improves Balance Control'. *Research & Investigations in Sports Medicine*, vol. 6, issue 1 (Crimson, 2020), pp. 474–6.

The ability to problem-solve . . . Dr Peter Lovatt, *The Dance Cure: The Surprising Secret to Being Smarter, Stronger, Happier* (Short Books, 2020), p. 86.

Symptoms of stress . . . Anna Duberg, 'The Effects of a Dance Intervention on Somatic Symptoms and Emotional Distress in Adolescent Girls: A Randomized Controlled Trial', *Journal of International Medical Research*, 2020.

Bronwyn Tarr's work was reported in 'Dancing Can Bring People Together, Say Researchers', BBC News online, 16 June 2016.

Those who danced in sync with each other felt closer to their dance crew than to others . . . 'Synchronised Moves to the Beat Break Down Barriers Between Groups of Children', 15 June 2016, Oxford Institute of Cognitive and Evolutionary Anthropology.

BBC Radio 1Xtra DJ Tash LC was a regular . . . Emma Warren, *Make Some Space: Tuning into Total Refreshment Centre* (Sweet Machine, 2018), p. 75.

The CHICAGOxLONDON gigs formed the backbone of Makaya McCraven's 2018 mixtape *Where We Come From* (International Anthem/ TRC). Paul Bradshaw reviewed the night for his blog *Ancient to Future*, 25 October 2017.

Fresh Roasted is run by Alejandro 'King Hippo' Ayala, who hosts a bi-weekly show, *QC*, on Lumpen Radio in Chicago.

The International Anthem crew took me to the Back Alley jazz festival on 14 July 2018. It was a free community event led by Chicago artists Fo Wilson and Norman Teague, in collaboration with the Hyde Park Jazz Festival and the Hyde Park Art Center. Ben LaMar Gay performed. Jumaane Taylor was performing with saxophonist Greg Ward, Jeremiah Hunt (bass), Gregory Artry (drums) and poet Preston Jackson.

Notes and References

The South Side drummers who meet every Sunday by the beach . . . The 63rd
Street drummers have been meeting weekly at dusk for the last four
decades. 'There's no organisation,' said drum teacher Rick Taylor, in
Place Making Chicago, summer 2008. 'They just know to come.'

An 'ecological nerve centre' . . . Dhanveer Singh Brar, *Teklife/Ghettoville/Eski:*
The Sonic Ecologies of Black Music in the Early 21st Century (Goldsmiths
Press, 2021), p. 80.

Adesola Osakalumi was talking about house-music circles during
choreographer Camille Brown's *Social Dance for Social Change* lecture
series, episode 25. Aired on Zoom, 5 February 2021.

'Teklife, b2b After-Party with The Era' took place at the Promontory on
19 July 2018. DJ Spinn, DJ Taye, DJ Gant-Man, DJ Manny, RP Boo,
Traxman, Boylan, DJ Tre, Heavee, Sirr TMO and DJ Phil played. It
followed a live radio discussion with RBMA's Vivian Host, charting
how footwork, the music and dance genre, developed into a cultural
movement. I had a short interview with DJ Taye on my Worldwide
FM show on 1 November 2016. 'The Official Silver Room Block Party
After Show' was at the Promontory on 21 July 2018, 10 p.m.–3 a.m. The
DJs were Ron Trent and Joe Claussell. Trinidadian Deep warmed up.

Between 2014 and 2019 £200 million had been wiped off the UK club market . . .
Ben Hunter, 'Event Horizon', *Knowledge Magazine 25 Year Anniversary,*
edited by Colin Steven (Velocity Press, 2019), p. 55.

By 2015 half of UK clubs had closed . . . BBC radio's *Newsbeat* compiled
a report on clubbing in Britain using figures from the Association of
Licensed Multiple Retailers. This revealed there were 1,733 clubs
in the UK, compared to 3,144 a decade earlier in 2005. Reported in
Mixmag online, 10 August 2015.

British–Ghanaian writer Caleb Azumah Nelson included a scene from the jam
in his best-selling debut novel Open Water . . . That Steam Down was
the music space in question was confirmed in email correspondence
with the author. Caleb Azumah Nelson, *Open Water* (Penguin Books,
2021). At the time of writing it still takes place every Wednesday at the
Matchstick Piehouse in Deptford. I can also recommend the Monday
night Orii Community jam at Colour Factory in Hackney Wick, which
is run by Fred 'Neue Grafik' N'Thepe.

'Britain's Black population is now about two million' . . . *Caribbean forebears* . . .
'Black Britons: The Next Generation', *The Economist,* 28 January 2016.

Over a million adults born in Africa . . . Tholani Alli, *Mapping London's African*
Community, 2016. https://africanculture.blog/2016/07/15/mapping-
londons-african-community-2016-demographic-dilemmas-discourses/.

The Mayor of Brent . . . Mayor Michael Adeyeye made the comment during
a visit to the mayor of Lagos in 2013. Monsur Olowoopejo, 'Over 1
Million Nigerians Live in London', *Vanguard,* 4 May 2013.

Notes and References

Val Wilmer, *As Serious as Your Life: Black Music and the Free Jazz Revolution, 1957–1977* (Serpent's Tail Classics, 2018), p. 209.

Siviwe . . . runs gumboot-dancing classes . . . Siviwe Mbinda developed the Happy Feet dance programme into a successful employment and resilience programme, alongside the highly respected Siviwe Tours, which he runs around his home area of Langa, Cape Town. He also runs the iThuba Innovation Hub, which includes an after-school STEM programme for children.

Deptford Royal Dockyard, which (between 1513 and 1869) built and refitted warships and vessels designed for exploration . . . Nathan Dews, *History of Deptford* (originally published 1884; republished by FamLoc, edited by Michael Wood, 2015), lists 164 ships that were built at the docks, but many others would have been repaired or refitted. Pp. 246–50.

[Deptford Docks was] 'the cradle of the British Navy' . . . Jess Steele, *Turning the Tide: The History of Everyday Deptford* (Deptford Forum Publishing, 1993), p. 71.

Matthew Sheldon of the National Museum of the Royal Navy wrote that state-built vessels were a 'key guarantor of the colonial system' . . . Matthew Sheldon, National Museum of the Royal Navy blog post, 2020: https://www.nmrn.org.uk/news-events/nelson-pedestal.

making Deptford Docks a foremost location from which the British Empire sprang . . . Historian L. M. Bates described Deptford Docks as 'the ground from which, more than any other, grew the British Empire' in L. M. Bates, *The Spirit of London's River* (Gresham Books, 1980), p. 53. Professor Joan Anim-Addo shared Bates's opinion and focuses on the legacy of empire and enslavement: 'On several counts, Deptford was central to the African–Caribbean trade and the black presence in the south-east London area.' Joan Anim-Addo, *Longest Journey: A History of Black Lewisham* (Deptford Forum Publishing, 1995). Anim-Addo also wrote that the famous abolitionist Olaudah Equiano was abducted from Deptford and forced to work on Caribbean plantations, until he bought his freedom and returned to London (ibid, p. 51). There were local industries that sprang up around these realities: Greenwich warehouses supplied materials, and the owner of one of these, ironmonger Ambrose Crowley, was wealthy enough to own 23 merchant ships, 'some of which must have been used on the Atlantic run', according to John Charlton in *Hidden Chains: The Slavery Business and North East England, 1600–1865* (Tyne Bridge Publishing, 2008), p. 100.

Including the East India Company . . . Anthony Francis, *The Deptford Royal Dockyard and Manor of Sayes Court, London: Excavations, 2000–12* (Museum of London Archaeology Monograph 71, 2017), p. 33: '*Trades Increase* and *Peppercorn* were both built at Deptford 1609–10 for the East India Company.' Also: '*A location which exists as a centre of business because of the activities of the East India Company . . .*' W. G. Sebald, *The Rings of Saturn* (Harvill Press, 1998), quoted in 'Deptford, Opium and the East India Company', Transpontine, 6 August 2005.

Naval officers who 'desire and direct' that men be press-ganged . . . Letter dated 11 May 1689, ADM/A/1762, in letters and orders received by the Navy Board, Caird Library, National Maritime Museum, Greenwich.

I wrote about the luxury flats being built on the site of Deptford Docks and the community fightback, focusing on Voice 4 Deptford: 'There Will Be No Reference Left of What Was Here', *The Developer Magazine*, 1 June 2022. This section was previously much longer, and could be a whole book in itself. I have included only a tiny taste of the powerful stories that exist in this location: stories about the creative resistance of communities in the face of royalty, wealthy merchants and other profiteers, and of the local workings of the enslavement trade. The grass-roots and volunteer-run Museum of Slavery and Freedom is attempting to locate and share these essential histories through regular walks and have published a map, *Walking Deptford's Legacy of Slavery* (MōSaF, London, 2022).

Gill Clarke, 'Mind as in Motion', first published in the spring 2007 edition of *Animated* magazine and reproduced by permission of People Dancing: Foundation Community Dance. All Rights Reserved. See www.communitydance.org.uk/animated for more information.

Bibliography

Abdurraqib, Hanif, *A Little Devil in America* (Allen Lane/Penguin Random House, 2021).

Adofo, Christian, *A Quick Ting on Afrobeats* (Jacaranda Books, 2022).

Anim-Addo, Joan, *The Longest Journey: A History of Black Lewisham* (Deptford Forum Publishing, 1995).

Arnone, Anna, *Sound Reasoning* (Arandora Press, 2017).

Atherton Lin, Jeremy, *Gay Bar: Why We Went Out* (Granta, 2021).

Augur, Ali, *Floor to Wall: Plastic People Flyers, 1998–2003* (Blurb, 2009).

Bates, L. M., *The Spirit of London's River* (Gresham Books, 1980).

Belle-Fortune, Brian, *All Crews: Journeys Through Jungle/Drum & Bass Culture* (Vision Publishing, 1999).

Branfman, Suchi (ed.), *Undanced Dances Through Prison Walls During a Pandemic* (Sming Sming Books, 2021).

Breathnach, Breandán, *Folk Music and Dances of Ireland* (The Mercier Press, 1971).

Burrows, Jonathan, *A Choreographer's Handbook* (Routledge, 2010).

Charlton, John, *Hidden Chains: The Slavery Business and North East England, 1600–1865* (Tyne Bridge Publishing, 2008).

Cook, Georgina, *Drumz of the South: The Dubstep Years, 2004–2007* (Drumz of the South, 2021).

Cullinane, John, *Aspects of the History of Irish Céilí Dancing, 1897–1997* (Dr John Cullinane, 1998).

Davies, Bernard, *From Voluntaryism to Welfare State: A History of the Youth Service in England, Volume 1, 1939–1979* (Youth Work Press, 1999).

Davis, Thulani, *Nothing but the Music* (Blank Forms Editions, 2020).

Davis, Tony, *UK Rave 1991* (Café Royal Books, 2021).

Denby, Edwin, *Dance Writings* (Alfred A. Knopf, 1986).

Dews, Nathan, *History of Deptford*; ed. Wood, Michael (FamLoc, 2015).

Ehrenreich, Barbara, *Dancing in the Streets: A History of Collective Joy* (Granta, 2007).

Ellis, Simon, *Some Things About Dance* (LeanPub, 2020).

Frost, Jumpin Jack, *Big, Bad and Heavy* (Music Mondays, 2017).

Gallagher, Robert, *The Dance Floors of England* (Diabolical Liberties, 2019).

397

Bibliography

Gerraghty, Geraldine, *Raise Your Hands* (Boxtree, 1996).

Gerrard, Bill, *The Devil at Dances* (Redemptorist Record, 1954).

Goetz, Rainald, *Rave* (Fitzcarraldo Editions, 2020; first published 1998).

Greenlaw, Lavinia, *The Importance of Music to Girls: A Memoir* (Faber & Faber, 2007).

Greenlee, Sam, *The Spook Who Sat by the Door* (Richard Baron Books, 1969).

Hanna, Judith Lynne, *To Dance Is Human: A Theory of Non-Verbal Communication* (University of Chicago Press, 1979).

Haring, Keith, *Dance* (Bulfinch Press, 1999).

Haslam, Dave, *Life After Dark: A History of British Nightclubs and Music Venues* (Simon & Schuster, 2015).

Henry, William 'Lez', *What the Deejay Said: A Critique from the Street!* (Learning by Choice, 2006).

Hind, John and Mosco, Stephen, *Rebel Radio: The Full Story of British Pirate Radio* (Pluto Press, 1985).

Ignatiev, Noel, *How the Irish Became White* (Routledge, 1995).

Isoardi, Steven L., *The Music Finds a Way: A PAPA/UGMAA Oral History of Growing Up in Postwar South Central Los Angeles* (Darktree, 2020).

Jackson, Lee, *Palaces of Pleasure: From Music Halls to the Seaside to Football, How the Victorians Invented Mass Entertainment* (Yale University Press, 2019).

James, Martin, *State of Bass: The Origins of Jungle/Drum & Bass* (Velocity Press, 1997).

Joyce, P. W., *A Concise History of Ireland from the Earliest Times to 1908* (M. H. Gill and Son, 1913).

Kid, The Fandangoe, *Tender Hearted Bold Moves* (Rough Trade Books, 2020).

Kirk, James T. and Fingers, Two, *Junglist* (Boxtree, 1995).

Knowles, Mark, *Tap Roots: The Early History of Tap Dancing* (McFarland & Co., 2002).

Kwesi Johnson, Linton, *Selected Poems* (Penguin, 2006).

Laban, Rudolf, *The Mastery of Movement* (MacDonald and Evans, 1960).

Ladinsky, Daniel, *Love Poems from God: Twelve Sacred Voices from the East and West* (Penguin Compass, 2002).

Leeds Craig, Maxine, *Sorry I Don't Dance: Why Men Refuse to Move* (Oxford University Press, 2014).

Leeson, D. M, *The Black and Tans: British Police and Auxiliaries in the Irish War of Independence 1920–1921* (Oxford University Press, 2011).

Levey, Paula, *Dancing in London* (New English Library, 1981).

Ling, Kate and Nicholls, Jon, *All of It* (Agnes Kirk, 2020).

Lovatt, Dr Peter, *The Dance Cure: The Surprising Secret to Being Smarter, Stronger, Happier* (Short Books, 2020).

Bibliography

Macalister Brew, Josephine, *In the Service of Youth: A Practical Manual of Work Among Adolescents* (Faber & Faber, 1944).

McNeill, William H., *Keeping Together in Time: Dance and Drill in Human History* (Harvard University Press, 1995).

Malin, Jola, *Carry a Whisper: Mourning a Suicide, Finding a Language for Loss, and a Search for Healing* (Yew Tree Press, 2018).

Mayhew, Henry, *London Labour and the London Poor* (Charles Griffin & Co., 1865).

Noon, Jeff, *Vurt* (Ringpull Press, 1993).

Nott, James, *Going to the Palais: A Social and Cultural History of Dancing and Dance Halls in Britain, 1918–1960* (Oxford University Press, 2015).

Oliveros, Pauline, *Deep Listening: A Composer's Sound Practice* (iUniverse, 2005).

Olusoga, David, *Black and British: A Forgotten History* (Pan Macmillan, 2016).

Paxton, Steve, *Gravity* (Contredanse Éditions, 2018).

Raboteau, Albert J., *Slave Religion: The 'Invisible Institution' in the Antebellum South* (Oxford University Press, 2004; first edition, 1978).

Salkind, Micah E., *Do You Remember House?: Chicago's Queer of Color Undergrounds* (Oxford University Press, 2019).

Shange, Ntozake, *Dance We Do: A Poet Explores Black Dance* (Beacon Press, 2020).

Shange, Ntozake, *Wild Beauty: New and Selected Poems of Ntozake Shange* (37 Ink, 2017).

Shelton, Syd, *The Battle of Lewisham, August 13th 1977* (Café Royal Books, 2021).

Singh Brar, Dhanveer, *Teklife/Ghettoville/Eski: The Sonic Ecologies of Black Music in the Early 21st Century* (Goldsmiths Press, 2021).

Smith, Michael, *Unreal City* (Faber & Faber, 2014).

Smith, Zadie, *Feel Free: Essays* (Penguin, 2019).

Steele, Jess, *Turning the Tide: The History of Everyday Deptford* (Deptford Forum Publishing, 1993).

Steven, Colin (ed.), *Knowledge Magazine: 25 Year Anniversary* (Velocity Press, 2019).

Taylor, Joelle, *C+nto & Othered Poems* (Westbourne Press, 2021).

Walker, Alice, *Hard Times Require Furious Dancing* (New World Library, 2010).

Waplington, Nick, *Safety in Numbers* (Booth-Clibborn Editions/*Dazed & Confused*, 1997).

Ware, Vron and Back, Les, *Out of Whiteness: Color, Politics and Culture* (University of Chicago Press, 2002).

Wilmer, Val, *As Serious as Your Life: Black Music and the Free Jazz Revolution, 1957–1977* (Serpent's Tail Classics, 2018; first published, 1977).

Bibliography

Wolfe, Tom, *The Pump House Gang* (Black Swan, 1992; first published, 1968).

Yashere, Gina, *Cack-Handed* (HarperCollins, 2021).